Tristan

by

Suzanne Schuurman

GEORGE RONALD

OXFORD

GEORGE RONALD, Publisher
46 High Street, Kidlington, Oxford, OX5 2DN
© SUZANNE SCHUURMAN 1987

British Library Cataloguing in Publication Data

Schuurman, Suzanne
   Tristan.
    1. Brain-damaged children—Biography
    I. Title
    362.3   RJ496.B7

    ISBN 0-85398-248-1
    ISBN 0-85398-249-X Pbk

Printed and bound in Great Britain by
Biddles Ltd, Guildford and King's Lynn

Foreword

A LETTER dated 16 October 1981 from the Spiritual Assembly of the Bahá'ís of St. John's, Newfoundland, Canada, setting out a few facts about Tristan Schuurman's life, first brought him to my attention: 'Tristan was born in 1964, while his family were pioneering in a remote settlement in the Canadian Arctic. As an infant he suffered a raging fever and, with incredible difficulty, was taken to where he could be flown out to a hospital in southern Canada. His parents were told that he would never walk or talk, that he would be nothing but a vegetable.

'Anyone who has attended Canadian Bahá'í National Conventions can testify that Tristan walked and talked, laughed and loved, and believed in Bahá'u'lláh with a devotion that inspired all who knew him. We remember him at Conventions, going from table to table, visiting with friends, uplifting them with his radiant spirit . . . Beyond the veil of physical afflictions lived a soul brilliant with the gifts of God; we have been blessed to know him.'

From the moment I read the letter, Tristan has lived in my consciousness as a vivid presence. He reinforces my understanding of how 'Abdu'l-Bahá exhorted us to live: in full commitment to the delights and responsibilities of our humanity and the earth we inhabit, and simultaneously in profound recognition that our world is an *ash-heap*, a *dung-hill*, a place of preparation for spiritual realms which *bestow only joy*, and in which *there is no separation*.

The deaths of children are the most poignant deaths – they turn our thoughts to blighted promise, the vulnerability of youth, wasted potential, lost beauty. 'How unfair!' we protest in our human frailty, all our bright hopes dashed, and tremble to remember that none withstands death's marauding. We might wish for Tristan a longer life, especially for the sake of

v

his parents, but we could not have imagined for him a richer existence than that which he created out of the circumstances presented to him. Through his ability to understand, accept and rise above his physical limitations and sufferings, he became a spiritual adept: his seventeen years were crammed with 'life' of the highest order. Longevity is a poor substitute for his attainment.

Tolstoy in his late diaries remarks, 'One must always live as though a favourite child is dying in a room nearby. He is always dying – and I am always dying.' There is wisdom in this epigram: the innocent is always with us as a most eloquent symbol, is ever being sacrificed, and ever holds up to our distracted gaze the world's real prize: spiritual consciousness. And far from being a morbid concept it may be seen, as Tristan Schuurman's story demands to be, as an affirmation that, wonderful and absorbing as life is, there await, in Bahá'u'lláh's words, *Worlds, holy and spiritually glorious . . .*, and that we may, even as Tristan did, long before reaching them, thrill to their impulses, breathe their air, move to their harmonies, feast on their fruits.

Roger White
3 April 1986

Acknowledgements

THIS BOOK owes its existence to many people. The idea of writing about my son did not occur to me, it was inspired by a series of interconnected circumstances.

Betty Birse sent me a copy of *Blessings* by Mary Craig. I was so moved by Craig's account of her experiences with her handicapped sons that I sent the book on to several friends.

Early one morning I had a call from Elizabeth Rochester in St. John's, Newfoundland. Elizabeth had just read *Blessings* and suggested that I write about Tristan because, she explained, the spiritual progress of the handicapped and their contribution to family and community were issues not usually treated in literature about the disadvantaged.

It so happened that that very day the teachers of Newfoundland and Labrador went on a *withdrawal of selected services* that meant in effect that the teachers were at school but the students were not. Sitting in my empty classroom I began the outline of *Tristan*.

In most projects there is a turning point. One day I sat dejected wondering whether I was up to the task I had undertaken. I studied Tristan's photograph on my desk. My eyes strayed to the books of poetry by Roger White beside the photograph. I hold Tristan himself responsible for the flash of inspiration that prompted me to send Roger a few chapters and request an unbiased opinion whether it was worth continuing. Roger White's encouragement and help have made him *Tristan's* godfather.

Finally to Don Maclean my special thanks for his careful work on the manuscript compensating for my abhorrence of commas and for herding my stray adverbs towards their rightful verbs and other deeds of grammatical virtue.

Wolfville, Nova Scotia
October 1986

This book is dedicated to all those whom Tristan loved

Chapter One

WHAT did I wish for that May day so long ago? I can still remember the feel of the warm spring sun and the smell of the lilacs but I can't remember what I wished. Ottawa was floating in the scent of lilacs. The bus was late. I picked a cluster of blossoms from a lilac bush nearby and called to my two small daughters. They left their study of a bug crawling on the pavement to answer my invitation to inspect the lilac bloom. They closed their eyes and nuzzled the blooms, crinkling their noses.

'Can baby smell the flowers?' asked one.

'No, I don't think so but perhaps it can feel the warm sun,' I answered.

Two small hands cautiously touched my protruding belly and felt it warm in the spring sunshine.

'Do you want to make a wish?' I showed them how to hold the individual lilac bloom in the crease of the palm and swing the arm around over their heads.

'What shall I wish?' thoughtfully demanded the elder.

'You might want to make a wish about seeing daddy soon. Do you remember that we are leaving tonight for Frobisher Bay? And you must wish in your head and not tell anyone.'

'Not even you, mummy?'

'Not even me.'

'What, mummy, what?' demanded the little girl in the stroller.

The eldest took it upon herself to explain. There was much giggling and whispering. Finally Mousie and Bonie, as the little girls were nicknamed, were ready. Amidst much laughter both blooms fell out on the count of two.

'I won't tell you what I wished,' Mousie confided conspiratorially. 'Now you wish, mummy!'

'Mummy wish?' queried Bonie's treble from the stroller.

I

Yes, mummy wished; I flourished my arm in an arc above my head. One . . . two . . . three. The bus swung around the corner. We were a confusion of children, a stroller reluctant to fold, and an awkward pregnant lady trying to board the bus.

We were on our way to the Carlingwood Shopping Mall. Only the day before a dear friend, Gale Bond, who had gone to the Arctic with her husband as a bride, had come over to say goodbye and share some advice.

'Go out every day no matter what the weather is like, no matter how much trouble it is to bundle up the children. Otherwise . . .' she seemed to hesitate before pronouncing the ultimate indictment in the north, 'you'll get bushed.' She had looked off into space for a minute, as if seeing a long procession of white days. 'You will need lots of rainy-day toys and presents for the children to take as gifts to birthday parties.' It was this last injunction that we were on our way to fulfill at the shopping center.

In the Simpson's Sears toy department we bought coloring books, paint by number, foldouts, punch-outs, rub and see pads, magic slates and magnetic toys. On the way down the escalator I saw a wool sale. Memories of my husband came flooding over me. What did I have for Hubert's birthday? I would knit him a sweater! Then, on the spur of the moment I bought some blue and white baby wool.

'Is it going to be a boy?' asked Mousie, looking at the blue wool.

'I don't know,' I answered seriously. 'We thought you were going to be a boy.'

'But I'm a girl!' she affirmed categorically.

'Yes, and I'm glad you are you.' I smiled at her wide blue eyes.

'Are you glad Bonie is a girl?' pursued Mousie.

'I like little girls.' The silence that met my last remark made me aware that something more was needed.

In the aisle between the wool counters, I squatted down until my head was level with Mousie's and Bonie's. With my arms around them both I said in intimate tones, 'I love you both very much, and dad and I are grateful that God gave us such wonderful children.'

'And the baby. . .' Mousie pursued insistently, 'will we love the baby too . . . very much?'

2

'Love baby . . . love baby . . .' Bonie began to sing.

Mousie turned to her younger sister and said, out of bitter experience, 'When the new baby comes, you won't be the baby anymore.'

'Happy baby,' sang Bonie, oblivious of the dire prediction, 'happy baby . . . happy baby.'

Amused shoppers smiled at the little brown-haired tot with the beatific smile singing 'Happy baby' and at the intense little girl helping to guide the stroller through the crowds.

That evening, at the Montreal Airport, and far from the scent of lilacs, we boarded the D.C. 6 that flew twice-weekly to Frobisher Bay.

I woke in the gray light of early dawn. Across the aisle, the cargo, fastened with wide strapping and covered with gray canvas, groaned and strained at every movement of the aircraft. Bonie slept on a bed of parkas at my feet, and Mousie lay with her head on my lap. The denuded rolling white landscape told me that we had passed the tree line. As one looks at a well-loved face after an absence of many years, so now I looked at the Arctic landscape of mountains and frozen lakes.

Traveling by train from Hamilton to Winnipeg with my mother, immigrants from warring Europe, I had watched for the first time this unfolding panorama. Grudgingly I grew to admire the immensity of Canada's wilderness. Although it took years for me to appreciate the vast northern forests that cast their elongated shadows on the snowy wastes as the true gothic of my adopted land.

Lovers can recall the exact day they fell in love. I know to the minute when I caught the lure of northern adventure. It was on a hot sultry summer's day in Winnipeg. Near the corner of Portage and Main ran a side street where a movie marquee advertised *Nanook of the North*. To a schoolgirl's eye it had looked like a cool alternative to a very hot afternoon. In that air-conditioned theater I had caught a chronic infection that manifested itself in a lifelong love affair with the North. That fascination had led me to Northern Labrador where I had met Hubert. My thoughts now turned to him with longing. Was he getting ready to meet us?

I have wakened in Thy shelter, O my God, and it becometh

3

him that seeketh that shelter to abide within the Sanctuary of Thy protection and the Stronghold of Thy defense. Illumine my inner being, O my Lord, with the splendors of the Dayspring of Thy Revelation, even as Thou didst illumine my outer being with the morning light of Thy favor.

I prayed silently. The words, that usually filled my heart with calm, today precipitated vague apprehensions that had been stirring within for some time. The morning prayer and the uncompromising landscape led me to an awakening realization that my misgivings centered on my motives for coming North.

At the time that Hubert finished his Master's program in sociology, we had read in *Bahá'í News* that pioneers were needed in the Arctic. Our reaction had been spontaneous and simultaneous. This was our special challenge, our field of service. We spent a year in Ottawa while Hubert attended the government-sponsored Northern University program that helped prepare northern administrators to cope with the Innuit language and the intricacies of government departments and policies. It had also been a time of inner preparation and of studying the *Tablets of the Divine Plan* by 'Abdu'l-Bahá, and of discussion with other pioneers. I could not hide from myself, however, that it was also the existentialist craving to explore the *outer boundaries* and the *inner frontiers* that had drawn me here and that my desire to teach humanity that 'We are all the leaves of one tree and the flowers of one garden' came a pale second.

God, you see how unworthy I am, and how shabby are my motives. It's no use hiding from You that I would love to go to this northern post even if it were not a goal of the Plan. Yet I do want truly to be Your servant and to do Your will in all things. Please help me to purify my motives. And O God, please keep my family in the palm of Your hand.

Gray swirling snow swept by a cold wind whipped around us as we stumbled off the plane. Blinded by the snow we hugged the parkaed shape that enfolded us in his arms. Drifting snow everywhere blocked out the view as we drove from the airport in the government station wagon. We passed barracks and rows of identical houses shrouded in snow-drifts – all that comprised Frobisher Bay proper, we were told. Then over a scarcely visible road we drove several miles till another smaller settlement appeared. Hubert informed us that this was Apex Hill, and that it would be our home. There was not much of a hill but our house stood on what apex there was. It was one of a series of row houses built by the government to house its northern employees. Below these houses stood small dwellings of different colors that had been built for the Innuit. As the wind died down, we could see that the land sloped gently to the shores of a frozen bay. The view was majestic for far across the bay we could see the rocky snow-covered distant shore, and above, the scudding gray clouds on the far-stretching horizon.

'Well, what do you think?' exclaimed Hubert with a note of pride in his voice.

It was certainly the biggest house we had ever had, with three bedrooms, a living room and a large kitchen furnished in the various shades of Canadian maple that I would come to know so well in all government housing in the North. There was a large storage room lined with shelves on which were rows of canned goods, big boxes of dry milk powder and bags of flour and sugar.

'Just like a store,' was Mousie's comment. I noticed with relief that the chocolate chips were on the highest shelf.

'What do you think?' Hubert asked again, putting his arm around me.

'It's wonderful!' I answered with a smile, fighting down a feeling of loneliness and dismay that engulfed me like a wave of the morning sickness from which I had suffered so often during this pregnancy.

'There's no bathroom!' Mousie announced stomping into the kitchen as we were preparing to have a cup of tea.

'Mousie, Bonie, come let me introduce you to a honey-bucket!' Hubert said, laughing as he led them to the garbage-bag-lined bucket that constituted toilet facilities in the north. I could hear loud protest.

'I won't do it in there!' said Mousie with loud finality.

'You can use Bonie's potty.'

'I'm too old for a potty. I just won't go!'

Within the next few days, the box of toys and my sewing machine arrived. Hubert, who saw that we had met our neighbors and were comfortably settled, prepared to return to his posting in Igloolik. He would come back to us in August, and after the baby was born, we would return with him to Igloolik.

Igloolik! On the map, it looks so big. Actually there are only several hundred people in a hundred-mile radius. Igloolik is the trading center. 'Tell me about it,' I asked Hubert. Patiently, he explained about the ridge-backed island in the Heckla and Fury Straits, just west of the great land mass of Baffin Island. Land and sea are not so definite up there as the sea is frozen over for most of the year, he pointed out. I could see he was keen to get back. For my young husband the great northern adventure was calling.

'Cloudy this afternoon, but becoming sunny after midnight . . .' the announcer's voice read the weather bulletin in a matter-of-fact manner. I laughed at the idea of it being 'sunny after midnight,' but it was commonplace for northerners for in the spring and summer the daylight endures into the night. Suddenly, I realized that clear weather meant Hubert would be leaving. Another separation, I thought, and my heart seemed to move with pain. But, no, it was the babe, moving languidly within me. *You are certainly not a kicker like your sister Mousie. Well, my little northern baby, in August you will be making your appearance. I hope your daddy makes it back in time.*

Spring in the Arctic does not allow itself to be ignored. It is not the soft warming season of temperate climes. Rather it is a time when the sun struggling to break the bonds of ice and snow drowns the land in incandescent light. The power of light wins and the snow begins to melt. Great rivulets of rushing water carve intricate, ever-changing patterns in the banks of ice and snow. I watched the children sail home-made boats in the temporary lakes that formed around the houses from the spring run-off, and remembered my own childhood when as a refugee child in France I had sailed miniature sail-boats in the baroque fountains of Paris under the watchful gaze of my nanny.

Despite the endless light that poured down on us both day and night, I made efforts to keep regular hours. Tacking up old army blankets over the windows I continued to put the children to bed at seven every night. This was not the pattern of life among our Innuit neighbors.

A knock. It is the middle of the night. Groggily, I struggle into a bathrobe that will no longer close over my stomach. As

6

I reach the door I check my watch. It's two in the morning. I see no one through the window in the door but the knocking persists. I open the door and see three smiling Innuit children.

'Can Avinga and Bonie come out to play?' the oldest one whispers shyly. Avinga, a common girl's name in the area, was the translation of the nickname 'Mousie'.

Trying to keep the edge of sleep out of my voice, I answer. 'It's the middle of the night. They are both asleep. Come back in the morning.'

They whisper, in Inuktitut, among themselves. Then the oldest one asks wonderingly, 'When is morning?'

My years as a student of anthropology have not prepared me for this sort of cultural impasse and I find myself saying what I know to be ridiculous: 'At nine o'clock . . . after breakfast . . .' They look at each other, giggle, and go away.

So much for cultural relativism! As I think of what would have been an appropriate answer to my night visitors, I fall asleep.

The enormous area of the Canadian North has but a small population which forms an intimate, and often interrelated, community. Soon after arriving in Frobisher Bay I found people who were relatives of good friends in Nain, Labrador, where I had taught for several years before meeting and marrying Hubert. After mentioning how much I had missed game meat on moving South, choice cuts of game and fish began to appear at unexpected times on my kitchen table. Often, that prize delicacy, seal liver, made up my supper menu. My doctor pronounced my blood count good; there was no problem with anemia during this pregnancy!

The mother of my early-morning callers was becoming less shy and agreed to cut out an amaut for me. An amaut is a marvelously designed, traditional Innuit garment that permits mother and child to enjoy each other's warmth. Contrary to a common misconception, the northern baby does not ride in the mother's hood, but rather in a pouch on her back. The hood of the amaut is enlarged, however, so that there is an area of warmed air for the baby's breathing.

I sewed the amaut myself out of white duffle and decorated it with colorful braid. As a wind protection all amauts and parkas in the north have a cover of Grenfell cloth or heavy cotton drill. At that time these were traditionally white.

7

Longing for more color I broke with custom and made a bright red cover. Little did I realize how close to tragedy that choice would later lead me.

One night after I had set out the bread to rise, written a letter to my mother in Zaïre, and sewn up the sweater I had made for Hubert's birthday, I went to bed early. Deep within the well of sleep I heard a door bang, the heavy stomping of feet and more doors banging. Had some drunks wandered in? I sat up in bed slowly adjusting my bulky abdomen.

'Is anybody home?' called a familiar voice.

In no time I was in the kitchen hugging a figure in a ragged parka that smelled strongly of fish and kissing a beloved face that bristled with a prickly growth of beard. On the kitchen table a shape in a black plastic bag flopped against the surface. My stomach turned.

'I brought you a fish,' Hubert explained with a boyish grin, and added, 'I caught it myself.'

In the light night, over tea at the kitchen table, Hubert recounted his adventure. Someone from his office had seen me and reported that I looked as though the baby would be born any moment. News had gone out over the radio-telephone to get Hubert back to Frobisher Bay right away. A plane was dispatched. The Hudson Bay factor had relayed the information and Hubert had set out by dog team to the edge of the ice, which was still several miles from shore. The plane had circled, but the water was too full of drift ice, and it could not land. He was to learn later that the pilot had started to fly back to Hall Beach, when the co-pilot noticed that the ice on which Hubert and the dog team were standing had become detached from the shore ice, and that they were in effect adrift on an ice pan. The pilot had turned back and this time succeeded in landing in the lead of water between the ice pan and the shore.

I clutched his hand to reassure myself that he was really there and touched his rough cheek with my fingers in wonder and relief.

'I'm sorry I couldn't shave, everything happened so fast!'

Before going to bed, we looked in on the sleeping children. 'You could believe that they are little angels if you did not see them when they're awake.' But there was a mist in his eyes. 'And this little one,' he said, gently patting my belly, 'will he mind if I sleep beside you tonight?'

8

'He doesn't kick like Mousie did. In fact he seldom moves.'

'But he's all right, isn't he?' There was a note of ill-disguised concern in Hubert's voice.

'The doctor says we are both in the pink of health,' I reassured him. That night the baby did move.

In the morning, through closed eyelids, I was aware of two little forms standing by the bed.

'Who's in bed with mommy?'

'Maybe it's a robber?'

'It looks like daddy. Let's see if he's in.'

I opened my eyes just in time to see Mousie lifting Hubert's eyelid. There was a rumbling roar. Two sets of feet pattered over to my side of the bed.

'It's daddy!' declared Mousie with finality. Soon they were all over the bed getting bouncy rides on daddy's knees and feeling his prickly face.

'Do they always wake up this early?' asked Hubert blearily.

'Always – don't you remember?'

'We must do something about this!' We did, by getting up and getting breakfast while daddy slept.

In the next few weeks everything about our life changed. The comfortable closed circumference of the life the children and I had lived was expanded by Hubert's presence. One evening was a particularly pleasant one. We had supper with friends at a club at the base in Frobisher Bay, then saw a private showing of a Peter Sellers comedy. I laughed till my sides ached. Later that night my pains started. I lay awake trying to imagine the new being that was soon to be born. We were coming to that divide when the life that had been in me must become separate. I sent my love to it and whispered, 'I dedicate what is in my womb to Thee, O God.'

The new Frobisher Bay Hospital had just opened. It looked and smelled of newness. An English lady doctor examined me, and an English midwife stayed by. I had brought embroidery and a book. The hours dragged. The other two children had both been born at exactly 7.20 in the evening. As the afternoon crept along I began to wonder if this baby would also choose that magic time. The doctor laughed at the suggestion and went home for dinner.

At six-thirty the midwife and I both realized it would not be long. At seven-twenty the baby was born and there was silence. I held my breath despite my desire to pant. Someone wiped the perspiration from my face. Then I heard a cry, reluctant at first and then gusty. A baby boy was laid on my abdomen.

'A very controlled birth, mommy,' came the clipped accents of the lady doctor. 'We had a wee bit of persuading to do to get your son to cry, but he is doing very well at it now.'

'My son!' a surge of pride, tears of relief, a sigh of love.

He lay glistening below my heart while the midwife bustled and spoke reassuringly. 'A big baby but we didn't have to cut.'

'I knew you would manage it so I wouldn't have stitches,' I said gratefully. We smiled at each other. I phoned Hubert as I was being wheeled by the desk. 'We have a baby boy, dearest. Our first son and so big, $9\frac{1}{4}$ lb.'

Was I well, he wanted to know . . . how was the baby? In my heart I blessed him for being no happier over a son than over daughters. I had read so much about men who craved a son that when our first two children had been girls I wondered in my secret heart if he was disappointed. Now I knew that it truly did not make a difference to him.

'Tristan,' said the doctor, 'Tristan . . . why such a sad name?'

'Sir Tristan was a brave and noble knight of the Round Table . . . and you know the Opera? If it had been a girl we had decided on Isolde.'

'Yes, quite. Will you call him Tris?'

'No, it will be Tristan, unless he gets a nickname like everyone else in the family.'

Chapter Two

FOR hours we had been flying over Baffin Island in a tiny single-engine Beaver. The red plane had looked like a mosquito on the tarmac of the military airfield; now it was a capsule that enclosed all that was dear and loved and safe in the immensity of an impersonal wilderness. The constant roar of the engine had a soporific effect on my two lively daughters. Baby Tristan slept in a ruffled basket at our feet. As Hubert leaned over to pick him up I instinctively reached out to support his head. Hubert's hand had already cupped itself behind the rolling head. Mutely, we looked at each other acknowledging in that one gesture that we were aware that this baby did not hold together but hung limp like a rag doll.

We were flying over the sea. Most of it was still frozen despite the advanced season, but this was not unusual. Cracks of open water were to be seen here and there but many of these were choked with drift ice.

'We're over Igloolik!' the pilot shouted back to us.

I craned to see out of the frosted porthole window. The radio crackled. The plane made a swooping pass over a handful of buildings.

'Doesn't look good. Lake still frozen!' he yelled over his shoulder.

Twice we circled low over the settlement. I said a prayer for the removal of difficulties under my breath.

'We'll try that lead over there!' The pilot handed the headphones to Hubert. 'Tell the guys to get over there with the vehicles. Doesn't look wide but we'll chance it.'

The plane dropped to what looked like a crack of blue in a field of white sea ice. I had flown enough with bush pilots to have developed an unbounded faith in their skill and an unmixed admiration for their ingenuity, but this feat surpassed anything I had ever seen before. I could imagine them telling the story tonight over beers with their buddies back in Frobisher Bay. 'There was nothing but this Goddam lead, no bigger than two fingers . . .'

The engine was running when the co-pilot jumped out on the pontoons. 'Pass me the kids,' he hollered over the roar of the engine. Hubert grabbed a little girl under each arm. 'Now the basket!' I saw the frilly basket covered over with a blanket tossed from the pontoon over the icy, gray water to the ice-floe.

'There's a baby inside!' I cried out, fighting down the panic.

'Oh, yah!' agreed the man on the ice pack who had deftly caught it.

The engine was revving up for takeoff as I stood hesitating on the pontoon.

'Jump!' someone bawled impatiently. The distance over the water seemed enormous. A hand reached out.

'The damn lead is closing in! Let's get the hell outta here!'

I jumped or was thrown by the moving plane. On the ice edge a smiling dark face appeared and a mittened hand helped me up. Ahead I could see Hubert and the diminutive shapes of the children hurrying to shore.

'My baby!' The man pointed and hurried me away, speaking in a dialect that was totally unfamiliar.

The plane was airborne. The lead had disappeared to a dark line as the ice-floe ground with a crunch into the shore ice.

A bombardier was waiting on the shore. Inside, the children sat wide-eyed and subdued. The basket was on Hubert's knees. I took out the baby and held him close as we bumped over the stones and shore ice. Hubert spoke and joked with the men in Inuktitut. After I had calmed down I began to notice that we were driving through what looked to be a carefully groomed Japanese rock garden. Only later did I realize that the island of Igloolik was composed of a series of raised shale beaches with a spiny ridge of rock as a sort of central backbone. It was over one of these beaches that we were now traveling. Eventually buildings came into view.

The first sight of habitation was incongruous. Outside a low-lying building stood a red-bearded man in a basque beret throwing shovelfuls of granular snow over enormous quantities of very red bloody slabs of meat. 'It's the Catholic priest,' Hubert shouted in explanation. 'That's the dog food for the winter.' A beautifully built stone church came into view next, then some hovels. Farther on I spied the familiar white clapboard construction of the Hudson's Bay Company trading post, flanked by a functional modern school. At last our vehicle stopped at a barrack-like building. Everyone clambered out. A few exchanges in Inuktitut that I did not understand and we were in the house. I stood in the kitchen looking around, my mind still spinning from all the new impressions. Hubert came in and put his arm around me.

'I thought of carrying you in over the threshold! This is our first real home. Welcome my darling!'

From outside the house looked like a barracks. It had originally been built as a bunkhouse for workers and was now divided into a three-bedroom house to meet changing needs. Later, Arctic construction became a specialty with certain architects, but our house predated such interest. When winter set in I was able to identify every nail in the walls, for they were white with hoarfrost. In the morning when I woke the girls I spent several minutes loosening their hair from the walls where it had frozen fast during the night. It was impossible to wash the floors in winter, for water froze instantly. We all wore woolen duffle liners and sealskin boots indoors and out, and the smaller children suffered more from the cold than the adults for they moved in the layers of cold air near the floor, whereas the taller people benefited from the warmed air that rose to the low ceiling. But all these discoveries awaited me. At that moment I only knew that Hubert had prepared this house for our arrival.

We said a prayer that our home might be a place of peace and love and that we might be of service to the community. It was 23 August 1964, ten days after Tristan's birth.

Igloolik was a quiet settlement when we arrived. It was in those days still very much a trading post and administrative center. The Innuit people lived on the land in small nomadic groups and came to Igloolik for supplies and on special occasions such as Christmas and Easter.

Next day, after Hubert went to the office I set off with the children to explore the settlement. Tristan rode comfortably in my amaut. We went to the Hudson's Bay store and invited the factor and his Scottish assistant for supper on Sunday. Our exploratory walk led us over the flat shale stones for a closer look at the stone church glimpsed on arrival. Lean scruffy dogs wandered everywhere. I remembered that in many places dogs are not fed in the summer when they are not working and have to forage on fish and offal as best they can.

The dogs seemed very interested in us and soon there was a mean-looking group close on our heels. Not a soul was to be seen. Every hair-raising story I had ever heard about children and women being attacked, mauled and killed by dogs raced through my mind. No weapon was visible but I stooped to pick up a stone. This was a movement that the dogs understood and they retreated briefly. 'Don't run!' I told myself, 'the minute you trip and fall they will be all over you, and the children won't have a chance.' Cautiously we walked back to the Hudson's Bay post. Twice I stopped and threw stones at the dogs when they came too close. Once I was lucky and clipped a dog on the rump. It yelped and retreated. Close to the trading post there was human activity and the dogs dispersed. Once safely home I let go the hands of the little girls that I had been clutching and found myself shaking. The little ones stood looking at me solemnly.

'Mousie, Bonie, listen very carefully. Never, never go up to any dog to pet it or even to get close to it. If any dog goes near you, throw a stone like you saw mummy do today. Never go outside to play without a grown-up with you. Remember . . . never . . . ever . . .!'

Hubert came in just then. 'Well, I hear you went down to the Bay. Nice little store isn't it? Not much left on the shelves this time of year of course. By the way, the factor mentioned to me that maybe you should get a white amaut cover like the other women. The only red that the local dogs see is meat and they might get the wrong idea.'

So that was it! We had been the victims of dogs with no color sophistication!

Beside the factor and his assistant there was red-bearded Father Fournier and the mechanic who were not Innuit. In the fall there would be more Euro-Canadians in the settlement, Hubert assured me. The teachers would soon be arriving, the mounties would be back from patrol and one of them had a wife who was now out on holidays, even a nurse had been promised. In the evening silent visitors would appear. The Innuit people never knocked or exchanged greetings. When I used the Labrador words for Goodbye – 'Aksonai', they smiled politely but were obviously mystified. They would come singly or in groups, look at magazines, talk to Hubert if he was in, drink tea if it was offered, play with the children and then silently leave.

After a week Hubert announced that he had to go on a trip to one of the nomadic camps on the western coast of Baffin Island. Seeing my dismay, he explained patiently that he was the area administrator and that it was an integral part of his job to visit the camps.

'But we have just arrived,' I wanted to cry. 'You can't leave me alone here by myself. I can only talk to two people in this whole settlement. I'll die of loneliness. Don't go, please! You are my only link with sanity, with the outside world.'

Was it pride that forbade me to say any of those things or some unexpected reservoir of courage that made me say instead, 'We'll be all right. Don't worry about us.'

But it was a gray day when I stood on the shingle beach waving to Hubert as their dory chugged off into the blackness of open water. Two days before the wind had shifted and the rotting sea ice had been cleared away. The boat soon became but a speck on the immensity of the Arctic Sea under the endless low gray sky. I stood desolately on the shingle beach till even the memory of the engine's chugging had vanished in the silence.

That evening as the little girls and I sat over supper a woman walked in silently and sat down with us.

'Would you like some lemon pie?' I gestured. She smiled and lifted her eyebrows.

The children went to bed without protest. I nursed the baby at the table, comfortable in the woman's companionship. She took out two pieces of sealskin that I recognized as the sole and tongue of a boot. She chewed the pieces to soften them, then sewed the sole with tiny delicate pleats to the tongue. My mending basket was full and we sewed in comfortable silence. At one point, she stopped and leaned across the table and spoke to me, pointing to the sea. I caught the word for husband and boat. In her eyes was a compassion that my heart understood. Unbidden tears clouded my sight.

'EEEE . . . eeee,' a long low expelled breath sound. I came to know it well.

At ten o'clock she left silently without a goodbye. Later I was to know her as Ujarak's wife.

Kneading satin-smooth dough made me think of the texture of a baby's skin! On the counter by the window sat six-month-old Tristan in a baby seat. A rattle hung within reach, on a wall can-opener. He did not reach for it. I went over to rattle it and his eyes moved reluctantly and slowly focused on the red discs. Just then, from the ice-porch, came the sounds of stomping feet. Hubert entered in a cloud of cold air.

'I'll be bringing six men over for mug-up in half an hour,' he said, giving me a kiss. I snuggled up to him delighting in having him home at unexpected times. With his arm still around me he turned to the baby.

'Well, if it isn't Moose-Foot himself!' Ujarak's wife had brought the baby beautifully embroidered moose-hide boots. Smoked moose hide is very fragrant and Tristan's sisters developed the habit of sniffing the air before asking, 'Where is Moose-Foot?' Moose-Foot, and later Moose, became Tristan's pet name.

Tristan's eyes moved in slow motion, from the rattle to his father's face. Like the sun coming out on a hazy day, a broad slow smile permeated his features.

'Come on up and play with old dad! Way up in the air we go . . . Whoop down again!'

I watched for a change in expression, for a squeal of delight. The same hazy smile hung on his face, although perhaps his eyes widened a bit.

'Well, I must be getting back,' Hubert announced, putting the baby back in the seat. 'When did the girls start reaching for toys?' he asked at the door.

'At about this age,' I answered, looking down at the dough I was kneading. Soon after there was a polite knock and Marjorie, the English nurse, came in.

'Just in time for a cup of tea before the crowd from the office arrives,' I said, welcoming her. As I made the tea I watched her talking to the baby.

'Here, take my finger!' I heard her say in her precise accent. As I put the cups on the tray I saw Tristan regarding her blankly. She placed his fingers around her index; after a moment the little hand dropped listlessly.

'Tea is ready. Come to the living room, I see the men coming with the ice. They have to leave the door open and it gets so cold in the kitchen.'

We took the baby and hurried away just as the skinbooted parkaed men began to load great blocks of ice into the heat coiled tank behind the kitchen. Ice, I had found out, takes a long time to melt. We had all learned to conserve every drop of water.

It had been such a relief when Marjorie had arrived in September. At last a woman friend to talk to! Her English reticence and my Polish effusiveness had finally found a balance. Ours, though not an intimate friendship, had a quality of warmth and mutual respect. We chatted about the affairs of the village comfortable in the knowledge that we both avoided gossip.

'I hear that we will soon have the radio-telephones installed. It will be such a help to be able to consult with the doctors in Frobisher Bay on some of the cases! Evacuations won't be so complicated either . . .'

'Once the darkness comes, evacuations are still going to be difficult. Planes won't land here without a runway. At any rate, Marjorie, anything you do here is better than what the people had before when there was only a lay dispenser.'

'You should have the baby checked when you go on holidays,' Marjorie volunteered with a certain embarrassment in her voice.

'Yes, of course we will. He does seem a bit slower than the girls, and I couldn't help wondering . . .' my voice trailed off.

'Not to worry,' Marjorie spoke quickly, and with a forced lightness. 'Not to worry at all!' Then as she put on her Fair Isle mittens she added, 'Lovely to have tea in a cup. It tastes so much better than in a mug.'

As the men came in with Hubert I excused myself to feed Tristan. We lay on the bed together. He nursed eagerly at first, then, seeming to grow tired, he dozed off. I stroked his cheeks to make him suck. There was plenty of milk, sometimes it would dribble out when his mouth grew slack in sleep. I stroked his fair hair and sang to him softly. At such times the golden strands of love fell, weaving us into their magic design.

There was something standing in the shadows of my heart.

17

Lurking on the periphery of my inner vision was a dark shape. I was troubled as I laid the baby in the basket. It would not have been safe to leave the girls in a basket at this age. They would have bounced and rolled out. Tristan lay quietly sleeping. There is a song in the opera *Hansel and Gretel* calling the angels to watch while the children slept. I tried to hum it . . . two at the head . . . two at the feet . . . two at each side. I tried to picture angels, heavenly beings. Could six crowd around this little crib? Dropping my pretense I called out to God in my heart, 'Help this little son of mine.' The strange shadow lurking in my mind stirred and stepped out.

There is something wrong with this baby!

But I refused to face that shadow. Quickly I walked out of the room closing the door on the little crib. (Did I leave it surrounded by angels or cooped up with the dark shadow of my dread?)

Isolation . . . the cold formed a cocoon around us . . . the darkness encapsulated us in a world without horizon . . . both cold and dark locked us in the islands of warmth and light that were our homes. But it is not isolation of the physical kind that brings the low-level anxiety that hums in the head without ceasing and makes some get cabin fever and others leave the north vowing never to return. It is the lack of a warm reassuring support group of family and friends; that can alone keep off the chill darkness.

The radio-telephone was installed in Igloolik that fall. For three hours a day over lines that crackled and faded we had a link with the outside world. It was through the radio-telephone that we got the message that Dr R. was coming. On the rare occasions that the medical officer visited the settlement Marjorie was in a flurry. She lined up all her cases and sent her interpreter on countless errands. To the question 'What on earth shall I feed him?' we responded with a dinner invitation.

Dr R., although of slight build, filled the room with his affability. At dinner we were entertained equally by Mousie and Bonie and by Dr R.'s jokes and stories. From our Frobisher Bay days, we knew this gruff bearded man who was truly interested in the welfare of the Innuit and fought the bureaucracy on their behalf. They, in turn, rewarded him with their confidence and affection.

At different times during the meal Dr R. glanced at Tristan who lay listlessly amid the toys in his playpen. To avoid the icy drafts that plague northern houses we had raised the baby's playpen on five big milk powder canisters, so he was chair height and we could easily see him from the table. After one of these inquiring glances I ventured, 'Tristan has had a bit of a cold.' Just then, the baby gave an odd whooping kind of cough. Marjorie looked uneasily at her plate.

'I'll come down to have a look at him after clinic tomorrow,' Dr R. said. He did not look again in the direction of the baby.

Next day he arrived toward noon. 'Now let's have a look at him!' he said in his gruff manner. Tristan lay motionless during the examination.

'What's the matter with his eyes?'

'I don't know; sometimes he looks up . . . as if to heaven,' I said lamely.

'Hmm. Have him given a full examination when you go out. When's your leave?'

'July or August.'

'Hmm. Well, I see my pilot going out on the ice. See you next time. The dinner was delightful.' He gave Tristan a troubled look. A slow radiant smile spread over the baby's face. Dr R. smiled back and was gone.

Now the dark shape of my concern stood out more clearly from the shadows. In the next two weeks Tristan's cold did not get better. The baby in his basket (six months old and still in his basket!) lay wide-eyed, inert. Only his eyes moved. They traveled as if on a track from the left upper corner to the right bottom, as if he were drawing a diagonal on the ceiling. Back and forth, back and forth, back and forth. It made me slightly dizzy to look at him and a feeling of nausea rose up from my stomach. Was it nausea, or was it fear?

My dread had no face but lurked constantly in the periphery of every waking thought. Hubert and I brought it up with Marjorie. 'The other children had turned over and reached out for things at this age. Why does this baby just lie there its eyes moving in diagonal patterns?'

Marjorie did not know, but she tried to be reassuring. Her precise English accent pushed back the dark shadow momentarily. While she spoke it retreated, but as soon as she was gone

19

it stood out more boldly than ever against the remembered forced cheerfulness. Her visits became infrequent. 'So busy!' she would say. She is uncomfortable with me because something is wrong with the baby, I thought.

In the evenings Hubert and I would sit and talk or read. The dark Arctic night had us in its grip. The plane that had brought Dr R. was the last that we would be getting till the light returned. At times the dark shadow would appear to us both and we would cautiously talk about Tristan's slow development. But what could we do? We were locked into immobility by the coldness and the darkness outside and within ourselves.

Chapter Three

IN the scythe-like wind we stood on the sea ice among the villagers watching the first rays of the sun fan out over the horizon. Was it cold or gladness that brought tears which froze instantly? Out of darkness into light . . . is that our soul's journey as well?

The return of the sun and the day that the last piece of fresh fruit is doled out are milestones noted on the calendars of northerners. That is why I will always remember the day, for on it I gave the last two oranges to Mousie and Bonie. They had gone off to share them with their friends and I was alone with the baby. I pulled the string of his music box before lifting him up to the changing table. The diaper was dry but filled with a chalky colored stool.

'Have the girls been feeding you chalk when they were playing school?' I babbled on cheerfully. But a cold chill passed over me.

Something was more than usually wrong. He did not nurse but cried with weak tired sobs. A bottle filled with diluted apple juice was no more successful than the milk had been. It seemed that he was too feeble to suck. But when I enlarged the hole and squirted the liquid in his mouth he turned his face away and lay limp in my arms.

Alarmed, I called Marjorie. The customary pallor of the little face seemed to have intensified; a complete lethargy had replaced his usual reluctance to exert himself. Next day was no better. Marjorie prescribed a broad spectrum antibiotic. By late afternoon she suggested, rather diffidently, that he should be evacuated to the hospital at Frobisher Bay. Another of her patients was going and the Mountie was also traveling out, so he could take Tristan. I told Hubert. He took the inert form and talked and crooned to it. With what appeared a great effort, Tristan focused on his father; another supreme effort brought a shadow of a smile. Then exhausted, he hung limp in Hubert's arms.

I expressed my milk and tried to feed him from a dropper. He threw up. Slowly, I began to accept that he had to be evacuated. All day I watched by him listening to his shallow breathing. *No, no I will not let this child go . . . I will not let it go out into that merciless cold . . . I'll never see him again . . . never . . . never. If he must go then I will take him out. He will not go without me*. Now that I was no longer a passive observer I felt a surge of strength. The bombardier would be leaving early in the morning, I had to pack not only for Frobisher Bay but for the possibility that we would go on to Montreal.

It was late before all the preparations were completed. Silently, I stole into the dim nursery to take another look at Tristan. Immediately on entering the room, I was aware of another presence; it was as though someone else were in the room. In the soft light by the changing table I could see the familiar orange crib, my sewing machine, all was as before yet the feeling of another person in the room was unmistakable. Tristan was awake. I took the baby and put him in the double bed, between Hubert and me. My grandfather's Ukrainian lullaby finally made his lids close.

Is there such a thing as an angel of death, I wondered as I lay beside him? I was still aware of the presence I had first encountered in the nursery. What was it? Was it the imaginings of an overwrought mind? Then as I began to relax I remembered . . .

We were living in a cottage by the sea in Newfoundland. It was evening and I had been brushing my long hair and counting the strokes, fifty-eight, fifty-nine. It had felt like a soft breeze through my hair, my brush had dropped to my protruding belly, for I was pregnant with Nadine, our first child. A warm loving presence felt close to me.

'Hubert, I have just had such a strong feeling of your mother's presence. Just as if she was right here with me. This will be her first grandchild. I wonder if she has been thinking of us just now!'

We talked of Toos, of her suffering for so many years with a spreading cancer. We spoke of her gentleness and loving qualities, and marveled at her patience. Later that night we had been roused from sleep by the insistent knocking of a neighbor. Since we had no phone in the cottage, the call from Holland had come to him. Hubert dressed and hurried out. There was no need for me to wait for his return to know what had happened. I sat up and began to read the prayer for the dead – for Toos.

It was that same gentle presence that I felt beside the baby now. Softly I breathed, 'Thank you for being here with Moose . . . thank you . . . Toos.'

The alarm rang. We were both surprised that we had slept. Tristan lay waxen between us, his breathing skimming the surface of life. I dressed in layers of warm clothing, then bundled the baby up the same way. Hot water bottles were filled and stuffed into the folds of the blankets and quilts that enfolded him.

When we were all ready to go Hubert looked critically at my boots. 'You'll be cold in those! Take my white army boots. They'll be too big but they'll be warm. Skin boots are fine for in the house and in the village but sitting in the cold for hours . . . you'll be more comfortable in something more roomy.' I compromised by taking my skin boots along with me.

Mousie and Bonie stood silent and wide-eyed looking at the preparations.

'We'll be brave, mummy!' Mousie announced and took Bonie's hand in hers for emphasis.

As I went out the door I caught a glimpse of the kitchen thermometer. Fifty below, at least there was no wind!

Heinz, the German-born mechanic, was driving the bombardier. Beside him I caught sight of the kind face of Ujarak half hidden in the wolf-fur of his hood. He was the elder of the village and the unerring guide on bombardier trips over terrain so flat, white and lacking in relief that most non-Innuit found it impossible to navigate.

The benches in a bombardier run along the sides of the vehicle and not across as in a car or bus. Across from me sat the Mountie resplendent in his 'dress' parka. Beside Ujarak sat a man I knew only as Jobie's father. Jobie was the little boy who lived across the way from our house and was a frequent visitor and playmate of Mousie's. In the corner sat a thin woman who was unfamiliar to me. This must be the medical evacuation Marjorie had told me about.

After half an hour of the most punishingly bumpy ride I had ever endured, I looked with new-found admiration at Heinz and Jobie's father who made this trip weekly for mail and spare parts. All my muscles ached from trying not to fall off the narrow seat and from holding Tristan in such a way that I would absorb the shocks on his behalf. It was bitterly cold, the kind of cutting, merciless, pervasive cold typical of the Arctic.

The Mountie shouted something across to me. It must have been that the rough part was over, for soon we were traveling over relatively smooth sea ice. It was still dark. Ujarak sat beside Heinz pointing first one way then that. I felt safe.

As though struggling against the weight of the intense cold, a faint light crept over the horizon. It was the first week in February, we would have a few hours of light and hours of dusk. Looking out of the porthole windows, I noticed the blowing snow. A wind was picking up. Soon the expanse of ice around us was a moving sea of undulating swirling white. The bombardier gave a lurch and began to climb onto land. Somewhere on this promontory, Hubert had installed a half-way hut for travelers. It was painted international orange. I strained to catch sight of it. A cup of tea and a chance to stretch our legs would be really welcome.

The bombardier came to a jarring halt. German expletives exploded into the frosty air. A glance out the window confirmed that we had not stopped for a mug-up at the cabin. Jobie's father and Heinz took a tool box from under the seat and went out. There were sounds of metal being banged and harsh voices. I thought it had been cold in the bombardier but the blast of outside air that attacked us when the door opened was marrow-chilling. The mountie came back announcing that the track had broken.

Under the blanket, Tristan's face looked so wan my heart froze. One tiny puff of condensation emerged from his mouth and his eyelids fluttered and opened.

All of us exuded clouds as we spoke and breathed. They looked like the little white clouds found in cartoon comics. I almost expected to see the conversation appear in black print in each one. Only from Tristan there was no white billowing breath-cloud. His was the thickness of three-ply knitting wool. With mittened hands I groped in the folds of the blanket for the hot water bottles. Two had frozen solid, one had burst. I discarded them under the seat.

The two men returned slapping their hands and smiling. The engine started up again. We were moving. Through the porthole window I strained for sight of the orange cabin. After ten minutes the bombardier lurched and stopped. This time Heinz sat hunched over the wheel muttering in German; then, as if having run dry in that language, he switched to English. The Mountie moved to the front and the four men had a long discussion in Inuktitut and English. Reluctantly, they took out the tool box and went out into the blowing wind.

I stole a look at the woman who sat at the back of the bombardier. She was huddled into the corner, eyes closed, withdrawn into herself. Instinctively, I recognized the wisdom of such a withdrawal to keep from using any unnecessary energy, hoarding what little heat remains to simply keep alive.

Ujarak reached under the front seat and drew out some tea, sugar, mugs and a kettle which he replenished several times with snow. He roused the woman in the corner, speaking to her sharply in Inuktitut and handing her a cup of steaming sweetened tea. Next he gave me a mug and looked a long time at the porcelain face of Tristan. He held my eyes and sighed, nodding his head. I felt strangely comforted. Heinz and his helper came in to warm their hands on the mugs of tea. With a sickening rush of empathy I felt how excruciatingly cold it was to work on the metal track. The wind howled like a hungry, patient wolf.

Next, Ujarak produced caribou skins from a back locker and proceeded to line the interior of the bombardier. Most of the wind's incursions were checked and even the dismal howl was muffled by the thick fur of the skin.

Jobie's father, then Heinz returned. Both looked dispirited. They would try once more. Maybe we could make it to the half-way shack, I heard someone say. As one body, we held our breath when the bombardier started moving, and exhaled it in a sigh, when it stopped a few hundred feet later. Heinz's silence was ominous.

Jobie's father and the Mountie began conferring. I noticed that he kept glancing at his feet, that were clad in a handsome pair of skin boots intricately inset with contrasting sealskin in geometric patterns. He came over to me. 'We're going to a hunting camp about two hours' walk from here. They have fast dogs there and they'll either come to get you or they can send word to Hall Beach. The only thing is . . .' he paused embarrassed and stole a look at Hubert's army boots.

'Look, would you like to wear these Arctic army issue boots? They would keep you much warmer than the fancy skin boots you have on,' I said, using Hubert's reasoning of the morning.

'Well, if you don't mind? Mine are on the small side.'

'No problem, I have my skin boots right here under the seat.'

As we changed boots he filled me in, 'Only have one liner . . . no way of knowing this would happen . . . Heinz did all he could . . . damn track keeps breaking . . . no way to mend it out here.'

The two men set off. I watched them disappear into the trackless whiteness. Like the woman, huddled into herself in the corner, I wanted to retreat into some inner space. My mind tried to calculate how much daylight remained.

Between Heinz and Ujarak there was a consultation after which Ujarak went out brandishing his wide-bladed snow-knife. He was back in a few minutes and with a brief word to Heinz put the knife away. 'Ujarak says the snow isn't right for a snow house, we'll be warmer here,' Heinz explained to me. Next they set to rummaging around in the side lockers of the bombardier and came up with several flares. 'Too early to send them up yet,' Heinz muttered, 'they won't have missed us yet. In a couple of hours they'll start looking and the flares will show up better in the dark.'

The warmth of Hubert's care seemed to envelop me. It was he who had requisitioned the flares, the primus and the skins as essential equipment for every bombardier making the Hall Beach run. The hours that followed were punctuated by the lighting of the primus and the drinking of countless cups of sweet tea. I had opened up my sweaters and placed the baby as close as possible to my bosom to get my body heat. I rubbed his back and chafed his little feet in the bunting bag. There was no response. Only the thin wavering line of his breath indicated life. All the bottles had frozen, but remembering how Innuit women feed their babies, I put my mouth up to his and squirted some warm sweet tea into his mouth. Most of it dribbled out but I saw several painful swallows, so I persisted as Ujarak looked on approvingly.

Time passed, it drifted by like the wind-blown snow, it covered over the tracks of our lives. There was no yesterday, no tomorrow, there was only survival now. Suddenly I laughed. So I had wanted adventure! I wonder, does God have a sense of humor?

Heinz and Ujarak went out to send out flares. They were gone a long time. 'We thought we should find a hill,' Heinz explained when they returned.

More sweet tea.

Movement outside. The door burst open and in tumbled two laughing figures dressed in the double-layered caribou clothing that is standard hunting dress of the Innuit in mid-winter. No, they had not come from the camp to which the Mountie and Jobie's father had set out. Their camp was south of Hall Beach and they were going to Igloolik to trade.

I noticed that their hoods had been made from the heads of the caribou and the animals' ears had been left intact. Some Innuit seamstress, with a real sense of fun, had made these men look like the god Pan in a northern version! They had materialized from the blank vastness and enlivened our tedium with their irrepressible laughter and jokes. Too soon their furry shapes rolled out of the bombardier and their shouts to the dogs faded in the wind.

I tried to picture Hubert at the radio-telephone. By now he would be wondering why we had not yet reached Hall Beach. I felt an ache for the worry and the sense of powerlessness he would feel. I had experienced it when, as radio operator assisting at an evacuation, all I could do was wait, relay messages and make calculated guesses about daylight, weather and chances of survival.

Light was leaving the sky like a sigh. How many flares had they sent up? How many hours had we sat here? I saw Heinz take out a flare and rummage around again. Was that the last one? 'Why doesn't Steward (the Hall Beach mechanic) get off his butt and get one of his chicken-wired machines down here!' I heard Heinz mutter. 'Well, the darker it gets the easier it'll be to see the flares!' he added. He went out with the last flare.

In the fading light I watched the thin line that was Tristan's breath go from the thickness of three-ply wool to that of two-strand embroidery cotton. Now it was a single thin strand that often broke, then came in a tiny puff like the dot after an exclamation point. By the time the men returned it was too dark to

27

see anything, and I sat mutely rocking the baby back and forth on the narrow bench.

Yet I did not feel despair. The warm close presence of Toos was still beside me. I could feel it more easily in the dark as my mind was emptying of all anxieties and of all hopes. At last I prayed. Out of the complete emptiness that was now inside me, I prayed humbly knowing myself to be a dot on the vast emptiness of the frozen Arctic, knowing I was holding a dying child to my heart, knowing that the long darkness was closing in.

Heinz's anger was like a light going on in the cabin. It woke me from my reverie, even the woman in the corner stirred. He rummaged and fussed. At last, in triumph, he emerged with a prize, a smashed up cardboard box. He took it with him and once more disappeared into the darkness. The wind had died down, the night was clear and even colder than the day.

Ujarak was making more tea. I refused the mug, but Ujarak forced it into my hand speaking insistently. Amazing what comfort flowed from that sweet tea. It did not reach my extremities, so I began to stamp my feet and rub my mittened hands. Ujarak put his face close to the baby's, hoping to catch the warmth of his breath on his cheek, for it was now quite dark. Outside the stars were out and there was a wisp of moonlight. There was a sound. Somewhere from that enormous Arctic emptiness, came a sound. It was not the wind. It was the sound of a motor. In the cabin of the bombardier no one moved; for a minute no one breathed. Then it was unmistakable. Heinz and Ujarak rushed outside.

It had been the burning box that the rescue vehicle had seen. I caught a quick glimpse of a panoply of stars and of a barefaced moon, as we were hurried into the other bombardier. The glow from the instrument panel cast an eerie shine into the cabin but I could not see my watch nor any breath coming from Tristan.

The rest of the trip was an ecstasy of discomfort. The cold had seeped into every crevasse of my being, and as we were jostled and bumped it seemed as though a thousand jagged ice crystals of pain broke in me at every movement.

Someone was saying, 'The plane has been kept waiting in the hangar. Not long now . . . can't you see the lights of Hall

28

Beach?' But I could not see the lights. It took every remaining ounce of effort simply to endure.

Looking down at his report the doctor said, 'You realize, of course, that the baby will not likely live through the night. There is danger of dehydration . . .' Then he looked up and asked in a tone tinged with compassion, 'What will you do? It's after midnight and it looks as if you had a rough time.'

My neighbors from Apex Hill were coming down to get me. I sat by Tristan's bed. He was awake and regarded me with serious eyes.

'You must get better, Moose-Foot. You must pull through. We love you so much. You must live.'

He closed his eyes wearily. I hummed Brahms's lullaby . . . 'may the angels watch over you'. Yes, now we need all those angels, two at the head, two at the foot and two at each side. As I left the ward I felt bereft of a presence. Returning for a moment I encountered it again. Toos was staying with Tristan. Heartened, I left the darkened ward. Even as we drove to Apex Hill I made arrangements to return to the hospital in the early morning.

At six o'clock I jumped up as if some internal alarm had rung. Weariness made me misdial the hospital number several times.

'Baby Schuurman . . . Oh, yes, admitted last night . . . an emergency. Yes, I'll go and check.'

The voice came back on the line and I could sense the hesitation. 'When the doctor comes in he will give you the full report.'

'Look, just tell me if he's still alive,' I heard my voice say in unfamiliarly harsh tones.

'Yes.'

'Thanks, I'll be right over.'

But I could not get right over. Snow had been falling all night in great heavy flakes. The wind was picking up. It was developing into a proper northern blizzard. The road from Apex Hill to the hospital was swiftly piling up with drifts. It was impassable.

I was back on the phone. The same nurse came on the line, her voice became defensive.

'I can't get over! The road is closed because of the storm.'

'You can rest assured that everything will be done for the baby,' came the patronizing reply.

'Have you given him a bottle?'

'Everything is being done . . .'

I interrupted with a bad grace born of desperation, 'Just tell me if you gave him a bottle.'

There was a hesitation, then, 'Just a minute and I'll check.'

'He wouldn't take it,' she announced, coming back on the line.

'His greatest danger now is dehydration,' I heard myself repeating what the doctor had said last night. Then out spilled the story of his illness, of our being stuck on the way to catch the plane. At last I paused, spent.

'I'll see what I can do. Where can I call you back?' Her voice was no longer brisk and patronizing but warm and caring.

In an hour she called back. There was no disguising the note of triumph in her voice as she told me, 'He took two ounces but I had to use a big dropper! I'm going off duty now, but I'll leave instructions for the nurse on the next shift.'

When I hung up the receiver my hands were shaking. My hostess put her arm around me. 'Was that the hospital?'

I nodded, unable to speak.

'My dear,' she said comforting me, 'he may never have grown up to be normal. You must see that it may be just as well.'

With an effort I steeled myself to answer. 'He's alive!'

All day the snow blew and the wind howled. It was an effort to go next door to visit friends who had invited me to lunch. I had to hold on to a line that had been strung between the two houses.

The doctor phoned in the afternoon. 'Assuming that he survives till tomorrow, we will fly him out to Montreal, for a complete analysis. As you know, the flight is cancelled for today.'

'What treatment is he receiving?'

'The nurse in Igloolik put him on a broad spectrum antibiotic. Until we can diagnose the specific problem, we are continuing that medication.'

At each change of shift I phoned the head nurse asking that they feed him with a dropper and tell me how much he took.

How long can a baby survive on sugared water, I asked myself, leaning my hot forehead against the double-glazed window. Outside was unleashed fury. Objects left outside were being hurled about by the gale-force winds. Inside I tried to find stillness. 'God, my God, look after my little son, please send nurses who will take time to feed him and hold him. Don't leave him alone, don't abandon him.' For a long time I prayed. The memory of Toos' presence was reassuring. When I awoke it was silent. The wind was no longer rattling the windows or tearing at the roof.

'Good news . . . the highway crew will take you back to the hospital on their first trip down on the snowplow.' Then, seeing my reaction my hostess added, 'It's good to see you smile again.'

I took the stairs two at a time up to the baby ward. There was lusty crying but it was not coming from his crib. From where he lay came a low wail like the plaintive mew of a smothered kitten. 'Moose, Moosey!' The tiny form looked smaller, diminished in the twenty-four hours separation. 'Moose-Foot!' I said more loudly.

He responded to my stroking by opening his eyes. We looked at each other. 'I'm proud of you, son. You made it! Now I am going to give you some formula, you'll never get your strength up on water and sugar.'

Morning dawned gray and cold but not stormy. Tristan was being sent to Montreal to the St. Justine Hospital. The tentative diagnosis was hydrocephalus. I asked for an explanation of the condition. Water on the brain? But his head is not particularly big! His body looks so small now because it is emaciated.

Chapter Four

THERE was gray slushy snow on the sidewalk and mounds of dirty snow piled up around the trees and near the road. But the wide steps leading up to L'Hôpital St. Justine were swept clear.

On the children's ward the little ones lay unmoving, in neatly made beds. The room I entered was immaculate. One crib was empty. The former occupant, a hydrocephalic baby, had been operated on yesterday. The other crib held a tiny familiar form tucked in tightly between snowy sheets. Gratefully, I lifted him up and pressed him to my thumping heart. Pale he looked as always, but today there was an aura of pain about him. I talked to him but he responded as if drugged.

A starched nurse came in and announced that the head nurse wanted to see me. She frowned at the disturbed bed but said nothing. Only when the strictly observed visiting hours were over and the second chime had rung did I put Moose down. His eyes followed me part of the way to the door, then closed.

The head nurse was a nun and formidable. I had been brought up in a convent school and I had since then weighed many of my childhood experiences there in the balance of life and found them wanting. No longer was I easily intimidated. So now I took the lead in the interview. My French was halting on medical subjects but adequate.

'Is it not strange,' I inquired, 'that Dr M. still has not consented to see me and discuss the condition of my child? It is four days since my son was admitted.'

The chart was lowered and the head nurse spoke through thin pressed lips, totally ignoring my question. 'Dr M. has seen the baby and consulted with other physicians. They no longer think it is a hydrocephalic condition. Yesterday they did an encephalogram.'

'Please explain, I don't know these medical terms.'

She paused to look me in the eye. I had a feeling that had I been a little girl again I would have been completely cowed and speechless. Her eyes were dark and cold. I felt as though I were looking into a deep well in the summer, and the unexpected damp chill made me shudder. As she gave me the results of various tests, I repeatedly interrupted her for explanations. It was still not clear to me. Something of the stiffness in her manner relaxed. She paused as I stood trying to assimilate the information.

'Imagine a bowl of porridge,' she said in an altered voice, the voice of a gifted teacher taking up the challenge to instruct a slow student. 'Imagine that someone takes a pepper shaker and shakes small specks of pepper all over the porridge. Not too much, but all over. At one spot the pepper shaker slips and a lot of pepper spills out. In that place the porridge is gray, with pepper specks close together. That bowl of porridge is like Tristan's brain; there is damage all over. The black specks are the dead brain cells. The cerebellum has a good deal more damage than the other areas.'

'What does the cerebellum control?' I asked, vainly trying to recall the various parts of the brain and their functions from my psychology course.

'Several things . . . mainly motor coordination.'

'But why does the doctor never see me? Why does he never call?'

Her lips were once more a thin straight line. 'The doctor is very busy,' she announced with hauteur. Then relenting, she added, 'I have given him your message and your telephone number.'

I did not see the mirror-bright floors, nor the well swept stairs as I left the hospital. I did not notice the dirty snow in mounds around the trees, nor the slushy gray snow on the pavement. In the middle of the block I stopped rooted to the spot by the sound of children's voices. For long moments I listened to the shouts, the laughter, and the calling back and forth. From deep within me surfaced the realization. 'Your son will never be like that . . . He has brain damage . . . brain damage . . . brain damage . . . He will never be normal, he may not live . . . brain damage, killed cells, black pepper dots over white porridge . . . never . . . never . . . never . . .'

Gradually, the gray winter day came back into focus. With

new interest I studied the faces of the people I passed. Young faces laughing – still untouched by shadow; an elderly square woman with flat slavic cheek bones – she would understand for she has suffered; a carefully groomed man in a business suit – would he know what it is like to experience . . . NEVER.

A policeman on the corner gave me directions on how to get home. 'It's a long walk, lady, over three miles. Are you sure you're all right? There is a bus you can catch on that corner . . .'

I walked home thinking of Buddha. A woman had come to him grieving and inconsolable after the death of her son. Lord Buddha had sent her out to get a grain of mustard seed from a household untouched by sorrow. Everywhere she went in search of her grain of mustard seed she found human misery and heartbreak. She returned without a grain of mustard seed but cured of her obsessive grief. One great tear rolled down my cheek onto the gray snow, a tear for the woman without a grain of . . . mustard seed.

The apartment was silent and empty. I took off my coat and boots and stood in the kitchen barefoot. On the table was my prayer book. I opened it and read. A clock ticked on a shelf.

Dispel my grief by Thy bounty and generosity, O God, my God . . . did God, the God I had prayed to and talked to all these years, see my pain, know my grief?

And banish mine anguish through . . . Thy might. The radiator hummed. My anguish – is it this feeling of pain all over? This dry-eyed pain – is that anguish?

Thou seest me, O my God, with my face set toward Thee at a time when sorrows have compassed me on every side. So it must have been like this for others! Bahá'u'lláh wrote this prayer knowing people would feel powerless – alone – their hearts breaking.

Thou beholdest, O my Lord, the things which have befallen me in Thy days! Now the flood-gates opened and tears, cleansing tears, washed away the anxiety, the anger, the frustration, the bitterness that had been gathering like suppurating matter within my heart.

'Do you read me? Over.' Speaking so loudly into the ivory telephone seemed incongruous. I tried to imagine Hubert sitting at the radio-telephone in the dining room. The children must be in bed now.

The line crackled. The voice barely recognizable except for the strong Dutch accent said. 'I read you. I read you . . . Over.' The static noises grew worse. The Montreal operator came on the line, 'We seem to be losing your connection. I will call you back.'

How will I tell Hubert the news over a crackling, fading telephone connection. Everyone else in the community will be listening in. I did not blame them for tuning in to the radio frequency but it did not give us much privacy.

Once more the phone rang. 'I read you loud and clear!' Hubert sounded elated. 'How are you, darling? How is the baby? Over.'

'The baby's condition is stable. He had an encephalogram. There is widespread brain damage. Over.'

Silence.

'Did you read me? Over.'

'I read you,' came a hollow-sounding voice.

'I can't get to see or talk to the doctor. It's really frustrating. How are the girls? I miss you so much. Over.'

'When can you come home?' asked the hollow voice.

'Soon, I hope! Soon my dearest. Over.'

Days passed, then weeks. I demanded to see the doctor, to get some definite report. Instead, I met the cold eyes of the head nurse. Finally, in desperation I announced that I was going home and taking the baby with me, unless I could be given some reason in writing why he had to stay. 'If you do that,' the head nurse warned severely, her eyes very black and cold, 'the hospital could refuse you any further treatment!'

My departure was carefully arranged to coincide with a charter flight from Hall Beach so that we would not have to hazard another trip by bombardier. A half hour before leaving the house to pick up Tristan at the hospital, the phone rang.

'Allo, Mme Schuurman? Ici Dr M.' I was so astounded to hear at last the voice of the mysterious and elusive Dr M. that I was speechless.

'Madame, si vous preferez que je vous parle en anglais . . .' mistaking my silence for lack of understanding he switched to a fluent idiomatic English.

Having recovered from my initial shock, I began to pay

attention to what he was saying. 'The tests were not conclusive. No exact diagnosis is possible. Would you bring the baby in to see me in the summer when you come south on holidays? So unfortunate that we were not able to meet. The discharge papers are signed and at the desk.'

I was putting on my boots when the phone rang again. Should I pick it up? I could see from the window that the car was at the front door. The plane for Frobisher was leaving in two hours and it was a long drive to the airport. I picked up the receiver.

'Je regrette, Madame . . . so sorry to inform you at the last moment like this. Your son has a high fever. There is an outbreak of measles on the children's ward. We cannot release him. You will not be able to visit him . . . How long? A week, maybe more . . . until it is all cleared up. You do understand our position, Madame!'

The usual chorus of dog howls greeted our plane's arrival at Igloolik. My amaut was empty. Immediately came the inevitable questions. 'Where's the baby? Where is Moose-Foot?'

In the next couple of days everyone in the village dropped in for a visit. They would peer at me curiously and studiously avoid asking about Tristan.

'How was Montreal?'

'Much milder than here.'

'Did you see any good plays or movies?'

'The visiting hours at the hospital ended at half past eight, so it was too late to go to a movie or play after that.'

'Too bad. I heard you got some good shopping in.'

I was incredulous and asked Hubert about it. 'They must be afraid to hurt your feelings,' he suggested.

'Hurt my feelings!' I exploded. 'It feels as if everyone in the settlement thinks I have murdered my child and is too polite to mention it!'

Even Marjorie avoided the topic of the baby. 'How are you? How was the trip back?' she asked in her clipped brisk way. 'No, I simply can't stay for tea. So many people down with this nasty flu. Must run . . .'

A great aloneness enveloped me. Only Ujarak enquired

about Tristan. As the tension and anxiety built up in me, I became a fountain of tears at the slightest provocation. When another week had gone by without any word from the hospital my agitation became extreme. Hubert bundled up the little girls and took them out visiting. 'You need some time alone,' he said as they left, 'to do some praying.'

'To do some praying !!!' I fumed, 'What I need is a clear line to the hospital. I need some information about my son. I need a doctor that does not play cat and mouse with me but tells me what is wrong. I need friends who will talk to me and not pretend that my baby does not exist . . . and he tells me to PRAY!'

Northern houses are not good for fuming in. There is no hall to pace. You can't break the dishes because they belong to the government and can't be replaced till next sea-lift. So after banging a few books around I fell onto the sofa. I felt as though great waves of sea-green water were crashing over me, blinding my vision, rushing in my ears. My breath came in gasps.

'God, help me! I'm going under!' I yelled into the silence of the empty house. Like someone drowning I flayed my arms and clutched the arm of the sofa where Hubert had left his prayer book. The lines moved and swayed before my eyes as if under water. It was a familiar prayer and memory supplied the words my eyes could not see.

'*By God! Should one who is in affliction or grief read this Tablet with absolute sincerity, God will dispel his sadness, solve his difficulties and remove his afflictions.*' The words were a life-raft on my sea of despair and agitation. Again and again I repeated them. My turbulent sea subsided. 'If my child is dead . . . help me to accept it. If he is alive, please teach me patience,' I prayed from the heart.

Calm at last, I became aware of a presence. This time I recognized it immediately. It was Toos. She is no longer with Tristan, I thought. Does this mean he is dead? I closed my eyes, the better to be aware of her. She was comforting me and then she was showing me something. As in a dream, when you see something and instantly know its significance, so now I saw that she was showing me a gleaming, golden tablet that represented Tristan's soul. It was blank yet I knew intuitively his life would be written on it.

37

That night there was a call from St. Justine Hospital. Tristan was coming home on the next Montreal flight. Despite the static interference, I recognized the voice of the head nurse. I could imagine the black eyes growing less dark as she said, 'I knew you would be worried. I had tried to call before but could not get through.'

Next morning, I was in the bombardier in my amaut. The days were warmer now and full of light. Soon after we left, the sun grew hazy and a low wind began to move the loose snow in great drifting sheets. By the time we had crossed the first stretch of sea ice and were on land again we were in a condition known as a white-out. Ujarak guided us through the atmospheric milk, but the bombardier was several hours late. Hubert was on the radio-telephone when we stepped into the nursing station. His relief at our safety was palpable.

Next morning the silver plane touched down in a flurry of snow. I was the first one to board. 'A baby?' The stewardess was perplexed, 'I know nothing of a baby returning to Igloolik. I am very sorry, if you give me your name, I will phone the hospital.'

Twice more in the weeks to follow, we were told that the baby was coming only to be notified at the last minute that he was not.

A television crew came to Igloolik and proved a welcome distraction. Every morning at sunrise they were on the roof, trying to catch a perfect shot of a dog team coming out of the sunrise. One day the director came in as Mousie and Bonie and I were sitting together, looking at a picture book. 'Look at Billy Goat Gruff,' little Bonie said to our visitor, pointing to a goat sculpture by Picasso.

'Why, that is the book on Picasso by my friend Duncan!' exclaimed our guest.

'It's one of our favorites. You know the photographer?'

How pleasant it was to discuss art. My mind luxuriated in the talk as my body would have responded to a soak in a hot tub of water.

Unexpectedly the radio crackled in the dining room. 'Igloolik, do you read me . . . Do you read me, Igloolik . . . Do you read? Over.'

This was not my scheduled time to be on the air. I must have forgotten to turn off the radio after my sched. an hour ago. I

38

rushed to the phone.

'This is Igloolik . . . I read you loud and clear . . . Over.'

It was the hospital of St. Justine. The head nurse sounded triumphant. Baby Schuurman was going on the night flight leaving Montreal tonight. Would someone be there to pick him up at Hall Beach? The escort was . . . but here the line faded. Yes! Yes, someone would pick him up, I interjected. The head nurse's voice came on clearly again.

'Madame Schuurman, I wish to say . . . ' but whatever it was that she had wished to say I never knew, for the line crackled, distorted and died.

'My son is coming home . . . tomorrow.'

'I had no idea you had another child!'

'He's been in hospital since February the fourth.' My cheeks felt wet. 'Could you stay with the girls for a minute, I must run and tell my husband.'

'Yes,' the stewardess said beaming, 'your baby *is* on this flight. And so sweet, such a lovely smile!' I walked down the aisle, my heart thumping furiously. An elderly lady was struggling to get an infant into a bunting suit.

'Thank you so much for looking after my baby.' The words sounded dry and stilted.

'Oh! You must be Madame Schuurman, I was just wondering what to do if you didn't come. I'm going on to Resolute Bay and I don't know anything about babies. He was so good at first but today he has been restless.'

'Did he take a bottle?'

'A bottle? The hospital did not send one . . . and you know, Madame, I have no experience with little ones.'

The flight had left the night before; it was now two in the afternoon. The baby had not been fed or changed in over eighteen hours.

'Moosey, Moose-Foot!' A broad smile spread over the baby's face and stayed there as I finished dressing him and slipped him into my amaut.

'Bless you!' I said with feeling as I hurried off the plane.

On the tarmac a bush pilot came up. 'I'm flying a charter into Igloolik for the Catholic bishop. He seems like a nice gent. Bet if you went up to him and gave him a big smile he would let you come along.'

The bishop was a courtly gentleman with a neat goatee and a black Breton beret. He bowed slightly and said it would be a pleasure.

It was the kind of pearl-like day the Arctic sometimes produces in early spring. The milky whiteness was opalescent, the sky was madonna blue and the sun painted smiles on every face. Igloolik looked like an illustration in National Geographic – in kodacolor. From the hunting camps many had come for the bishop's visit. The voices of the dogs from visiting dog teams blended with those of the resident dogs – some fifty strong – in an Arctic symphony of welcome. The bishop's party disembarked, the crowd dispersed and I jumped into Hubert's waiting arms. My amaut was full.

Chapter Five

MOUSIE and Bonie rushed into the house excitedly calling, 'Grampa's coming! Grampa's coming!'

Hearing the door bang, I dried my eyes and made an effort to compose myself. Their excited prattle was interrupted as Hubert came in and added, 'That is not all the good news!' He paused then offered, 'We are being transferred to Frobisher Bay!' When he did not see the expected reaction, he continued, 'Well, aren't you happy? Isn't that what you wanted?'

Before their noisy entry I had been studying our nine-month-old son. In a crib filled with bright toys, some hung up at eye-level, some dangling within arm-reach, he lay without moving. Only when picked up would he laugh or give an expansive, radiant smile. He ate, but without relish; he slept, but woke as lethargic as before.

Hubert relished the responsibility of area administrator of this vast area; he was exhilarated by the travel it necessitated by boat, dog-team and plane to the nomadic camps; he savored the long discussions his growing competence in the Inuktitut language enabled him to have with the visiting hunters; he responded to the challenge of planning the development of this frontier region; he craved the boundless variety the position offered, dog-officer, coroner, welfare officer, registrar of vital statistics, justice of the peace. The versatility of his personality and the strong love of change and adventure were perfectly met in this isolated place. My heart read all this easily, yet since Tristan had returned I lived in dread that he would once more be seized by an inexplicable illness. I had begged Hubert to request transfer to a place that had a hospital. So, at his news, my feelings warred with each other. On one hand, I was relieved for Tristan's sake, on the other hand, I painfully regretted pulling Hubert away from so much that he thrived on and condemning him to a desk job at Frobisher Bay.

'It will be great to have Grampa here!' Hubert said, putting his arm around me, 'He will absorb the children, so you'll have time to pack, and maybe even cheer you up a bit . . . What is it love?'

'Just look at him, Hub,' I said turning to the crib. 'Hour after hour he just lies there . . . like a . . . like a vegetable!'

We stood side by side, looking at the blank little face and the long limp body in its white terry cloth sleepers lying amid the brightly colored toys.

'Look at it this way,' Hubert said, taking my hand and stroking my hair. 'We have him home, he is not sick, he eats and sleeps well – By the way, Dr R. just came in on the plane. He said he wants to see Tristan. Maybe he can give us some advice.'

That afternoon there was a clinic for pre-school children. After seeing Mousie and Bonie and pronouncing them fit and healthy, Dr R. said, 'I'll walk back to the house with you if you offer me some coffee and one of your famous cinnamon buns.'

As we had our mug-up Dr R. filled us in on news from Frobisher Bay. Then he said, 'I've just been at a conference that dealt with the effects of children like this (here he glanced at Tristan lying inert on the couch) on their families.'

He paused to swallow the last piece of cinnamon bun, then proceeded. 'My advice to you is . . . when you go out this summer . . . find a good nursing type of institution and leave the child there. It will be well looked after.'

I looked at him incredulous.

'Look, Suzanne,' he said forcefully, sensing my reaction, 'you are a young woman. If you keep this child your marriage will suffer. You won't be able to be a proper mother to your healthy children.' Here he indicated Bonie and Mousie playing tiddly-winks on the white polar-bear rug.

I dropped my eyes, unable to answer.

'In five years time, you will still be carrying him around. He'll never be able to do anything . . . Look at him . . . he's just a vegetable!' Then as a final volley he shot out, 'I've read the reports from St. Justine . . .'

I took the tray to the kitchen. From the living room I could overhear his voice saying to Hubert, 'You'll really have to talk to her. It's hard for mothers to be rational, to see that there is only one way. Put him away. Forget that you ever had him, and get on with living your life.'

As Dr R. left he shook my hand and looked intently in my eyes. I closed the shutters of my soul and called upon a long tradition of hospitality and courtesy to carry me through the goodbyes.

We were alone. Dr R.'s words hung between us. In silence I picked up the baby. In silence Hubert and I sat looking at him.

'This is my son,' I said firmly. 'I could no more put him away and forget that I had him than I could put away my heart and tell it to stop beating.'

'We'll look after him,' Hubert said, weighing his words. 'He'll get better.'

Ujarak had slipped in silently during Dr R.'s visit. Hubert consulted him in Inuktitut. 'Ujarak thinks the baby will get better!' he announced jubilantly. We nodded at each other, sharing our understanding that love is a medium in which hope grows.

Several weeks later, Grampa was sitting at our dining room table. 'There sat this gray-haired gentleman with a goatee just ahead of me on the plane,' Grampa expounded. 'Now why would an old man like that be going to the far north, I asked myself?' Grandfather continued with a twinkle in his blue eyes as he looked across our dining room table at the white-haired goateed bishop facing him. The bishop guffawed and slapped the palm of his hand on the napkin.

'I had been thinking the same thing!' the bishop confided. 'Why is *that* old man gallivanting around the north country?'

Amid much laughter, the two compared ages and found that they were born within a month of each other. Little Moose, carefully held up on Hubert's lap, joined in the laughter and flapped his arms as if he were a pinioned bird. The vague beatific smile lit his face as he tried to focus on his Grampa.

Henk Schuurman's hair had turned completely white by the time he was twenty-one. This had been a distinct advantage during World War II as it permitted him to falsify his age and work in the Dutch underground. Now in his mid-sixties, Henk was smooth-faced and irrepressibly cheerful. He had just retired from the tax department and was now fulfilling his lifelong ambition to travel. What better way to start than to visit his son in the far north?

On arrival at Frobisher Bay we were assigned an apartment in a former nursing station that stood apart from the rest of Apex Hill. Years later we were to learn that the building rested on a natural deposit of radioactive material. Subsequent inhabitants of the house had to wear buttons measuring the degree of radioactivity they were absorbing. During that year Tristan's condition began to improve.

We attributed this improvement to the purchase of a jolly-jumper. A jolly-jumper is a large spring that can be hung from a door frame; on an adjustable rope is fastened a cross-piece from which in turn hangs a chair-sling in which an infant may be placed.

When Tristan was thus suspended for the first time, he hung limp. He *did* like being near his sisters' play area. We placed him in the jumper for a few minutes at first, then for longer periods. Hubert encouraged the rolling eyes to focus on the toys. Placing the dragging legs in a jump position, he would pull on the spring, simulating the bounce that Tristan was eventually able to achieve. Around him cavorted the ever-active girls. It was an incentive for him to keep his head up to observe their games.

It was not long before he learned to turn around, and within a week he knew how to jump. His sisters would set up a tower of blocks not far away and urge him to jump towards it. When his flaying arms demolished the tower there was applause and shouts of encouragement. Back in the playpen he no longer lay immobile but turned over to look at what was going on around him or to play with a toy. The long period of complete passivity was over.

Eagerly I looked forward to our visit with the elusive Dr M. An appointment with him was first on our summer holiday agenda. With pride, I anticipated showing him my pudgy, healthy baby.

Hubert and I arrived early at Dr M.'s office, which was in a very French part of Montreal. Tristan was alert and beaming. Dr M., with considerable Gallic charm, ushered us into his dark wood-paneled office and showed us to leather chairs.

'Most unfortunate that we were not able to meet before – such a charming mother.' My hackles rose at such blatant hypocrisy. I watched silently as he examined the baby. Hubert talked on about Tristan's improvement in the jolly-jumper, but soon he too grew silent.

Dr M. drew the tips of his fingers together to form a steeple and leaned his elbows on the polished desk. His chin rested on the peak of the steeple as he spoke, looking past us into some invisible distance. 'The Chinese have a cure for children like this.'

Through my mind flashed a confusion of thoughts about the probable difficulties involved in seeking medical help in China, but hope pushed all obstacles aside. We would manage somehow. I was completely unprepared for what came next. In a meditative tone Dr M. continued, 'They leave them on top of a mountain . . .' Incredulous, my mind supplied the missing words . . . 'to die.'

It had fortunately taken Hubert a moment as well to realize the implications of the doctor's statement. We looked at each other over the abyss of dashed expectations and rose to go. I gathered up the compliant form of my son and, hugging him tightly, walked out of the office leaving Hubert to take care of the formalities.

A gray cast had come over the day. I shivered. Even when Hubert put his comforting arm around me, the coldness did not go away. It lay deep inside, like some ponderous foreign object. Many, many years later the place where it had lain remained bruised and dented.

When did I face the reality that I had a handicapped child? To that I can answer only that it was a slow process with many setbacks like the emergence of spring in the Arctic. There were days when it was quite evident, like a deceptively warm day in June, but then would come days of retrenchment that like late snow flurries would set up defenses of negation and my heart would cry out, 'No, no!' Certainly Dr M. had brought it home with bruising bluntness, but that very harshness had brought with it a strong antidote of hope. The soul struggles for an equilibrium, and the blow had been counterbalanced by an even fiercer trust in Tristan's progress. If one were to ask me on what that hope was based, I could only answer that it was built on – love.

When I had gone to Montreal with Tristan in those first days of his illness, I had wired my mother asking for her prayers on his behalf. Now on her first visit to us in the north her acceptance of our son was as complete and loving as it had been of the other children. Unlike my mother, who was an active Bahá'í, Henk, my father-in-law, was a Sufi (a movement of Eastern Mysticism introduced to the West by Innayad Khan). Grampa had added Tristan to the list of people for whom his group prayed regularly; his expectations of Tristan's progress were unswerving.

After our holidays life quickly settled down to a routine. Every laundry day, Henk played with the older children while I took Tristan to the laundry room that was shared by the two apartments. On this particular day, I put Moose into a big galvanized tub on the table beside me. This arrangement supported his back, for unlike most children his age he could not sit up unassisted. Whenever he lost his balance, he would slump over.

As I worked on the wringer-washer I sang and talked to him. Water was delivered to the house by truck so conservation measures had to be taken and I carefully saved the rinse water to use again. As I leaned on the old washer waiting for the water to fill up the reserve sink I saw Tristan reach over for a toy that had fallen in front of him. He retrieved it and sat forward, his back not touching the side of the tub. He was sitting up, alone!

'Oh! Pooser! I am so proud of you! You can sit up all by yourself!' I rushed past Grampa on the living room floor playing a game with the girls and phoned Hubert to share with him our son's triumph. This was the first step away from the vegetable state that had been forecast for him. Alas, when I returned to the laundry room I found it inundated. A memorable day indeed!

A few days later Tristan, whose nicknames had multiplied to include the appelation Pooser, in a little suit, his blond hair slicked back, sat all by himself in front of his first birthday cake. Very deliberately, he put his hand right in the middle of the pink icing. But, I thought proudly, he also had the good sense to lick it. Each of us made a wish and Bonie helped him to blow out that first flickering candle.

It was September and a particularly fine grainy snow had fallen. Grampa had gone back to Holland for the winter, promising to return to Canada the following summer. With Pooser growing daily heavier and more awkward to carry in my amaut, I set off to visit a newcomer to Apex Hill.

46

It was traditional in the north to welcome new arrivals with a loaf of homemade bread. In those days, there were no commercial bakeries in the north and it took people some time to get themselves organized sufficiently to bake bread themselves. The door I knocked on was opened by a gaunt and sad-eyed, although smiling woman. She did not ask us in. I gave her the bread and, despite the cool reception, asked her over for supper the next day. It takes time to learn northern ways, I reasoned.

The Jamiesons, a couple in their forties, came the next evening. He was a tall convivial man who talked to Hubert at great length about different government departments. The sad eyes and polite smile of Mrs Jamieson were not very communicative. When she offered to read a story to the two girls while I bathed the baby, I felt relieved.

I brought in Pooser, rosy after his bath, to the living room. I could see that she was noticing the way he tilted his head to look at objects, and the way he would flap his arms as if they were wings. Hubert went to tuck in his daughters and Mrs Jamieson held out her arms to hold Tristan. Her polite smile was completely gone and was that a tear I saw in her eye? Pity was not something I was used to yet. 'It's time I put him to bed,' I said firmly. She handed him back without a word but now unmistakably there were two tears.

Perplexed at my guest, I took my time tucking in the baby. When I returned the men were in an animated discussion and Mrs Jamieson was glancing at a magazine. I sat down beside her and took out my sewing basket. She asked me bluntly about the baby's condition. I answered candidly, and something prompted me to relate Dr R.'s advice and what Dr M. had said. Her face assumed a far-away expression and she began to relate her own story.

Mrs Jamieson (Agnes she asked me to call her) had had two normal healthy children, a boy and a girl. Her husband had a good job, they lived in a nice suburb of Montreal. She stopped as if suddenly struck by a thought. Strange that you don't realize when you are happy – only on looking back! Then when she was forty she had another child. This child was not normal, it was constantly sick, drank only a special formula, fussed all day and cried most of the night.

As if on cue a whine came from Tristan's room. I sprang up

47

to check. When I returned it was as if she had proceeded with an inward narrative during my absence. I sensed that I had missed part of the sequence. She had become a nervous wreck. The doctor had put her on tranquilizers. The other children felt neglected and got into trouble. She was always so tired that she could not be a proper wife to her husband. The men had stopped talking and I was aware that Mr Jamieson felt compelled to monitor the intimate details his wife was pouring out. She was always tired, Agnes continued. Mr Jamieson expelled a long slow breath. Hubert shuffled his feet. To forestall more private communications Mr Jamieson entered the recital.

They had found a really nice place for their son, in Ontario near Smith Falls. There the sickly baby had care and medical attention from professional staff. He turned to Hubert as to a man who should understand these things, explaining that his wife simply could not have managed anymore. Hubert said something suitably reassuring.

As if from another room I heard my voice ask, 'How did it feel to leave him?'

She turned to me, the polite smile no longer masking the pain in her face. 'I tried to think that he would miss me, but when we went to visit he . . .'

As her voice trailed off her husband broke in, 'Of course he did not *know you! He's just a vegetable* and far better off where he is well looked after.' He turned to Hubert again but I could see that he was struggling to suppress a deep anger. 'It was too hard for Agnes to keep going there to visit. It's a long drive and then there's the added expense of overnighting in Ottawa.'

'So you came here?' Hubert asked.

'Yes,' Mr Jamieson replied defensively.

Agnes was staring vacantly and her nose twitched. 'It always smelled of urine on the ward.'

Angrily her husband interposed, 'You were keeping him so clean you were killing yourself.'

They left soon after. Mr Jamieson said some gruff goodbyes for both of them, for Agnes still seemed to be off in some remembered time.

Hubert and I returned to the silence of the living room. Without speaking we picked up the empty coffee cups. Over the sink we looked long and silently in each other's eyes.

Hubert took me in his arms. As he held me, great tears fell, for Agnes, for ourselves, for our children, but most deeply for the incomprehensibility of it all.

The following week I tried to call on Agnes in an effort to introduce her to her neighbors and involve her in community activities. She did not open the door. Regularly I made attempts to visit her. Often I could see her inside her little house, but she would not answer my knock. Once in October with the snow swirling around I knocked insistently; I was cold and needed to come in and get warm. At last she answered. She stood as before, her eyes sad, her mouth smiling, but the smile was decidedly tipsy and her movements clumsy. She did not ask me in and when she slurred her refusal to come to tea to meet her neighbors I caught a strong whiff of whisky.

Before Christmas Hubert informed me that the Jamiesons had left. 'Logic can never convince the heart,' I murmured on hearing the news.

'Do you know that people think Pooser is a battered child?' I asked with mock horror as Hub and I sat over coffee one winter night. 'What a disgrace and you a Justice of the Peace!' We laughed but there was a sadness as we looked at our son. His many falls as he navigated the apartment in his walker left ugly bruises. Certainly he had been progressing well. Even now he was sitting in a high chair trying to drink from a cup. Oops! it spilled. No matter, he would do better tomorrow.

But tomorrow came and I could barely rouse him. Groggily he took a bottle, developed a nose bleed and as soon as the bleeding stopped sank back into sleep. In the next few days we could barely keep him awake for four or five hours out of the twenty-four.

At the hospital in Frobisher Bay the doctors suspected meningitis and did a spinal tap. The test was clear and no one could come up with an explanation for the sudden lapse into sleep. His nose bled as often as three or four times a day. After about five weeks he began to spend more time awake but he was listless and whiny. All interest in the walker and jolly-jumper had vanished. Most of all he liked to sit on our knees and have us talk to him or show him pictures in storybooks.

My conviction grew that we simply had to move closer to a medical center. We still had no diagnosis of his condition and we were in the dark about any prognosis for his future. Reluctantly Hubert agreed to take educational leave. There was his M.A. thesis to finish and a Ph.D. program at McGill (combining sociology and anthropology) looked interesting.

Once more when the summer holidays came a medical appointment was on the top of our list. This time Montreal Children's Hospital had been recommended. Grampa was again on hand to help us move. This time we were moving south, first to Ottawa and in the fall to a place close enough to Montreal for Hub to attend McGill.

'What are those big green things?' Bonie asked as the plane was landing.

'Trees! Silly!' Mousie answered.

It was a sunny summer. The children tanned quickly and bloomed. At a family consultation we had decided that it was time for the older girls to drop their nicknames. Nadine would replace Mousie and Hedy would be called Bonie no more. 'After all, I am starting school in the fall,' Nadine pointed out. Pooser it was agreed would still be Pooser or Moose, 'He's still a baby,' Hedy said with an air of superiority.

Yes, he certainly was still a baby. He could stand when assisted and moved about awkwardly but hardly could it be termed proper crawling. Luckily he was small and everyone simply mistook him for a much younger child.

It was midsummer when I took Tristan to Montreal by train for an assessment at the Montreal Children's Hospital. The thin manilla file started that summer was to grow into a hefty tome in the following years. Throughout the day various doctors came in, asked questions, took samples of blood or urine and requested X-rays. There seemed to be no clear explanation for his illness or present condition. Could Tristan stay in the hospital for the week for observation and further tests? When tired out from tests and examinations he fell asleep. I slipped out and caught the evening train back to Ottawa, promising to return in two days.

On my next visit I again waited for him to fall asleep before I left to catch the train. On my subsequent visit I had expected to take Tristan home but I was informed that Dr Silverstein, the liver specialist, had detected a very enlarged liver and spleen. This was the only clue the doctors had to go on, and they wanted to run some more tests. Once more, hoping to avoid a traumatic scene, I waited till my son slept before leaving the hospital.

At home in Ottawa Nadine was very sick with a high fever – 'Measles', the doctor informed us. There could be no question of visiting Tristan in the hospital while she was ill. I nursed Nadine and worried about Tristan while a week dragged by. As I was to learn later, there had been an outbreak of measles at the Montreal Children's Hospital as well.

Ten days later after Nadine had bounced back to good health we had a disquieting phone call from the Montreal hospital. The ward nurse informed us that we were to pick up Tristan right away. We had been advised that we could not even visit. Why now the sudden change? The nurse replied that she was not free to give any details, but we were to come right away.

Hubert took the day off from work and we drove down to Montreal. On the ward, we were met by a doctor who explained that Tristan was regressing. I did not stay to hear more, but hurried to his room. There, in the crib, lay a hunched up little form in fetal position. I could see, at a glance, that he had lost weight. I called softly . . . 'Moose? Pooser? . . .' There was no response. I touched him, but there was no movement.

The doctor and nurse were beside me. 'Is he sick? What's happened?'

The doctor lifted the baby's eyelid. It gave me a shock to see only the white eyeball. 'He is withdrawn,' the doctor answered.

'What's wrong with his eyes?' I heard Hubert ask with concern but I did not hear the answer because I lifted up the little form and went to sit on a rocking chair by the corner window. Lovingly I touched the little body. I whispered in his ear and rocked back and forth, singing my grandfather's Ukrainian lullaby. As I stroked the cold skin, one of my tears fell on his face; I saw a twitch and then the eyelids struggled to open. Once more I saw only the frightening white globe of eyeball and neither iris nor pupil. Mercifully the lids closed again but the body relaxed out of its fetal position.

'Let's get him home!' Hubert said, coming over to the

rocking chair.

On the drive home, I talked to Pooser until his body lost its rigidity. Eventually he opened his eyes and looked at us. It was as if he had gone a long way away and it had been hard coming back. But at last he focused and saw us. Hubert pulled up on the side of the road and we each in turn held him and talked to him. The thinnest of little smiles wafted across his stiff face. After that, his body began to feel more normal, and he clung to my neck and whimpered. At last he took a little milk from a bottle and fell asleep, but not into that state of absence that he had been in before.

The sleep must have refreshed him. By the time we arrived back in Ottawa, he awoke and smiled at his eager sisters. It was months, however, before he regained lost ground. His ability to stand supported had vanished; he could no longer drink from a cup, but went back to the bottle; and his limited vocabulary of sounds was reduced to a couple of grunts. It was at nighttime that the extent of the trauma he had sustained was most evident. Since I had left the hospital only when he was asleep, he would not now fall asleep unless he was lying on my chest and, he seemed to have reasoned, unable to get away from him. Even after several weeks, when normalcy had returned, he insisted on placing his head over my heart before he would fall asleep.

'This must stop!' Hubert announced one night. 'He must learn to fall asleep on his own; otherwise, we will never be able to go out or to lead a normal life.'

Upstairs the crying went on and on. My mind agreed, but my heart was being wrung. The crying would stop as, exhausted, Pooser would fall asleep and topple from his standing position in the crib. But the fall to the mattress would wake him up again. After two hours, weariness overcame Pooser, he fell down, did not get up, and slept.

When I got up to make tea I dropped the teacup. As Hubert helped me I realized that he too was shaking. After that night we had no more problems with Tristan's going to sleep.

Chapter Six

RAWDON is a small town in the Laurentian Mountains, north of Montreal. It has a cosmopolitan ambience, for although in the midst of a French-speaking region, many English-speaking cottagers go there for the summer. Hubert and I had come to know the town when we attended the Beaulac Bahá'í Summer School, not far distant. It was largely for this reason that we chose to live there while Hubert attended McGill University in Montreal.

In the center of town, there is a little jewel-like lake. Its beach was deserted in September. I loved to dream there through the golden autumn afternoons while the children built sand castles. Flaming maple and golden birch leaves fell on the water and sailed like Viking ships on the surface of the lake. Across the water I could see the steeple of the United Church and the roof of the comfortable two-storied white-clapboard manse that we were renting. I threw a pebble into the smooth water and watched the expanding rings. A family arriving in a small town makes rings like that, I thought.

The first ring must be the immediate family circle. How idyllic our first weeks had been. Hubert had spent time raking up mountains of golden and scarlet leaves and the girls had jumped in the piles with whoops of joy. Tristan had received a present that made the yard and its golden leaves accessible to him. It was undoubtedly the most memorable gift he was ever to receive: a yellow Volkswagen convertible pedal-car. Pooser's car became his mode of locomotion over the uneven terrain of the big yard, where the walker could never go. He would follow Hubert around as he raked and, with the same delight that his sisters took in jumping on the leaves, he would drive into the piles.

On one day he seemed to have vanished from the yard. My frantic search brought me to the small graveyard near the

53

church adjoining our house. I saw him before he spied me. He was parked behind a tall tombstone surrounded by wreaths left on the newly dug grave. I caught a look of rapture on his face as he smelled the flowers and then looked upwards to the incredibly blue sky. When I got him home he still had a chrysanthemum clutched in his little hand.

Then there is the second ring, I thought as I tossed in another pebble. It is a larger circle, the family in the immediate community. Nadine was going to the English-language school two blocks from the house; she had her circle of friends, as did outgoing little Hedy.

The first week we moved to Rawdon I had set off with Tristan in his stroller to explore the town. I had stopped at the open-air fruit-and-vegetable stand two blocks from the house. The apples and plums smelled delicious. I looked up from the stall, remembering that at this time last year we had been battling a snowstorm in Frobisher Bay. Beside me, in the stroller, Tristan showed signs of fatigue, his head rolled as though the neck were a rubber stem unable to support its heavy burden.

Just then, the owner of the stand came up. One glance convinced me that I would be safe in speaking French. She wanted to know all about our family. The prime location and the loquacious disposition of my questioner made her a natural purveyor of information. Giving her 'the scoop' like this on 'the new arrivals' would surely make her an ally.

In mid-question she caught sight of Pooser. In his weariness he had grown slack-jawed and was drooling. His eyes, never in good control, were wandering to separate corners. The woman's face had been shrewd and assessing, but friendly; now her eyes narrowed, and she stepped back. In a jeering tone she made a comment that I did not understand. Realizing that my command of French did not embrace local idiom, she redeemed the situation by saying in a pleasanter tone and in heavily accented English, 'He is not right, the child?' She pointed to her head and made a circular motion with her finger. I mumbled that he was tired and that I must get him to bed. The short walk home was through a mist. My throat felt so tight it hurt.

With a sweet smile on his face, Pooser drifted off to sleep in his crib.

Downstairs I made myself a cup of coffee. Beyond the confines of the house and the fenced-in yard was a small town that I had to live in with a child 'that was not quite right'.

You are lucky, I told myself. It is a small town and soon everyone who is going to stare will have stared. The novelty will wear off. The madame at the fruit stand will tell everyone everything there is to know and that will be the end of it. How much better than facing a big-city supermarket where there would always be fresh stares, where hundreds of times I would have to watch the narrowing of the eyes, the look of revulsion, the withdrawal.

This tight pain in the chest and throat is only part of what it means to have a child like Tristan. A line from a prayer surfaced like a bubble in the memory tank of my mind. *But for the tribulations which are sustained in Thy path, how could Thy true lovers be recognized; and were it not for the trials which are borne for love of Thee, how could the station of such as yearn for Thee be revealed?*

But there was more. There was the entire expanse of the future. For every child there is a web of dreams and aspirations that the parents spin on their behalf. It forms the cocoon from which the child must emerge at puberty. For Tristan there was a great void. I longed to have him learn to walk and to talk, but there had to be something more to hope for, to aspire to.

In the silent house I sat and prayed for my little son, for this dearly loved child of my heart. There are lovely prayers for children. As I repeated them again and again, I realized with a winging feeling of relief that nowhere in the prayers do we ask that our child be physically strong, nowhere do we ask that he be able to run well, or be smart in school.

O God! Rear this little babe in the bosom of Thy love, and give it milk from the breast of Thy Providence. Cultivate this fresh plant in the rose garden of Thy love and aid it to grow through the showers of Thy bounty. Make it a child of the kingdom, and lead it to Thy heavenly realm. Thou art powerful and kind, and Thou art the Bestower, the Generous, the Lord of surpassing bounty.

You are certainly a child of God, my little one, I thought. You can attain to all the spiritual virtues we are told to pray for. You can grow up to be kind and loving, generous and unselfish. If you attain to those virtues, you will have attained your soul's goal in life even if you never run a race or win a spelling match.

Then there is the third wider circle, I continued musing. This circle has a less-defined perimeter. It includes all the people with whom we as a family interact, at the Beaulac Summer School and at the Montreal Children's Hospital.

Was it but last week that I was sitting just this way beside Pooser, at Beaulac listening to a speaker on prayer? I had become so engrossed that I was only marginally aware that one of the women beside me was staring at Tristan. During the question period she leaned over and asked in a not unfriendly way, 'Do you know that there is something wrong with the baby's eyes?' In this setting I had been unprepared for so blunt a question.

'There is a lot more wrong with him than just his eyes!' I answered just as bluntly.

'Well, as long as you know,' she added seriously. 'Many parents don't notice these things.'

I looked in her candid eyes and appreciated her motive, but it made me even more aware that her attitude was qualitatively different from what I had come to expect from the Bahá'ís who came from all over Canada to attend courses at the school. Here, Pooser was accepted with the same unquestioning love that was bestowed on Nadine, Hedy and all the children present.

I began to watch the reactions to my son at Beaulac. In a mysterious way he managed to establish relationships with some people whom he would always recognize. If someone called out a greeting, he would first move his head, much as older people with bifocals move to bring a subject into view in the appropriate part of their lenses. For Pooser, this involved the tilting of his head. Then he would focus his eyes like someone adjusting the distance on a camera. All the while, a slow glowing smile would begin to dawn, and with full recognition a look of pure delight would envelop both child and friend.

We had to exercise great care in selecting baby-sitters. One woman had raised six of her own children and helped look after several grandchildren, but her patience was not able to encompass Tristan and his condition. We came back early one day to find Pooser in tears sitting in a corner on a potty. She could not accept that a two-year-old was still in diapers.

Good fortune brought our way, however, a most unlikely baby-sitter. Miss Judd was a spinster of mild and unassuming manner. Although she had no previous experience with children, she possessed a boundless gentleness. Pooser took to her immediately and a strong attachment developed between them. Hedy and Nadine liked her because, as Nadine put it, 'She is fair and makes sweet desserts.' Miss Judd often dropped in to visit and soon it became clear that she had set herself the task of teaching Tristan to walk. If we felt that this was premature, we kept it to ourselves, so intense was her outpouring of love and involvement with our son and so responsive was he to her gentle encouragement.

As Tristan improved, our trips to the hospital were reduced to one a month. Armed with a plastic card that gave name and details of socio-economic status, we spent the entire day moving from one hard bench to another in the warren of outpatient clinics. Over a period of time we learned many useful things, not all of them related to medical practice. There was an inverse relationship between the benefits received from a particular clinic and the length of time that we had to wait.

Dr Silverstein was 'a short wait', yet it was he who first proposed (after a series of frightening blood tests when Pooser, wrapped in a sheet, howled with terror as a blood sample was taken from his neck vein) that Tristan had had toxoplasmosis. Toxoplasmosis is a condition caused by *toxoplasma gondii*, parasites found in some domestic and wild animals. It was possible that I had ingested the parasite when eating game meat in Frobisher Bay. Up to 50% of the world's adult population has antibodies for this parasite, so in all likelihood only the fetus was affected. *Toxoplasma gondii* infect the tissues of the central nervous system, and especially those of the liver, as well as causing certain specific damage to the eyes. By the time Tristan's system had fought off the infection damage was irreparable. But it was not possible to find any trace of the suspected parasite. The diagnosis would have to remain, forever, a hypothesis. Over the years, no one was to propose a more likely one.

Dr Silverstein was a kindly man who took time to explain. The liver biopsy performed when Tristan had been in hospital during the summer revealed extensive scar tissue. The liver, he took pains to explain, was an amazing organ. With even as little as twenty-five percent of healthy tissue, it could function reasonably well for a long time.

'How long?' I had wanted to know.

Dr Silverstein removed his glasses and polished them. 'It is impossible for me to say. Maybe into adulthood.'

'Is there anything that would help, like a special diet?' I wanted to know. 'I notice that he drinks great quantities of milk and eats fruit and vegetables but he does not care for meat or sweets.'

'Just let him eat what he wants. Don't *force* him to eat anything. The body is a great regulator, if it is left alone to choose from healthy foods.'

The physiotherapist was not 'a long wait' either. From her we received invaluable advice about how to teach Tristan to tuck in his lolling tongue and to control his drooling, as well as exercises to prepare him for walking.

It was the eye specialist, who, after 'a long wait', was always particularly trying. Although the worst of Tristan's erratic eye movements had ceased, I was still very concerned about the way he moved his whole head in order to look at something. At times Pooser's blue eyes would rotate in a most disconcerting manner. Doctors had a field day peering into his eyes with their little lights, and interns would be called in to see the damaged area on his retina. Pooser, usually a placid happy child, would become restless and irritable.

The king of the specialists was the neurologist. His waiting room was a vast antechamber with hard uncomfortable benches. His clinic began in the afternoon. We learned to pack a lunch so that we would get to the top of his list. The great man would arrive, sometimes as much as an hour after the official opening of his clinic, with a retinue of white-coated attendants. A hush would descend upon the long-waiting parents and their restless whining children, as the regal snow-maned figure swept into his office. The last audience that I received from this eminence was memorable indeed.

In earlier visits, the great authority had precluded the possibility that Tristan would learn to walk in any forseeable future. On this day, I carried in a limp and exhausted little figure. The doctor laughed good-humoredly when I reported that Tristan had learned to walk. Around him sat interns hanging on his every word, as knowingly he remarked about the folly of parental gullibility.

Turning to me, he said with heavy irony and condescension, 'Well then, let's see him walk! Stand him over there!' Then turning once more to his respectful audience he confided, 'Mothers are always willing to believe the impossible.'

I held Tristan up until he steadied. He was limp with fatigue. It was now three in the afternoon and we had been up since six o'clock. As he regained equilibrium, I left him and crossed the room to stand by the neurologist who held out a candy. I squatted down on my haunches and held out my arms to help bridge the space that yawned between us. It had taken three of my strides, and I estimated that it would take him at least ten steps.

'Come on, Pooser, come to mummy!' I urged. My eyes were misty as I saw him gathering himself together and, raising his arms, tuck his wrists under his armpits in the typical way that he had of using his arms like stabilizer wings. Splay-footed, he began to traverse the space. I could hear the room grow still. I kept my eyes on his, and it seemed to me as if I were reeling him in across the room on some strong invisible line of communication between us. He halted midway, distracted by something and suddenly became aware of the other people in the room. His balance, always so precarious, was on the verge of a fatal slump. I started to move towards him, but felt a strong hand on my shoulder holding me back.

'Pooser, walk over here. Walk, Pooser!' He found my eyes again, and the heavy swaying head came into line with his body. With feet wide apart, he navigated the last five steps. I closed my eyes as I hugged him to me whispering in his ear, 'Oh Pooser! I knew you could do it.'

Behind us, someone was clearing his throat. 'Well, I am always delighted when the mother of one of my patients manages to prove me wrong.' The words were gracious, but there was no smile in the eyes. The interns relaxed and nodded at the magnanimity of the great man. In the back of the room I could see the physiotherapist and it was to her that I turned. 'The exercises you recommended were great! I think they really helped.'

There was an awkward silence. Flushed with Tristan's triumph, I brought out a question that had been troubling me.

'Perhaps you could give me some advice,' I said, turning to the neurologist. 'As you know, Dr Silverstein thinks that I may have been the host to the parasite that caused Tristan's condition. Would it be risky for me to have another child?'

'My dear Mrs Schuurman, do you know what I recommend?' There was a dramatic pause. The interns poised their pens to capture a major medical pronouncement. 'I suggest that you go right home and jump into bed with your husband and don't worry your head about it!' Red suffused my face and seared my mind. Blindly I lifted my child in my arms. There were titters from some of the interns. I glanced around and in the back row, caught a look of compassion on the face of the physiotherapist.

'Our next case you will find interesting . . .' he was saying as we exited.

'Ba-ba, Ba-ba,' Pooser intoned, standing at my knee and contributing to our discussion about the new baby.

'What shall we call her? Baby Sally?' Nadine queried looking up from her Grade I reader about Puff and Baby Sally.

'You can borrow my dolly carriage,' Hedy offered magnanimously.

'Tomorrow, Miss Judd will come over and stay with you for two days,' I continued. Pooser banged his block on the arm of the couch to denote approval. 'When we come back with the new baby, I hope you will all help to look after her.'

'I know how to hold a baby!' Hedy announced, cradling her doll in her arms.

'I'll read the baby stories,' volunteered Nadine, who was even at that tender age showing unmistakable signs of becoming a bookworm. 'Was I adopted?'

'No, Mousie,' I said, reverting to her old pet name and hugging her close, 'You came out of my tummy, like Hedy and Pooser. But the doctor said that whatever made Pooser so sick as a baby may still be inside me and the next baby I would have might get sick too. That is why we are adopting a baby. Did you know we will be getting the baby on the birthday of Bahá'u'lláh?'

We returned with a ten-day-old baby girl, whom we named Lisa. The tiny red-haired wide-eyed baby was everything a mother could wish, alert and content. I would hold the compact little figure and remember the rag-doll feel of Pooser at the same age. Then she caught a little cold, and as she fussed and wailed in discomfort the bonding of needed love formed between us.

For Pooser, nothing like that was needed. From the start this was 'his baby'. He would rock her tirelessly in her pram and assist fascinated at each bath time. He seemed positively tuned in to her, in a psychic way. As his ability to communicate increased, he would tell us when she was wet or hungry.

That was the year we acquired two new members of the family; the baby and Auntie Hedda. Hedda had been a good friend of Hubert's during his bachelor days in Montreal and had been an important influence on me in my youth. Our little Hedy had been named for her. She suffered from Parkinson's disease, which made it impossible for her to live alone, and family circumstances made it uncomfortable for her to remain at home. So she was welcomed into our family to become a respected member of the third generation.

In the spring we all piled into a station wagon and drove to Lucerne, Quebec. We bought a new house that stood on an acre of land and had room for our expanded family. Ottawa, where Hubert was returning to work with the Department of Indian Affairs and Northern Development, was just across the river.

'Our student days, our northern experience, that is not how people ordinarily live,' Hubert explained in an effort to ease my transition to a more affluent way of life. 'Besides, we moved here to form an assembly.' Yes, that somehow assuaged my feelings of unease. Auntie Hedda, Hubert and I constituted the three additional adults needed to form the first Spiritual Assembly of the Bahá'ís of Lucerne.

'You must come over to a cocktail party and meet some of the people on the street!' exclaimed my neighbor as I was planting flowers in front of the house.

That evening Hubert nursed a ginger ale and discussed sailboats. The ladies around me were admiring a marquise diamond and talking about jewelry as a hedge against inflation. Our new environment felt as strange as had the silent social calls of the Innuit of Igloolik.

After the party I went in to check the children and was

61

alerted by Tristan's heavy breathing. His temperature registered at 105°F. In the yellow pages we located the closest hospital. The emergency department told us to bring him right in.

I drove along unfamiliar dark country roads trying to follow the directions I had been given. Lucerne was not a highly developed or populated area. At last I found a Pizza restaurant. The owner was counting his cash. As I pounded at the door he quickly closed the cashbox and reached under the counter. Perhaps he keeps a gun, I thought, moving into the light so that he could see that I was a woman and not dangerous. At last he came near the door, and I called out to him, asking for directions to the Sacre Coeur Hospital. He opened the door, looked at the limp child lying in the car, and in heavy Italian accents gave me the needed directions.

'Pneumonia, most likely,' the doctor surmised. I left Pooser under an oxygen tent and drove home in the early dawn on roads that were to become very familiar in the next week.

Our main concern after the crisis had passed was that Tristan not go into the serious regression that had beset him at Montreal Children's Hospital. We took turns visiting him three times a day and bringing toys and books that he loved. But it was a very limp and withdrawn figure that I chauffeured home ten days later. Soft rain was falling as we pulled into the driveway of our house on Castelbeau. In the big window the whole family had lined up and were waving. Nadine and Hedy had made a welcome home sign and painted pictures. The sun shone for all of us, when with visible effort the limp shape rallied as I carried him in. A smile, wan but happy, illumined us. We watched Tristan coming back to life, the gray lethargy dispelling under the bombardment of loving sibling attention.

Chapter Seven

THOSE were golden days, sunflower days. The clouds of
concern about Tristan's condition that had hung over us for so
long began to dissipate and we emerged into sunlight.

We were shopping in Ottawa one day when a grand-
motherly lady stopped, beamed at the children, and gushed,
'What lovely children! You must be so proud!' May God bless
her and send His bounties upon her for those kind words! I
looked with new eyes at Lisa, with auburn curls and intent
eyes, taking in everything around her. Behind her was the
golden head of Tristan tanned and healthy, a pleasant smile on
his face and the mouth at last trained to stay closed and not
drool. It was indeed a lovely sight, but it was more than that. It
marked the end of an era when every foray into a public place
meant running the gauntlet of intrusive stares.

In our Bahá'í community of Lucerne the adults were
outnumbered two to one by the children. Pooser, accepted
like the other children, was included in the various activities;
Sunday School, bowling parties, picnics and excursions. True
to the teachings of Bahá'u'lláh, community members stressed
kindness and service to others. When Tristan passed around
the paper napkins at the social part of the feast, everyone
beamed. Later when he learned a fragment of a prayer
everyone applauded.

In such an atmosphere of loving acceptance Pooser
bloomed. He learned that even strangers approached with his
lovely open smile responded with friendliness. Harshness had
no place in his world at this time. Anger, yes! The children
became angry with each other and quarreled as children will. I
grew exasperated at times, and a slap or two would be
administered. A spanked bottom was the ultimate but seldom-
used punishment. These flurries were like passing storm
clouds in those otherwise sky-blue halcyon days.

63

The sunflowers we had planted on the south side of the house became heavy with seed. I would hold Pooser close, and silently we would watch the chipmunks come stealing from the hedgerow and climb the thick stalks for the sunflower seeds. Birds alighted on the heavy flower heads and pecked greedily at the centers. On his face the wonder at the birds and the suspense at their balancing feat was reflected so vividly that I was torn whether to look at the sunflowers or at his expressive face.

As Nadine had once protected Hedy, so now Pooser was the guardian and boon companion of Lisa. It became evident that Lisa was an exceptional child. No one could remember teaching her to walk or dress herself. Difficult words were part of her earliest vocabulary. Yet even for such children there is unexpected peril, and the watchful care of a retarded child can be protective.

The phone was ringing as we entered the house. There was a meeting to be planned, and the phone conversation was protracted. Pooser and Lisa played on the floor behind the bags of groceries I had set down in my haste to answer the phone. Then I heard Pooser's voice rising in agitation, 'Ba-ba, no, no!' There was no sound from Lisa. Above a brown paper bag, I could see a serious concentrated look come on Tristan's face dispelling his usual smiling calm. 'Momma, wook, Ba-ba, no, no!' Pooser was tugging at my skirt, in his hand was an open bottle of aspirin. Lisa had an aspirin in her grubby little hand. The bottle was half empty.

I don't know if I even said goodbye to my caller. I knew the way to the hospital well. Pooser and I sat in the emergency waiting room while Lisa's stomach was pumped. I looked at the worried little boy sitting beside me and patted his hand reassuringly. 'She'll be all right, Pooser.'

It was impractical to travel to Montreal every time Tristan needed help. Finding a speech therapist in the Ottawa area was not an easy task. After many frustrating entanglements with red tape a hospital therapist agreed to take on Tristan. He hated walking through the antiseptic-smelling halls and meeting stretchers with their burdens of groaning bodies. Every session was traumatic.

Tristan was not the only one for whom speech difficulties were causing increasing frustration. Auntie Hedda's voice was becoming so low that it became impossible to carry on a normal conversation with her in a room full of people. Pooser seemed always to be aware of Auntie Hedda's particularly low times. Sometimes I would find him standing with his cheek pressed to her face, or holding her hand. There built up between them a form of silent communication. When Hedda's deteriorating condition caused her to drool occasionally, to her great embarrassment, it was Tristan who, without any awkwardness, would get up and wipe her chin and give her a hug.

When Tristan's sisters quarreled or were being punished for some misdeed, he would go to their side and sometimes simply stand behind them, with a hand on their shoulder, physically lending his support. On their part fierce protectiveness was mingled with a glowing pride at his increasing accomplishments.

Tristan needed a great deal of extra help. Learning to dress himself, to wash his hands, to brush his teeth, to put on shoes, all these were tasks of monumental proportions that took hours of careful training day after day. Everyone helped. Nadine with her precise mind studied the situation and devised mnemonic aids to help her brother distinguish between left and right shoes. I would hear her carefully explaining day after day. 'Look Pooser, do you see that the buckles face out. See these little flippy parts, they have to go away from you.' Pooser would bend his golden head in concentration and give his sister an adoring look.

The two older children became known in the family as 'the girls' and the two youngest as the 'little guys'. Hubert took 'the girls' downhill skiing while I stayed home with 'the little guys'. Hubert did chemistry experiments and built Meccano models with Nadine. He had Pooser help him with his carpentry and let him hammer nails and built boats with him. Hedy dressed up in different costumes, and was photographed as a model. Lisa mothered a succession of cats, who allowed themselves to be dressed in doll's clothes or carried around like a shoulder bag.

In the basement we built a big playroom with a raised platform like a stage. Here the children put on little plays. Pooser was often included in non-speaking parts. Hedy, who was the most social of the children and who was always involved in absorbing friendships, organized performances to which all the children on the street were invited.

Since the children could now be left with any competent baby-sitter, Hubert wisely insisted that we escape regularly from the absorbing family involvement for a night at the theater or a concert, preceded by supper at a good restaurant. At such times, removed from the never-ending demands of the family, we could reorient ourselves to each other and pursue our interest in the arts.

During our second year in Lucerne we managed to find a nursery school that would take Tristan. It was in Hull, and in French, but it was designed for children who, like him, were termed marginally educable-retarded. The teacher who ran the school, a truly gifted educator, was full of energy and inventiveness. With the help of two assistants she took the dozen children in her charge through the Peabody Pre-Primary program, translating it into French as she went along.

When any of the mothers came early to pick up their children we would congregate in the hall and exchange experiences. Soon we were making a point of arriving early in order to have a chance to talk over our problems. Of the dozen mothers, I was the only one not on valium or some other tranquilizing drug prescribed by physicians who handed out prescriptions rather than offering a listening ear.

Driving home, I pondered all this in my heart. Why didn't Tristan's condition raise the same problems for our family as for those of his fellow nursery school students?' In the rear-view mirror I could see Pooser's radiant smile. That was the most obvious answer. He was for me a source of joy! His warm smile, his presence, were a delight that was undimmed by the many malodorous chores. As I sniffed the air I realized that he would need to be bathed and changed when we got home. Although being toilet-trained was a prerequisite of attending the nursery school, Pooser had by no means a perfect record. Yet even that messy task was not particularly onerous.

Hubert, unlike the husbands I heard about at the nursery school, had endless patience with Tristan. He would sit and talk to him in the evening or read him stories, and on the weekends would welcome his clumsy help in any project he undertook. Pooser's desire to imitate his daddy was bottomless. During those times when father was reading the paper, and was not to be disturbed, Pooser would sit very still and imitate turning the pages of another section of the paper. Even though he might be holding it upside down, he would study it seriously and wait for the moment when daddy would turn to him, show him a picture, and say, 'Now what do you think that man is doing, Pooser?' Pooser would answer, 'Baa!' and point to the soccer ball. 'Yes, that's right, he is playing with a ball,' Hubert would respond, looking proudly at his son.

No, I concluded my musings as I pulled into the driveway of our house, I really do not need to take valium!

Our globe spun around. Black oceans and colorful countries swirled in bright patterns before my eyes. The globe stopped, and fronting us was the northern hemisphere and its great island of Greenland, pink on the edges and white inside to denote the icecap.

Hubert had just asked me if I would go with him to Greenland for a year. He had been given the task of writing a report on the government's implementation of its centralization policy. In collaboration with the National Film Board of Canada, he would also make a film on that little-known land. The week before, he had returned from a six-week exploratory trip. His eyes had glowed with excitement when he described the deep fjords into which the glaciers calved monstrous icebergs, and the herds of caribou that scattered at the noise of a helicopter. I realized, with a pang, how much he missed the challenge of the north.

As a young girl I had vowed to myself that I would be the sort of wife who followed her husband to the ends of the earth. Now I looked around our comfortable living room. Was I still detached? Would I be able to walk away from the comfort and security of suburban life?

'Well?' Hubert asked, returning with a tray of tea and crackers.

'There are two things we must discuss,' I answered carefully, 'Auntie Hedda and Pooser.'

'Auntie Hedda would have to go to a nursing home in the next year, at any rate,' Hubert pointed out. 'You are simply not equipped to give her the care she will need. It is barely manageable for you now.'

To this I had to assent. We both sat in silence reluctant to discuss Pooser's condition.

'Pooser has been so healthy these last two years,' I began tentatively. Hubert passed me a cup of fragrant Earl Grey tea. I could sense that he was giving me the lead in this discussion for it was I who had felt so strongly about coming south on Pooser's account. 'We also know that there is nothing medically that can be done now to help his condition.'

For some time we examined the issue carefully. Hubert summed it up, 'We must decide whether we are going to allow Pooser's condition to change the way that we would otherwise lead our lives.'

Suddenly I was aware that we were at a crossroad. Beside me I could feel the restless energy of my husband. Never would this man be satisfied with a routine comfortable existence.

'No!' I said emphatically. 'No! We must go ahead and not be held back by Tristan's condition. Let's decide right now that it will not be a determining factor in our choices; otherwise, we will come to resent him and the limitations that we impose on ourselves for his sake.' Hubert let out his breath. For a long time, we looked at each other.

It had not taken me long to realize how pointless had been our move from Frobisher Bay. No real medical help had become available. We still had only a tentative diagnosis of toxoplasmosis with the characteristic damage to brain, retina and liver. The damage was irreparable, but Tristan was now glowing with health and he was making steady and heartening progress. Many times I had regretted the lost opportunity to continue in our northern pioneer post. The comfortable life we were leading made me uneasy at times and I had wondered if we would become its captives.

'I think we made the right decision,' Hubert said as we finished off the tea and crackers and got down to planning the details of our move.

Chapter Eight

HUBERT and I were born in Europe. He was nineteen when his ship sailed down the St. Lawrence River; I was seven when first I saw the Statue of Liberty rising through the early morning mists at our port of entry to 'the new world'. We were returning now to a familiar world, but neither of us realized how thoroughly Canadian were our children. They were unprepared for all the differences, ranging from the small ones like the shape of electrical outlets and the eating of bread with a knife and fork, to the greater ones that involved language and established customs.

Hubert's family received us with warmth and unquestioning acceptance. It was an old family and welcomed with enthusiasm the additions of its youngest members. Uncle Hans, Hubert's brother, and Aunt Alice had two boys and the six cousins got to know each other despite language barriers. Tristan flourished in the bosom of the extended family.

The week in Holland sped by quickly and once more we were airborne, this time for Denmark. Hubert had considerable research to do in Copenhagen, so he installed us in the charming Hotel Marina, at Vejdbeck, on the sea coast and only a short train ride away from Copenhagen. It was then that we discovered Tristan's love of luxury. He entered the lobby like a disinherited prince returning to his rightful palace.

Not far from the hotel lived the first Bahá'í pioneer to Greenland, Palle Bishop. He was an executive of a large corporation, but his knowledge of Greenland was current and his interest and assistance were inexhaustible. Soon after our arrival, we were invited to his home for dinner. His Norwegian wife and their three little daughters were charming and soon the children were playing happily together.

It was at dinner that we fully realized how great a gulf

divides the European and North American methods of child upbringing. Our host's three children spoke only when spoken to, unlike our oldest who asked questions, not impolitely, but engaging directly in the general conversation. At the end of the meal, the three girls got up from the table and in a row went to their mother, curtseyed, shook her hand, and thanked her for the meal. Nadine guffawed with laughter and then, realizing 'it was for real', stopped in embarrassment. Subdued, our children asked to be excused from the table. To cover up for her social blunder, Nadine turned to the hostess and said with the aplomb of a nine-year-old, 'Your apple dumpling was delicious and the pastry was really flaky!' Hedy muttered that she really liked the apple juice. Pooser, getting into the spirit and ever a good imitator, went up to our hostess, shook her hand, bent over and gave her a kiss on the cheek, and then departed with a bow. Lisa was asleep, her red-gold curls on the plate amidst the remnants of the flaky apple dumpling. Hubert and I looked at each other in mock horror, but inwardly we were exploding with laughter.

Slowly our Canadian barbarians were tamed to European ways. They learned to shake hands. At different times, I saw them practicing curtseys, but they insisted that it was too sissy. Danish social graces call for many ritual phrases as well as patterns of behavior. We all learned to say 'Tak for mad!' after meals and the countless other courtesies that were considered essential. Pooser's civility seemed to transcend specific cultures. He would bring someone an ashtray when they lit a cigarette or a glass of water when they coughed because he saw the need not because of social custom. Watching Grampa, who was a quintessential gentleman, he had picked up many niceties such as pushing in ladies' chairs and opening doors. While still a little boy he had in his manner something gallant, and a special courtesy of the heart.

'Look, children, we're flying over the Greenland icecap!' Hubert exclaimed during what felt like an interminable flight. Across the aisle Nadine and Hedy were playing Snakes and Ladders with an amiable steward. Lisa was sleeping in my lap while Pooser was making his new Dinky cars go 'Vroom, vroom' over the tray in front. Even Lisa stirred as we craned to peer below at the unrelieved expanse of white.

'It looks just like any old bunch of snow,' Hedy commented disappointed.

'Yes,' agreed Hubert, 'but it is snow that lies over a mile thick in some places.'

'And it never melts,' added the steward.

'Not even in the summer?' Nadine inquired with concern.

'On the land near the sea the snow melts in the summer but not on the icecap.'

'Imagine a deep oval bowl, like the serving dish we use at home for vegetables,' I tried to explain. 'The oval dish is filled with snow; that is like the Greenland icecap. Then imagine the bowl floating in water, because Greenland is an island surrounded by the sea. Only the rim of the bowl is not covered with either water or snow. It is only on the coastal rim of Greenland that there is land and people can live.'

'Are we going to live on the rim?' Nadine wanted to know.

'Yes, Godthab, the capital, is right on the sea. If you go inland any distance you come to the ice fields,' Hubert explained. 'You'll see it more clearly when we get on the helicopter for the last part of the trip.'

'Is it cold?' pursued Nadine.

'Not as cold as Igloolik,' Hubert answered. 'The sea never freezes.'

The steward showed the girls a map portraying the land around the north pole. They found Igloolik and Godthab.

'But how come the sea never freezes?' Nadine wanted to know.

'The warm Gulf Stream current branches off there,' the steward pointed out. For the children, Snakes and Ladders became more absorbing than the never-changing field of white below them.

When we stepped off the plane at Sunderstrom Fjord we were met by a familiar presence. That sharp undercut of frigid air I would recognize anywhere! Once more we were in the Arctic, that land that one could at once love and dread.

Greenland . . . vast . . . beautiful . . . challenging. To each member of the family it presented a different challenge. For Hubert, there was a film to be made and information for a book to be collected. For the two oldest girls, there was a language to be learned and a new environment to be explored.

For all of us it was a rare opportunity to live in a little-known area of the globe.

'It's a great privilege for us as Bahá'ís to spend even this one year in a country that has been specifically referred to by 'Abdu'l-Bahá in *Tablets of the Divine Plan*,' I would often stress to the children.

On a weekend excursion into Godthab Fjord, as we all stood awestruck on the deck of the *Disko* watching the majestic cliffs mirrored in the smooth deep waters, I read to the children 'Abdu'l-Bahá's prophetic words:

> Perchance, God willing, the call of the Kingdom may reach the ears of the Eskimos . . . as well as Greenland. Should in Greenland the fire of the love of God be ignited, all the ices of that continent will be melted and its frigid climate will be changed into a temperate climate . . . that is, if the hearts will obtain the heat of the love of God, that country and continent will become a divine garden and a lordly orchard, and the souls, like unto the fruitful trees, will obtain the utmost freshness and delicacy . . . Should you display an effort, so that the fragrances of God be diffused amongst the Eskimos, its effect will be very great and far reaching.

'*Effort*, that means *trying*, doesn't it?' Hedy queried.

'Do you mean that if we try . . .' Nadine broke off, then started again with another question. 'How much effort will it take?'

'I don't know how much effort will change this land into "a lordly orchard",' Hubert responded, 'but I would imagine all our efforts will help.'

'Do you remember Bill Carr?' I asked the children. They nodded, but Hedy's face lit up, for he was a special favorite of hers. 'You know that he has lived in Thule, that is far to the north of here, for many, many years. Once he wrote the Guardian asking that same kind of question. He asked if what 'Abdu'l-Bahá had written was to be taken symbolically or literally.'

'You mean if there would be really, truly, orchards?' Hedy asked.

'Yes,' I answered.

'Shoghi Effendi, the Guardian, actually wrote to Bill?' exclaimed Hedy impressed. 'Wow!'

'What did the Guardian answer?' Nadine wanted to know.

'Bill told me that the Guardian had written that it meant both; that, in the spiritual sense, this area would become a bountiful orchard, and also that the actual climate would get warmer,' I answered.

Later I heard Nadine talking to Hedy, as they surveyed the mossy slopes where once Vikings had grazed their sheep. 'Can you imagine apricot trees growing there?'

Greenland had accorded us a hospitable welcome. The government had provided a beautifully furnished apartment for our use and had at every turn shown great care and consideration of us as Canadian visitors to their land.

To our delight we learned that there was another Bahá'í family in Godthab. Lotus, an American, and John Nielsen, a Dane, and their three children had moved to Greenland several years before. It had been a great struggle for them, and when we had heard their story we began to see how much 'effort' had already been expended. Our two families were the nucleus of the Bahá'í community in Godthab.

For the children, our first months in Greenland were a study in contrasts. Instead of a house and a big garden they had a fourth-story walkup apartment; instead of familiar English and less-familiar French, they heard Danish in school and Greenlandic on the playground; instead of a street on which each house was set on an acre of land, they lived in Block P with approximately three hundred apartments; instead of a society that accepted that children are noisy and rambunctious, they were confronted by expectations of formal politeness and decorum.

Both Nadine and Hedy adjusted to the Danish school system very well. At first they had understood more Greenlandic, which resembled the Innuit dialect they had picked up in Igloolik, but in five months they were fluent in Danish. When they were able to participate fully in the lessons at the school they attended, I stopped tutoring them with the help of texts we had brought from Canada.

For Lisa and Tristan I had obtained the same excellent Peabody Language Institute Kit that Tristan had started using in his Nursery School. Every day I prepared, with the help of a detailed manual, a diverse and stimulating learning experience, with cards, tapes, puppets, posters, figures that could be dressed in garments appropriate for the season, an assortment

73

of plastic fruits and vegetables, magnetic shapes and a magic wand that lit up at the right answer.

Tristan was six and we felt that he should have exposure to other children, so we enrolled him in a special-education class. The language difficulty, combined with his poor motor coordination, made the experience less than rewarding for him. Yet every day he manfully struggled out to school. By November it was dark night when school started, as well as bitterly cold. Clutching my hand he would navigate the five flights of stairs. The school was just across from Block P, but the distance was dark and forbidding in the blackness of Arctic night. A lone light shone at the end of the brick wall that sheltered the school playground from the prevailing winds. Towards this beacon Tristan would set off resolutely, while I stood under the lamp at the stairwell, waiting to wave him on when he turned to look back. No lady of olden days ever waved to her knight with more admiration for his courage and determination than I did then.

The skies lightened reluctantly by ten, and by noon there was a grudging concession to daylight. Lisa and I would stand on the balcony that connected all apartment entrances and wait for school to come out. As a backdrop for the scene stood Sermitsiak, the great snow-capped mountain that dominates the region in lore as well as on the horizon. Around the protecting wall of the school our knight would emerge, wave up to us, then hurry to climb the stairs where lurked the last of the dangers, vicious downdrafts and the occasional teasing child. We welcomed him home with cocoa and crackers. Then the fun would begin as we explored sights, sounds, shapes and textures guided by the puppet Peamony and his magic wand.

Hubert constructed elaborate Lego train systems with Tristan. He and Pooser would play for long periods, running an electric train across the level crossings where Tristan's cars and trucks lined up in all but forgotten traffic jams.

After some months we were offered a large house that had originally served as the American Consulate. We moved in, grateful to be spared the dragging of Hubert's heavy film equipment up five flights of stairs. In front of the house was a fish and game market where housewives came shopping for foods that constituted their traditional diet. Young men lounged against the fence or played a complex game in which

74

they threw coins into a design drawn in the dirt or snow. Oldsters came to sit and chat on the benches and a couple of them would play plaintive melodies on their harmonicas.

The activities of the fish market at their front door provided the children with endless diversion. At times Tristan would come home with a little bag of caplin, a tiny fish that washes ashore to spawn at certain times of the year, or Hedy would bring home a pair of caribou antlers that some hunter had given her. The children were always the first to pick up the news that a whale had been beached.

Our first exposure to a whale flensing left us gasping and choking at the odour. Despite this, the grandeur of the enormous hulk being rapidly desecrated had drawn us closer. Whale flensing is a festive occasion, songs are composed about it, everyone hurries to the beach in carnival spirits. In the past a whale stood for freedom from hunger for a long, long time. But I returned home from that first experience with the stench strong in my nostrils and a sense of awe at the demise of so gigantic a creature.

Across the street from the fish market stood a modern home for senior citizens. The girls first went there as part of a school project. They returned with Hubert, helping him to carry film equipment for a sequence he did in the home. The next time they wanted to take Tristan.

'They have other retarded children there,' Nadine said, looking me straight in the eye. 'The old people enjoy playing with them, because they have a lot of time on their hands.'

I watched them taking Tristan across the road. Nadine's remark made me aware that they were both beginning to assess their brother differently.

On two occasions Pooser had been screaming with frustration when Hedy's friends had arrived. 'I feel so ashamed when he acts like that,' she had confided to me after, 'I have to explain about him having been so sick . . . and they don't really understand.' In the harsh reality of life in Greenland the glow of love and tolerance that had surrounded Pooser in Lucerne was being replaced, in their eyes, by the cold judgment of their peers – their brother acted weird at times – he was retarded.

After his initial introduction Pooser often went on his own to visit the seniors' home. On the street he was regularly hailed by some elderly Greenlander who was obviously a good friend.

From his earliest days Pooser had a sweet and winning smile. As he grew older that smile attached itself to incidents that he found particularly amusing and a sense of humor developed that became a sustaining aspect of his personality. First a twinkle would appear in his eye, then a smile, then all who knew him came to realize that some sight or situation was appealing to his sense of whimsy. Yes, he would laugh at all the obvious things that everyone else found funny, but he would also be amused by sights and situations in which no one else could at first detect any comedy. In trying to explain it to the family he would have to re-enact the situation and often would laugh so hard and so infectiously that we would all be laughing heartily before we even understood the quirk that had precipitated Pooser's sense of fun.

Pooser became a mimic from necessity. His speech was so limited that in order to make us understand who he was talking about he would use the ploy of mimicry. If he came back from the fish market with a kroner (seventeen cents), he would try to explain which of the old-timers had given it to him. He would stiffen his right leg and drag it along till he came to a bench. He would ease himself down, adjust the rigid limb, reach into his breast pocket for an imaginary harmonica, close his eyes and pretend to play so realistically that not only did we know precisely who had given him the kroner but we almost expected to hear a plaintive melody come from his cupped hands.

November 1971; it was time to return to Canada. In the big rambling house by the fish market there were stacks of boxes and suitcases. Driving in the taxi to the heliport, we noticed that snow was beginning to blow, and by the time we reached the terminal large pellets of ice and drifting snow were slashing down. There was no need to ask if our departure would be delayed. We had said our tearful goodbyes and attended farewell parties; everything in the house was packed ready for shipment.

Hubert bundled us back into a taxi and as we sat in anticipation gave the destination to the driver, 'Hotel Godthab!' The children cheered and I relaxed, thankful not to have to unpack. As Tristan walked into the sumptuous, newly completed hotel, he stretched out his arms wide and exclaimed with a sigh, 'Ah! Luxury!' We had almost forgotten that sensuous delight Tristan took in first-class hotels. His pure joy broke the gloom of our postponed departure. At dinner I realized how much our children had been 'civilized' by the influence of Danish culture, yet when one of them hopefully asked for a hamburger I decided that they were still fundamentally North American kids. (They settled for a Polser, which resembles a hot dog.) At the end of the meal Pooser clicked his heels and saluted the head waiter, who, not to be outdone, returned the salute.

In five days the weather cleared. Hedy sat at the window seat with tears streaming down her cheeks, 'I'll come back to Greenland some day, I know I will!'

Chapter Nine

THOUGH Greenland lay behind us we were unable to return to our home in Lucerne because our tenant's daughter was being married in December. Luckily Hubert had some more research to do in Copenhagen. Once more we were installed in Hotel Marina.

Nadine and Hedy were fluent in Danish so we went sightseeing without the inconvenience of having to ask for directions and translations. How many castles we saw! How many art galleries! It was the evenings we all enjoyed the most, for Hubert joined us and we went swimming in a community pool.

The pool was marvelously designed. There were three pools actually; a large pool for serious adult swimmers; an intermediate pool for children learning to swim; and a small wading pool, bathtub-warm, on a raised platform overlooking the two larger pools. Pooser and Lisa delighted in the warm shallow water, and the location made it possible for them to watch their older sisters learning to swim in the medium pool.

One day, while I was playing with the two youngest in the warm pool, another mother approached with her toddler. She spoke to us in Danish, indicating that the intermediate pool was the place for bigger boys. I did not understand every word, nor did Pooser, but her intent was clear: the warm pool was only for babies and small children. Pooser and I looked at each other.

'Would you like to try the middle pool?' I asked, smiling encouragingly. I knew he would not. He hated cold water and was terrified of the deep, yet I could see in him a great struggle to conform to expectations.

As we got up to go, the mother who had spoken to us must have caught the awkwardness of a movement, the telltale gait, that bespoke of Tristan's handicaps. I could see in her eyes the dawning of recognition, and she spoke soft conciliatory words, withdrawing her challenge.

It was too late. Pooser was steeling himself for the scary unknown. Clinging to his father for dear life Pooser entered the intermediate pool. Hedy and Nadine splashed up with words of encouragement and praise; nonetheless, for Pooser it was a cold and terrifying experience and we went home soon after.

Next evening he did not want to go to the pool at all, and it took a great deal of coaxing to get him to come. He kept looking at his older sisters in the intermediate pool where other boys his age were splashing fearlessly. Whenever anyone came by he would get out of the warm water and sit on the edge, pretending to be merely playing with Lisa.

When Hubert's research was completed we flew to Holland. One evening Grampa brought over a Sufi friend who had been in a prayer group that had adopted Tristan during his illness in infancy. She was a big-boned woman dressed in sensible tweeds and oxfords. When she shook hands her penetrating eyes bored into the eyes of the one she was greeting, and she leaned forward as though to follow her gaze into the very depth of the soul. She was certain that she would recognize Tristan by his vibrations; she had felt them all the years she had prayed for him.

When our visitors arrived Tristan and Lisa were playing in their bedroom. Lisa was usually a restrained child, seldom making friends at first acquaintance, yet this time it was she who greeted the new arrivals. Tristan, usually the outgoing one, drew back and was reluctant to shake hands.

Our visitor was visibly confused by the two children. 'Is this really Tristan?' she asked, clutching his hand and gazing intently at his face. Then, altering her strategy, she closed her eyes the better to get 'a reading' on his vibrations.

Tristan threw me a look of 'Help, mom!' I could see that this was one of the rare people to whom he did not respond in his usual outgoing way. I smiled encouragement to him. Inwardly I tried to beam him a message, 'Please be polite, Pooser. It's important.'

Meanwhile the look of concentration was deepening on our visitor's face, and her hand still held Tristan's. Finally, dramatically, she opened her eyes wide and proclaimed. 'Ah, yes, I have it now!' As soon as she released his hand Tristan darted back to his trucks.

We served tea. Normally Tristan delighted in passing out serviettes and cakes, but he was not to be seen on this occasion. When Grampa and our visitor rose to leave, we called to the children to say goodbye. Tristan was not to be found, but the bathroom door was locked so we made his excuses.

Only after the front door had closed did I go up to the bathroom door and whisper, 'Come out! The coast is clear.' A very sheepish-looking little boy emerged. I gave him a reassuring hug.

St. Nicholas arrives in Holland in early December. Our children received presents from Black Peter, and from their cousins they learned that bad children get a bundle of willow switches with which their parents can punish them. It was all exciting and different, since as Bahá'ís we had never celebrated Christmas, but rather gave gifts at the Days of Há at the end of February.

On one day during our week's stay in London we went to visit the grave of the Guardian of the Bahá'í Faith, Shoghi Effendi. It was a day that pearl gray light filtered through layers of mist. We stopped at a corner florist to get flowers. By the time we reached the gates of the cemetery the flowers and we were beaded in fine mist droplets. The hushed calm of the place enveloped us, as silently we walked under the great trees till we found the grave of Shoghi Effendi, marked by a white column topped by a golden eagle. The children marched with their flowers as close to the column as possible.

'How will he know it's from us?' Lisa wanted to know.

'He won't, he's dead,' Hedy explained.

'Let's take them home, then,' Lisa suggested.

'It's a tribute,' Nadine explained. 'See, lots of other people brought flowers. I bet people from all over the world come and bring flowers, because he was the Guardian.'

Pooser went up to various pots of flowers inhaling their fragrance. We called him back and together said prayers.

'O Gow, gui me, pwote me, make me a shiny stalk . . .'

Pooser struggled through his rendering of the prayer. I imagined him a flower on a stalk nodding mist bedewed beside the memorial to Shoghi Effendi. I was startled to hear Lisa reciting a prayer flawlessly. Yet one more thing she had learned to do well, seemingly without effort. As we turned to leave Pooser turned and blew a kiss to the golden eagle.

Our return to Canada made me think of science-fiction stories in which people enter different time-warps. Much had happened to us, yet it seemed to us that the friends we had left in Canada drinking tea were but replacing their empty teacups on the table.

Tristan's adjustments were exacerbated by his speech problems. Nadine was his chief interpreter. When he could not make himself understood he broke out into tears and rages of frustration. Friendships at school were truncated by his inability to speak clearly.

Then something happened that manifested a working of providence so remarkable that it constituted a major landmark in Tristan's progress. Nadine came home from school very excited one day. She spoke so quickly and so breathlessly that at first I did not get the gist of her story. Then slowly and more calmly she told us what had happened.

'I went to this girl's house after school. She's a girl who never used to have *anybody* over to her place . . . maybe because she had a brother a bit like Pooser.' Nadine stopped and hesitated at that point, then continued. 'He had a great deal of trouble at school and everyone thought he was really retarded. Then he began going to a speech therapist.' She paused to unfold a piece of paper that she had clutched in her fist all the way home. 'I have her name here. I made her mother write it out to be sure it was correct, and the phone number too. You will phone, mom, won't you?' Nadine's eyes were brimming with tears. She sniffed self-consciously and continued, 'Well, her brother talks just fine now, and it turned out he wasn't really retarded; it was just that he couldn't talk. I had a great old discussion with him . . . and I thought, wouldn't it be great if Pooser could talk too!'

That evening I phoned Mrs Rose Fletcher, whose name was on the crumpled piece of paper. She agreed to see us, but would not guarantee that she would be able to help. She had very few openings in her schedule and a city bylaw forbade her to teach in her own home, which was in a residential zone. She had to rely, therefore, on the use of a room in a church basement which was available to her a few hours a day. Before

I hung up I recounted to her how highly recommended she had been, and the interesting way we had heard of her after having tried all the other available speech therapists in the city.

A few days later in the church basement we met Mrs Fletcher, a small, serious, intense and rather formidable lady. Usually, she had children read something, but at seven years of age Tristan still could not read. A tape was made of Tristan in conversation.

She telephoned a few days later. Tristan had very few sounds at his disposal, she stated. His blends were non-existent, and he dropped all terminal consonants. To our great relief she agreed to work with him. He was a challenge for her.

And so began a twice-weekly speech therapy schedule that was to last over two years and to change the course of Tristan's life. We took any time slot that was available, even if it meant missing school.

In the church basement, sitting before a mirror propped up with books, Mrs Fletcher worked with Tristan. The limp ham-like tongue that came out of Tristan's mouth was not the pointed tip Mrs Fletcher wanted. She stood behind him, showing him how to move his reluctant piece of pink ham from one side of his mouth to the other. No wonder the other therapists had not succeeded with Tristan, I thought, watching. It was not lack of effort or willingness on his part. The muscle development of his tongue was not up to making the necessary movements to produce the desired sounds.

'Every day, work on these exercises,' she directed.

'Tongue up, towards the right eye,' Mrs Fletcher commanded. 'Tongue up, towards the left eye. Now, tongue behind your lower teeth, tongue behind your upper teeth! Pucker up your mouth in a fish kiss!' The tension was broken as the reluctant piece of ham disappeared behind both upper and lower teeth, and Tristan exploded with laughter.

From that day we worked on the flat inert tongue with a daily series of tongue and lip exercises. And slowly, so slowly that it was virtually imperceptible at first, the tongue muscles began to respond.

One day Rose Fletcher instructed, as she had so many times previously, 'Tongue behind the lower teeth! Say YELLOW!'

Miraculously, instead of the usual LELLOW, Tristan enunciated a clear beautiful – YELLOW! 'YELLOW' became the favorite color at our house. 'Yes' came soon after. From then on progress was constant.

Rose Fletcher had an imposing array of games, toys, cards and puzzles. 'You can't just sit and talk to a child for half an hour,' she would say. 'You have to give him something to talk *about*.'

He worked on color-learning games, number games, matching shapes, telling-the-difference-between-shapes games, telling-time games. Always the games were accompanied by suitable phrases or explanations. For half an hour Tristan talked to her and to his partner in situations that were intriguing and absorbing.

This remarkable speech therapist was a hard taskmistress. She insisted that the parent be present at every session and that there be daily practice sessions at home. But once convinced of commitment she was most helpful in suggesting games to be used at home to supplement the work being done at the therapy sessions.

One of the first (and perhaps the most popular) games she recommended was *The House that Jack Built*. I believe that it was put out by an English toy firm, for it was not easy to find in Canada at the time. The dice had colors instead of numbers on the side. You had to first roll white, for that was the color of the framework of the house. At each roll you could acquire another item for your house provided you rolled the right color. The roof was red, the window shutters green, and so forth.

'Oh! How lucky! I rolled red. Just what I needed for my roof,' I would enunciate clearly.

'Lucky for me!' Tristan would say, carefully putting his tongue behind his upper teeth to come out with a clear 'L' sound. 'I have gween now!' The blends were still hard and 'GR' would come much later, Mrs Fletcher assured us. 'I can get the shuttews.'

We played that game till it literally wore out!

This exciting time, when Tristan was emerging from the isolation that his hitherto unintelligible speech had imposed on him, also marked a period when the amount of time I had to spend with him became significantly out of balance with what was left for the other daughters. The twice-weekly sessions at the therapist meant that the older children had to baby-sit Lisa.

They also had to learn patience, for though Tristan's speech was so much improved it was still halting. If he was interrupted, he would have to begin all over again, for he was unable to pick up the thread of thought after an interruption. Even if someone passed the butter in front of him, it would be a distraction and he would start all over again from the beginning. Despite these problems, he became more and more the raconteur and his special humor emerged despite all his speech difficulties.

'A piece of wilderness is what we need,' Hubert announced one night after supper. 'How would you like to have a cottage on a lake? The children should be learning to swim and to use boats. It would be a great thing for the family.' The log cabin we found was all we had dreamed of while away from Canada, an authentic piece of wilderness.

For Tristan the summers at the cottage were high adventure. He did the usual things like paddle in the warm shallow water by the sandy beach, watch minnows through the cracks of the small wharf, guard the toads and frogs Hedy caught and eat marshmallows at the cookouts with the children of our neighbors recently returned from Thailand. But there was a world for Tristan at that lake that only he could enter, and this was a magic world.

At the wharf jutting out from the beach we had several boats tied up. The oldest girls used the rubber dinghy for their swimming excursions, Hubert and I went out in our canoe every evening after supper, but there was also an old flat-bottomed rowboat that leaked a little. It was this craft that Tristan claimed for his own. It was secured to the wharf by a long piece of rope so that Tristan could row for hours, in great circles.

We would hear him talking, giving orders, scampering from bow to stern and rowing, rowing, rowing. In the warm sunny days his hair bleached white, his body tanned golden brown and the muscles of his thin arms and shoulders began to develop. Was he a pirate, sailing the Barbary coast? Sometimes we would see him hoist his shirt as a sail or flag on a spare oar. Was he Leif Ericsson discovering new lands? At times he would stand, hand shielding his eyes, looking out over the water. At other times he would cast a plastic bucket over the side and haul it up as he had doubtless seen fishermen hauling in nets in Greenland.

On his return from these long sun-drenched afternoon voyages of his, Tristan was happy and relaxed. At supper he ate ravenously. At dusk he and Grampa would wait for the family of loons to swim by, and in the gathering dusk listen to their haunting calls across the lake.

Peaceful were those days and evenings by the lake. Yet our conversations often turned to war. Both Hubert and I had been deeply scarred by our childhood war experience. World peace was not for us some remote dream, it was a need made real by experience of war, a craving that had led us both to espouse the Bahá'í Faith.

Grampa had worked in the Dutch underground movement. He had turned prematurely gray in his twenties and was able to pass for a much older man; his code name had been De White. The older children, who had been reading about the war, were impressed that he had known Corrie ten Boom. Around the camp fire they heard tales of courage and heroism in the face of danger. As these concepts emerged like the leaping flames of the fire so too did the dark concepts of cowardice and betrayal.

At night I heard snatches of their conversations from their bunk beds. 'Let's make up a code word,' Nadine suggested in a whisper. 'If there is an emergency you can send me the word and I'd come to your aid.'

'Yeah, let's think of a secret word,' Hedy's sleepy voice would answer. 'Do you ever wonder if you would be brave . . . or . . . just scared?'

Chapter Ten

THE family and the Bahá'í community were still central to Tristan's life when most other children fell under the sway of a peer group. The feeling of acceptance and unconditional love that he experienced from Bahá'ís, the enduring friendships that he maintained, the sense of belonging in a world community, were all real and meaningful.

He absorbed the spiritual teachings of the Bahá'í Faith much as some people absorb music. Loving, courteous interactions among the members of the Bahá'í community created in him a sense of harmony. Later he would feel disunity, much as one would recognize a jarring false note. For Tristan the allegros and andantes of spiritual life fitted into a pattern. Intuitively he could assume the main solo part or be an accompaniment or blend in with the orchestration of spiritual harmonies.

Seven to ten were his cloudless years. The visits to the doctor were few, and only with the common childhood ailments. He looked like a normal child a few years younger than his chronological age. With his fine gold hair, and a delicately molded face sensitive and responsive to humor, he would, at first glance, appear slight but well built. Only the practiced eye would at second glance pick up the slight awkwardness of movement and the splay-footed walk. His speech was slow and deliberate, every syllable enunciated. If one were to pick up the telephone and hear him speak for the first time, one would suspect an impersonator.

Then, as throughout his life, he was more comfortable with adults than with children. A native charm of personality, added to the courtliness of manner learned from his grandfather, produced a polite and winning child.

Tristan's good health allowed us greater involvement in Bahá'í administration. Many Bahá'ís visited us en route to distant continents and remote islands. All through his life

Tristan would delight in this vast network of friends.

We held weekly firesides at which Tristan loved to play host, opening the door, taking coats, ushering in arrivals. After refreshments there were often songs. This was the best part for the children. Tristan's favorite was the negro spiritual 'He's Got the Whole World in His Hands'. He loved to suggest names to be included in the verse 'he's got you and me brother in his hands, He's got . . . in his hands,' often suggesting the name of some shy person in the group.

This was the boom time of the *Back-to-the-Land* movement in Canada. Hubert and I were deeply affected by it. Both of us had experienced great food shortages during the war in Europe. We had a young family and we struggled to balance our long-range efforts for world peace through the Bahá'í Faith with the need to provide practical security for survival. So it was not really surprising that on a canoe trip that we took in the summer of 1974 we should see a plot of land on one of the Rideau Lakes that beckoned us to an agrarian life.

Grampa and the children were enthusiastic. So we sold our house and moved into a rented town house while we built a Georgian-style brick house on our farm. Grampa stayed with us late into the fall that year. One of the reasons for his delayed departure, I suspected, was that he had struck up a friendship with a diminutive English lady with bouncing white curls and sunny disposition. Our children fondly called her Auntie Bea but were puzzled that white-haired people could still be romantic.

Auntie Bea and Grampa were opera lovers. The day that Grampa was to take Auntie Bea out for supper and to the National Arts Center he looked over his wardrobe and bemoaned the fact that he had only summer clothes and nothing suitable to wear for an evening in town.

The dry cleaner's truck was passing by so he gave me a jacket to give to the cleaners. Then we stood on the front step in the autumn sunshine discussing who would go to meet Auntie Bea at the bus stop. I had just found a wad of bills in his shirt pocket while doing the laundry that morning.

'Your money doesn't need to be laundered,' I teased. 'You come by it honestly.'

As I spoke he paled and the same look of concentration came into his eyes that I had noticed in Hubert's when he tried to remember something.

'The opera tickets!' Grampa exclaimed, 'I left them in my jacket pocket!'

The dry cleaner's truck was rounding the corner of the street when Grampa started sprinting. Tristan got off the school bus just in time to see Grampa running down the street waving his arms and calling after the disappearing truck.

'It's a good thing the Schuurman men kept in good shape,' I said, greeting Tristan fondly. 'Not many men his age can run that fast.'

Tristan watched with that special glint of fun that illumined him when something struck him as particularly funny. I could tell that at the supper table we would be treated to a good-natured impersonation of Grampa.

'Grampa tells me you are really doing well in yoga, Moose,' I said proudly. 'You keep it up and you too will be able to fly down the street when you're seventy.' As I said those words something caught at my heart. Would there be an old age for my son?

Grampa came back puffing but holding up his opera tickets triumphantly. Auntie Bea would never know how close she came to spending another evening at home listening to records.

Tristan was the only one of the children who listened to opera with Grampa. The new stereo system had a tape deck which permitted Tristan to play his favorite tapes. (Before that his poor fine motor coordination had played havoc with records and needles.)

One day we taped a program from the radio that was to become a beloved favorite with Tristan and with the whole family. It was a concert with Rabbi Schlomo Carlbach. Typical of the Eastern European Hassidic tradition in which Rabbi Carlbach grew up, his songs were variations on the theme of man's dialogue with God. As relief to the heartwrenching, tear-brimming songs, he would launch into finger-snapping, foot-stomping rhythms of a hora. How often I have seen Tristan put on that tape and listen rapt to the songs and stories that spoke directly to God of the perennial afflictions of mankind, and how often I have seen him rise and lift high his arms and clap his hands above his head while he danced hypnotized by the hora's beat.

Later in the fall Tristan told us that he was in trouble at school and had been sent to the principal's office. I stared at him incredulous. It turned out that he did not know what had gotten him into trouble nor had he been able to communicate with the principal. He broke down and cried, not from contrition but because the aura of 'being in trouble' was upsetting him.

After he had been comforted and tucked into bed I sat for a long time thinking. All too well I knew, from my years of teaching, how easily blame accrued to the shy, the reticent, the slow of speech.

Early the next morning I called the school in Bell's Corners where Tristan attended the special-ed. class, and made an appointment to see the principal and his homeroom teacher. I dressed carefully, remembering how quickly and indelibly first impressions are formed.

The vice-principal who saw me was very understanding. It had actually been the little boy with whom Tristan had been playing who had broken the school rules but Tristan had stood by his friend. We talked about how difficult it was for some children to absorb all the rules, especially if they were new to the school. Next, I explained about Tristan's speech therapy and why it took him so long to formulate and then articulate answers, especially under stress.

Finally, I went to the portable which housed Tristan's classroom. A gray-haired teacher met me at the door. The face is not unkind, I thought.

'It can't be easy to teach a group of children all of whom are at different levels. Some of your students no doubt have multiple handicaps!'

She sighed and smiled. I could almost see the mantle of many years of conscientious teaching heavy on her shoulders. Gradually she began to tell me of the various emotional problems of the children in her class.

'Well, Tristan's problems are mainly physical,' I explained, 'and I am very concerned that they don't become emotional as well.' Then I went on to tell her about how heavily 'being in trouble' had weighed on my little boy. She asked about the nature of his illness and I related some of his story, stressing the importance of his speech therapy and of his teachers. We parted friends and I knew that I had an ally who would be truly interested in Tristan's progress. The rest of the school year passed peacefully and happily for Tristan.

There was, however, another cloud on his horizon. Lisa, who had always been *his baby*, was growing up, going to kindergarten, forming her own friendships. They still shared the same bedroom and often played happily together, but more and more Lisa would seek out her own girlfriends and play with dolls and dress up. On weekends, when we went to our land, the old closeness would return, but once we returned to town the rift between them would widen again. We made sure that in the new house there would be separate bedrooms for all the children.

There were several active Bahá'í communities around the Ottawa valley, and though generally they functioned autonomously, at Naw-Rúz, the Bahá'í New Year on the 21st of March, the communities combined to have a joint celebration.

Unlike many boys, Tristan loved to dress up. That year he had received a navy blue velvet bow-tie at the Days of Há. When he emerged from his room, ready for the Naw-Rúz festivities, all his sisters exclaimed how handsome their brother looked! Indeed, in suit and bow-tie, his light blond hair worn long in the style of the day, he cut a dashing figure.

While the girls headed for the laden supper tables, Lisa stationing herself strategically beside the desserts, Tristan was busy socializing. Throughout the evening old friends came up to tell me how much they enjoyed talking to him. When dancing started Tristan was truly in his element. He was one of the first on the dance floor and managed to dance with all the prettiest girls. Yet often he would approach some shy wallflower. Who could refuse him?

Only when Lisa had hung limp and sleepy in my arms for over an hour did we manage to get him away from the dancing and into the car for the drive home. The older girls talked of the boys they had seen and danced with, Lisa dreamt of lovely desserts, but Tristan sat wide awake, still in the glow of the dancing and the music.

'Oh! How beautiful the lights are!' he exclaimed, looking out at the city of Ottawa and at the Ottawa River shimmering in the darkness. 'How beauti-ful!'

Chapter Eleven

MANY HANDS MAKE LIGHT WORK. Tristan stood looking at the sign in the big dining room of the camp at the Ontario Bahá'í Summer School. A light bulb had been drawn and colored yellow, around it were several hands reaching out to the bulb. 'Ma–ny ha–n–ds make light work!' He sounded it out.

'How do they do it, mom?' Tristan asked puzzled.

'How do they do what?' I asked, my mind still engrossed with the logistics of assigning beds in the cabin that we were to share with another family.

'I thought light worked on 'lec–tri–s–ty,' Tristan pursued.

'That's right, Moose, light bulbs work through electricity,' I answered absently.

'Then why does it say . . . "*Many hands make light work*"?'

'Oh, that's just a play on words. Look, there's Nadine, she'll explain it to you. Remember how she explained about "the fork in the road"?'

Nadine's help was enlisted, and I returned to the cabin to straighten out the disagreement over bunks between Hedy and Lisa.

Since the children were wee infants we had taken them to Bahá'í Summer Schools. For all of us it was the highlight of the summer. Tristan was transformed by the total acceptance that he experienced among the Bahá'ís. There was no hanging back with the family here.

When I returned, the big dining hall was filling up with people. Tristan had been put to work setting the long trestle tables to illustrate that, in effect, *Many hands make light work*! As he saw old friends again he would leave his paper napkins and run out to greet them effusively. Anyone welcomed by Tristan was left with a distinct feeling of wellbeing. His welcome was not exclusively for those he already knew from other summer schools or conferences; if anyone entered the room hesitantly or stood shyly by the wall, Tristan would set out as the one-boy welcome committee to take them by the hand and introduce them around.

We scarcely saw Tristan during the days that followed. At meals he sat with *his* friends. The children's sessions lasted all morning. He participated and never gave the impression that he felt out of his depth. Only during the afternoons, when everyone went to the sandy beach on Lake Huron, did we keep an eye on him. Since he was the most cautious of children we really were more in a position to observe his socializing.

It was the summer he turned ten. His humor and charm were at their apex that year. The mischievous twinkle in his eye was as yet undimmed by pain. A cap of golden hair, that bleached to platinum in the sun, framed delicate features, tanned and clear skinned. It was with the eighteen to twenty-eight crowd that he was most popular.

At one time I overheard the handsome sports director asking Tristan, as he came up to him among a bevy of lovely young girls, 'What have you got that I haven't got?'

'Brains and personality, brother, brains and personality!'

The repartee came from a Pete Seeger record that the children knew by heart. Interspersed with the songs were stories told by Pete Seeger. One had to do with two maggots that had fallen off a spade. One had fallen on the carcass of a cat and had fed and fed. Another had fallen into a completely empty rain gutter. When the two met a couple of days later the starving maggot said, 'Hello brother, you look so sleek and fat! To what do you owe your good fortune?' To which the other maggot replied, 'Brains and personality, brother, brains and personality!'

Nancy, who at last year's summer school had been on crutches, was now in a wheelchair. Tristan was often with her and was most solicitous. We were well into the week before I realized that it was Nancy's room-mate, Joannie, who had captivated Tristan's heart in a special way. At the closing party, everyone dressed up. Tristan danced with Joannie and looked as if he were in the seventh heaven. Joannie was a young woman in her early twenties, slight of build and graceful of movement, with red-gold lights in soft flowing hair. She was sweet and kind to the smitten little boy, and promised to write.

On the long drive home we played word games to pass the time. Only when someone used the expression, '*Many hands make light work*', did Tristan emerge from his brown study.

'Joannie showed me how that works!' he exclaimed. 'We used to wipe the tables together after supper!' From the glow on his face I wondered if her presence had also made light his task.

How strange, I mused, so many things come naturally to Tristan. Thoughtfulness of others, sensitivity to needs of those who are handicapped or lonely or shy. Yet other things are incredibly difficult for him, like the ten number facts. He still has to use a number line to figure out five and four.

Just before the end of summer we moved into our new house at Westport. From the front windows we could see the Upper Rideau Lake spread out before us and watch the pleasure boats come into the harbour at Westport. From our back windows we had a pastoral scene of rolling meadows separated by hedgerows of hawthorn and apple trees, rosebushes and raspberries. Our Georgian-style brick house lay a half-mile out of the village on an expanse of meadow which, when freshly mown, masqueraded as a lawn.

Full of idealism and enthusiasm we embarked on our new rural life. The garden we had planted in the spring was yielding a rich harvest.

There were problems, however. When we had made the decision to move to the country, Hubert had been on a flexible-hours program. We expected that he could work longer hours during the week and have most of Fridays off. After a few months he found the seventy-nine-mile drive twice a day too tiring. We decided to buy a small one-bedroom condominium in Ottawa where he could stay overnight. He returned to the farm on Wednesdays and of course on the weekends. The children missed him and so did I but they did enjoy staying at 'dad's pad' on trips into town and swimming at the apartment's pool.

On Monday mornings the farm was like the hub of a wheel and we, the six spokes, all radiated out from its center in different directions. Hubert drove to work in Ottawa. Lisa, starting grade I, and Hedy in grade VII went to the local school just outside Westport; Nadine, entering Rideau District High School, traveled by bus; I had begun teaching again half-time and drove to Delta; Tristan had the longest bus ride to reach his school at Sweet's Corners.

When we had first moved to our 'farm' the younger children had felt lonely for their friends. Between Lisa and Tristan there had been a resurgence of their old closeness. Lisa's bedroom was finished first and she asked Tristan to share it while his was being completed. During that time Lisa, who had learned to read on her own, taught Tristan the prayer, 'Blessed is the Spot . . .'

I could hear them at night after they had gone to bed. Lisa, sitting on her bed with the illustrated children's prayer book on her lap, would prompt.

'. . . and the house and the place . . .'

Tristan, enunciating slowly and carefully after his two years of speech therapy, would repeat after her. It took about a week and a half of daily coaching for him to learn the prayer. We were all very proud of him. But that joint venture also marked the final waning of their special relationship. For it was Lisa who had been the teacher, it was she who could read now, it was she who had corrected him, shown him the accompanying pictures and done the explaining. The old days when he had been her protector, the older brother, had somehow inexplicably been overturned, distorted. Tristan found it difficult to forgive her for surpassing him.

Lisa was the quietest child. In her room she read for hours, worked at puzzles, threaded beads. The outbreaks of Tristan's frustrations at her and himself were hard to understand and accept. There were times that Tristan was mean to her, times that family feelings ran high about Tristan's special privileges, about the time I spent with him doing speech therapy.

When I tucked them in at night I would try to explain to them separately, for they were now in their own rooms, why there were the differences.

Hubert was growing restless. Despite his busy schedule at the farm planting trees, working on the garden, building shelves around the house, he was reaching out for a new challenge. The film on Greenland had been well received; the book (*Northern Neighbors*) that he had written on the same subject was at the printers; a circumpolar display that he had organized was touring Europe. It was only a matter of time before he would come up with another new idea. Yet when he asked, 'How would you like to go to Lapland?' I was not prepared.

I stifled the cry that rose in me, 'But we have just moved!'

As if guessing at my unspoken objection, Hubert reassured me, 'It will take at least a year to arrange it all. I would have to get permission from the native organizations to make a film about the reindeer herders.'

Hubert packed for an exploratory trip to Norway and Sweden to undertake the arrangements for a film that would explore the old and the new modes of life of these northern people the Lapps, or Sames as they called themselves.

Tristan watched his dad pack his suitcase, kiss everybody goodbye and drive off to the airport. The house seemed mournfully quiet after his departure. I settled down to do some mending and was not surprised to see Tristan dragging up a big suitcase from the basement. He loved to play 'going away'.

Passing by his room, I asked, 'Packing just like daddy?'

'I'm going far away,' Tristan affirmed.

Later the suitcase went bump, bump, down the stairs. When I went outside to check, Tristan was sitting in my station wagon, his suitcase in the back seat, making vroom, vroom noises at the steering wheel. I made sure the handbrake was on and went back to my sewing, knowing that he could amuse himself for a long time in games of make-believe.

It was with a start that, some time later, I looked up to see a police car come up the circular drive. I ran to open the door to a very young police officer.

'Do you know this child?' he asked gravely. Tristan, with a broad if sheepish grin, was getting out of the police car. 'We found him walking down the road with that suitcase. Would he have any reason for running away from home?'

'Were you going to see the Dances?' I asked Tristan, making a great effort to hold back my laughter.

Tristan nodded.

'He said that he was going far away,' the young officer said, consulting his notebook.

'His father just left this afternoon,' I tried to explain.

'I see, a family break-up!' said the young officer, brightening.

'Oh no, just a business trip!'

The policeman scrutinized us. Tristan was not doing very well hiding his grin behind a serious mien. I wondered if I was doing any better.

'Well, I guess it's all right,' he said, starting to go back to his car.

I dropped down on my knee to give Tristan a big hug. Over his shoulder, I could see the young officer glancing back at us and shaking his head in disbelief. I broke into helpless laughter.

'Well Moose, you really did it this time!' I said laughing, 'I bet you were pleased as punch to get a ride in a real police car.' Tristan beamed from ear to ear.

His sisters had been watching and now they spilled out of the house and surrounded him with questions. Instead of relating the details, Tristan went to the phone to call up his friends the Dances.

Horace and Ellida Dance were a retired couple who lived down the road towards the village of Westport. Horace was a mild-mannered man who used to work on the railroad that once serviced Westport but of which only a deserted station and a high embankment running near the Dances' land remained. Tristan loved to visit the couple and their dog Tippy. Nobody made chocolate cake like Mrs Dance, I soon learned. Whenever Mrs Dance went away to visit her daughter, Tristan would inform us and we would invite Horace over for supper. If one of them were sick, Tristan would call every day to check on their progress. Always the conversations ended by a question about Tippy's welfare.

'I specialize in corners,' Tristan declared, one day out of the blue.

'What do you mean?' I asked, puzzled.

'First Bell's Corners,' he said, naming the school he had attended before our move, 'and now Sweet's Corners!' the name of his present school.

'How do you like the school?' I asked, realizing that lately he had not been talking much about school.

'It's great,' Tristan answered. 'It's open house tomorrow. Will you come to meet my teacher?' he added with intensity.

Sweet's Corners School had been built as an 'open concept school', but the special-education room had been enclosed and set back. We had been admiring the room for some time when a tall slim lady with an Afro-hairdo and intense intelligent eyes walked in.

'I'm Jolleen Hopwood,' she introduced herself. 'I don't get too many visitors on parents' night, so I was in the library.' Jolleen Hopwood was an inspired teacher, and in Tristan she had a devoted disciple.

Often, while I was sitting over coffee, after supper, Tristan would talk about things that were on his mind. One evening as the two oldest bickered in the kitchen over whose turn it was to do the dishes, Tristan brought up the subject of his illness.

'You know, mom, you talked to me about the brain . . . my brain was hurt when I was a baby . . .'

'Yes,' I answered thoughtfully.

'Well, do you know how the brain works?' Tristan persevered.

I looked at him steadily, 'It's rather complicated.'

'Well, *I* know!' he said.

'Tell me,' I said softly.

'The brain is gray and all folded up. Different parts do different jobs. They all have names . . . I'll show you my picture,' he volunteered with enthusiasm.

In his science notebook was a clear diagram of the human brain, labeled in Jolleen's neat script.

'Can you read the names of the different parts?' I asked, impressed.

He could and did. When he came to the cerebellum I stopped him. 'This is where you lost most of your brain cells,' I explained. Then remembering the head nurse's description, I asked Tristan to bring a clean plate. On the plate I sprinkled pepper, then on one section of the plate I sprinkled it very liberally. 'The dark spots are the dead brain cells, but here in the cerebellum,' I pointed to where the pepper lay more thickly, ' . . . in the cerebellum you have more damaged cells. The parts that aren't hurt still work fine but this is the reason you have to go to speech therapy.'

Jolleen ordered films on the subject of his interests. 'I just can't understand it!' Tristan exclaimed one day after supper. 'I watched that movie about the circulation of the blood all by myself. The other kids didn't even care how the blood gets all around us!'

We retired to the living room where we looked up the

anatomy section of the *Encyclopaedia Britannica*. By now Tristan knew the volume at a glance and without hesitation found the page where over a basic outline of the body transparent overlays could be placed showing the circulatory system, the digestive system and so forth.

'How fascinating!' he exclaimed, enunciating the word with relish.

Then suddenly something caught in my chest and throat, and I rushed upstairs. With the door of the bedroom closed, the spasm of sobbing broke out and my brimming eyes overflowed.

'My God,' I prayed fervently into my pillow, 'don't let me think of what *might* have been. Just let me be grateful for what *is*!'

Question followed question. 'How are cars made?' I let Hubert field that one. Next he was carting off to school my huge pictorial history of Japan.

When Tristan's social studies notebook came home some time later I looked through it with amazement. Jolleen was writing, illustrating and researching all the answers to his questions. Tristan could name the main cities in Japan, and read off the figures for the population and talk intelligently about the country's industries. On the weekend when Hubert joined us after supper Tristan told us about the film he had seen on life in Japan.

'The people looked like . . .' he was hunting in his mind for an apt comparison, ' . . . like Greenlanders!'

'We must have this remarkable teacher over!' Hubert exclaimed.

It was close to the end of the year before our schedule and hers made that possible. When Jolleen and her husband arrived for tea Tristan fairly glowed with pleasure. He passed around the serviettes, the cookies. It was plain to see that he hung on every word his teacher spoke and when on leaving she gave him a hug, his happiness at our praise of her and the success of the visit was complete.

A small shadow appeared that year on Tristan's horizon. He began to itch. At times, when he put on his pyjamas, I could see the scratches on his chest and arms. We went to the doctor, who sent us to the dermatologist. We tried creams; we tried baths; we tried oils in the bath; we tried oatmeal preparations in the bath; we tried three baths a day; we tried no baths at all. Still Tristan itched. Someone suggested a home-made cream with sheep tallow and bear grease. It worked better than any apothecary cream but still . . . Tristan itched.

Many times that year he was troubled by unexplained tummy aches often accompanied by diarrhea. After a particularly bad bout the local doctor suggested that we take him into the newly built Eastern Ontario Children's Hospital, in Ottawa.

We could not have chosen a worse day. As the December daylight waned a freezing rain started to fall. Tristan sat beside me unusually silent.

'Are you worried that you might have to have an operation?' I ventured. At our last consultation with the local doctor he had suggested that Tristan might be suffering from appendicitis.

'No,' he said thoughtfully, 'I won't need an operation.'

'Well, I certainly hope not for your sake, my Moose!' I said, trying to sound cheerful.

'I won't,' he asserted again calmly and quietly.

I glanced at him from the corner of my eye. 'Moose, I know you have been in hospital more than most boys your age and I know that you don't like it, but if you need your appendix out it's better to get it out.'

'Don't worry, mom, I won't.'

There was something about his tone, the quiet certainty in what he said, his effort to comfort me, that made me silent. The next question I asked in humility. 'How do you know?'

'I don't know how . . . but I know *for sure*,' was his reply.

'Does that happen to you often, Moose . . . that you know things *for sure*?' I asked gently.

The following silence was so protracted that I was beginning to regret my prying question, when at last he answered, as if from a distance, 'Sometimes.'

For a long time we traveled without speaking. I had to reduce speed. The back road we were driving on began to glisten like a dark mirror as the freezing rain encrusted it in ice. There was little traffic on these secondary roads, but I was worried about sliding off into the ditch. Before leaving we had called Hubert; he would be expecting us for supper at the apartment.

Outside Ottawa we stopped at a garage to phone Hubert and assure him of our safety. All motorists had been warned to stay off the roads, he informed us. I promised to call again when we reached the hospital.

Tristan was hot and I suspected his fever had started rising again.

The Children's Hospital was like an oasis of light after our hours on the dark slippery roads. As we were processed by the reception desk I realized how many halcyon years had passed since Tristan had last checked into a hospital. It was after nine-thirty, and although our local doctor had phoned ahead of our arrival, still we had to sit and wait to be seen by a doctor. Tristan began to wilt. At last we were ushered into a cubicle. Another half-hour wait. A white-jacketed figure came in to take down Tristan's medical history. Midway he left, task unfinished. After twenty minutes a doctor came in and started taking down the medical history all over again. There were endless questions. He wanted to look in Tristan's eyes. Another doctor was called in to look at the interesting phenomenon. After numerous delays still another doctor came in and started asking the same questions all over again.

By this time I had had enough. We had left home at four, driven in impossible conditions to the hospital; it was midnight and my child was obviously sick! The last doctor listened to me and said, 'I'll admit him but I don't know what he has, I doubt that it is appendicitis.'

I thought that once on the ward I could finally put Tristan to bed. I had not counted on the intern. In his brightly lit office, he wanted to hear Tristan's medical history from the beginning. In my arms Tristan's limp body grew heavier, my own eyes were drooping, and my mind was growing sluggish. Despite fatigue I perceived that this young intern considered that *he* would be the one to find the answer to this otherwise puzzling case. His questions became more intense, and obviously he was warming up to this game of detective while we grew more desperately tired. At last he closed in. He had, he knew, isolated a rare mineral deficiency that must be the cause of my son's condition.

I looked at his eager face, the excitement of a brilliant diagnosis already bright in his eyes. The sick form in my arms was invisible to him and my tiredness immaterial. I explained, as evenly as I could, that the test he was suggesting had been given to Tristan several years ago. I watched the excitement drain from his face. Was I sure, he wanted to know. Yes, I was sure. He walked out, slamming the door in his disappointment. For another quarter of an hour we sat in the office, forgotten. Tristan had fallen asleep in my arms and I was too numb to move. Eventually, I found a nurse who showed us to a room and Tristan was tucked in.

The rest of Tristan's stay at the hospital was happy. He was not too sick to enjoy the little TVs, attached on an extendable arm to each bed. There were playrooms with fascinating toys for ambulant patients. The doctor that finally took on Tristan's case was Dr McKee, a senior doctor, who explained to me several things that were puzzling about Tristan, including his high sedimentation rate and enlarged spleen. They wanted to keep him under observation.

One day as I was leaving the ward a young woman in a lab coat ran up to me. 'I'm so glad to see you, Mrs Schuurman!' she exclaimed rather breathlessly. 'I wonder if you could tell me a little about Tristan's eating habits.'

'Well, he eats like a horse most of the time,' I replied. 'Everyone in the family wonders how he stays so skinny.'

A frown came over the pretty face. 'You see, he only marks off tea and toast on the menu sheets.'

'The menu sheets?' I asked, perplexed.

'Why yes, didn't you see them?' She handed me a long menu sheet that would have shamed many a restaurant. 'We send out a menu sheet once a day and the patients can mark off what they would like for each meal,' she explained obviously proud of this new concept in catering to young patients. 'But you see sometimes Tristan doesn't tick anything off . . . and I was wondering . . .'

'Did it occur to you that . . . that he might not be able to read it?' I asked gently.

'Not read it . . .?' She looked at me flabbergasted, then came sudden realization, quickly followed by embarrassment. She blushed, 'Oh, how stupid of me, I never thought of it . . .'

'Perhaps if you or one of the nurses could come in and read it to him and mark it off . . .' I suggested tentatively.

'Yes, of course, but . . . it's just that I realized that there are others who may also have that same problem . . .' she hurried off down the hall.

I had to leave to go back to Westport and my teaching duties. Hubert visited Moose daily, and instead of coming home on the weekend suggested that we all come down and camp in the apartment.

The girls were very much impressed by the beautiful new hospital. Hubert had arranged for Tristan to go out Saturday night with the family. He had purchased tickets for a Christmas children's play at the National Arts Center.

All the nurses on the ward stood by as Tristan, resplendent in suit and velvet bow-tie, left for his night out on the town. The head nurse reminded him smilingly that, just like Cinderella, he was expected back before midnight.

There was an Italian restaurant, Imbro's, on Rideau Avenue. The children loved to go there and it was here that we took the family in a festive mood. Tristan always put on a performance eating spaghetti; that night he was irrepressible. Even the head waiter came up to tell us how much pleasure it gave him to see someone who *so obviously* enjoyed his meal.

The foyer of the National Arts Center is both spacious and imposing. A wide red-carpeted stairway sweeps up to the level of the opera's entrance. Tristan, like an Ariel released from hospital captivity, started up the staircase his arms spread as if a bird in flight.

'Ah! Freedom, freedom!' called the ascending Tristan.

Hubert and I, standing at the foot of the stairs, watched as our son sped up the red expanse of carpet. Nadine and her sisters stopped their examination of the massive sculpted doors near the foyer. Nadine's eyes brimmed with tears.

'It's all right, mom, I'll go up after him!' she offered, following her brother more sedately up the wide staircase.

Afterwards, in the foyer at intermission, she confided to me, 'The people who watched him were somehow moved . . . he was so . . . so beautiful. I thought I would be embarrassed that he was making a scene, but it was . . . right somehow . . . almost part of the performance.'

We did not stay till the end. Soon after the intermission, Tristan began to itch and get tired. We left and drove him back to the hospital. It was almost with relief that he checked back in at the desk on his ward.

'I came back before I was changed into a pumpkin!' he said

to the head nurse with a wink.

Tristan was released from hospital the next week. At home we teased him about his rest cure in a luxury hospital. Dr McKee saw Tristan as an outpatient and sent him to see several specialists. The internist took time to explain the possible effects of the badly damaged liver. None of the dermatologists had a cure for the itching. The rest of the year Tristan remained healthy.

The trip to Lapland was on! Preparations began in the spring. Hubert was surrounded by cameras, batteries and black 'spook bags', as the children called the big black bag used for loading film in the magazines. There were trial shoots and long-distance calls to make arrangements.

Kautokeino, which is in Norwegian Lapland and is the home of the Same Institute, was to be our home base. Hubert described the town to us and showed us slides taken during his Easter visit.

In *Bahá'í News* we read that Canada was responsible for sending two pioneers to Norway. 'Marvelous! We can fill a pioneering goal!' Hubert exclaimed.

'Only for one year,' I pointed out.

There were no secondary schools in the area, so we had to make arrangements for Nadine and Hedy to attend Ontario Ladies College in Whitby, Ontario. The last week at Westport passed in a state of excitement. The house had been rented for the year, the children's bags stood around half-packed, the phone kept ringing, last-minute arrangements had to be made. When Tristan called me urgently to his room one evening, I went in, but my mind was elsewhere.

'Look, mom, look!' Tristan pointed excitedly.

Nadine was standing on a chair changing the bulb in his overhead light. Beside her, Hedy held up the lamp shade. Lisa was standing at the light switch.

'Don't move!' Tristan commanded. His sisters froze in mid-movement, puzzled. 'Well, mom?'

'Moose, I'm sorry I don't understand,' I had to admit as I surveyed the tableau.

With delight, Tristan exclaimed, 'Many hands make light work!'

Chapter Twelve

PHYSICAL pain is a country apart. It was only years later, when I had become much better acquainted with the foreign land of pain, that I realized that Tristan had been traveling deeper and deeper into that hostile terrain. While Hubert, Lisa and I were passing customs in Italy (where we picked up a Fiat car at the Torino factory) Tristan was being admitted to the borders of *discomfort*. The three of us were awed by the splendour of the Alps. Did Tristan at the same time confront the enormity of his isolation in pain? The alpine meadows, lovely Vevey, the Black Forest, the drive along the Rhine, in later years Tristan remembered none of that. And we in our blindness did not recognize the sad devastated terrain he was traversing alone into that inhospitable land of pain.

At Vevey on the serene Lac Leman we stopped for a break. Tristan looked on as we bought fruit at the open market, watched as Lisa threw crumbs to the swans on the lake. Slowly he began to unwind and return to us. 'What beautiful flowers!' he said, admiring the red geraniums in the flower borders by the lake.

'Tristan has the same taste in flowers as the Guardian,' I said, laughing, and explained to the children that all through the Bahá'í gardens in Haifa there is a predominance of red geraniums.

Moose needed a break from traveling. Sores had developed where he had scratched. Many places we stayed overnight did not have bathtubs, and he had not yet become accustomed to showers. The sponge baths and hurried applications of his creams were not keeping the itching under control. More and more time in the car was spent fidgeting and scratching and being miserable. I could see how much effort he expended controlling his distress, but sometimes by late afternoon if we did not stop in time, the discomfort and frustration would erupt in tears and loud protests, all the more vehement for having been bottled up for so long.

Hubert and I praised him for carrying on so nobly and enduring so patiently. But a grim set to his face and a new gauntness was evident. Was he losing weight? I wondered.

So when we arrived in Holland on a raw rainy day, it was none too soon. Tristan revived visibly and in a day was back to his cheerful self. The presence of beloved Grampa cheered us all. The warmth of Hubert's family restored us.

Oslo was bleak in haze and rain when we arrived. The Canadian *chargé d'affaires* had booked us into the luxurious Hotel SAS. As soon as Tristan stepped into the vast carpeted lobby, and spied the gold-braided uniforms of the doorman and bellhops, he spread out his arms, half-closed his eyes and inhaled deeply.

'Ah! Luxury!'

The rooms were, indeed, luxurious. Tristan immediately wanted a *real* bath. Later when I dried him I noticed how irritated and red were large patches of his skin.

The children came back from their exploration of the hotel shopping plaza bright with excitement. They had gone into a boutique on the lower level of the hotel. Lisa had inspected the Icelandic sweaters and had commented to Tristan that mom could knit as well as this. When the clerk had asked if she could be of assistance, Lisa explained that they were just looking but that when her parents had been in Iceland for a Bahá'í conference, her mother had purchased wool and knit everyone in the family a sweater.

'I was at the same conference!' the sales lady exclaimed, 'I'm a Bahá'í too!' This chance meeting transformed the city for them.

Moose hated to leave Oslo. He stooped down and patted the rich carpet in the foyer, 'Goodbye, Luxury,' he mumbled.

Norway was arrayed in autumn finery as we drove north. When we crossed the border we found that the Swedish forests were fragrant and mushroom-rich. This was familiar landscape reminiscent of the great Canadian forests we had left behind.

But what of Tristan? He looked more and more peaked. Every morning he would get back in the car with a grim resignation. Determination prevented him from scratching during the prayers we said at the outset of every day's driving; after that he fell into the well of discomfort. I could see that had he been offered the option of stepping out of his skin and living only in his bones, he would have gladly taken it.

At the heart of Swedish Lapland lies Jokkmokk. In this charming town we stopped to make contact with the Same organizations and the Same Folk High School with which Hubert hoped to collaborate in making his film. In this town lived our closest Bahá'í neighbors.

Our first evening there, they came to our little hotel room. Ola Okfors, long-haired, wearing one golden earring, was a male nurse at the local hospital. The children loved him on sight. So many 'hippie'-type Bahá'ís had passed through our home that the children always associated them with music and relaxed good times. Gail Ross, with dark curly hair, was also a sixties' flower child from Canada who eked out a living by craft production. She arrived at our hotel room smelling of wood smoke, for she had been dyeing wool with natural dyes on the shore of a lake. Both Ola and Gail were to become our bosom friends in the year to come.

Just a day from Kautokeino, our destination! We had crossed the Arctic circle before reaching Jokkmokk. The farther north we drove the more the trees thinned out and the more the umbers and ochres of late fall replaced the fire-blazing colors of the south. The three countries, Sweden, Finland and Norway, interlock like jigsaw puzzle pieces above the Arctic Circle.

It was Friday evening and the short Arctic day was rapidly drawing to a close. It was too dark for Lisa to continue reading and Tristan had scratched himself into exhaustion. I could ill-disguise my disappointment that we would arrive after the Same Institute had closed for the weekend, for I expected, recalling our Greenland experience, that an apartment would be waiting for us. The film Hubert would be making was to be in collaboration with the Same Institute. Ah well, a weekend in a hotel is not the worst thing that could happen. How nice it would be, though, to have a place of our own after weeks of traveling.

It was dark when we arrived in Kautokeino. Hubert had been there before on his exploratory trip, and was able to drive us straight to the Fjel Stua or Lodge. It was an architecturally interesting wooden building and the managers, the Petersons, who belonged to a missionary movement, were kind and helpful. They guided us to a room and went back to help Hubert with our bags. It was not Hotel SAS! Tristan and I stood in the bare room. We looked at the four bunks along one wall, the small rough wooden table, the three chairs by the window and the small white sink on the opposite wall. Then we looked at each other.

'Mom, can I have a bath before supper?' Tristan asked plaintively.

We inspected the bathroom facilities. There was a rough cement shower.

'I'll wait till tomorrow,' reconsidered Tristan, trying not to sound disappointed.

'What about a rub-down with a soft wash-cloth and a fresh application of cream?' I suggested as cheerfully as I could.

The dining room was closed but the manager's wife would prepare something. We had sandwiches and tea.

'*Breakfasts* are great here!' Hubert assured us.

Back in our room we sat on the three chairs, with Tristan on dad's knee, and said a prayer of thanks for having reached our goal safely.

It was a dispiriting two days. Sunday turned cold, and snow started swirling around. I thought of Vevey surrounded by vineyards. 'We are five hundred miles above the Arctic Circle and at three hundred meters elevation above sea level,' Hubert explained, 'so it is not unusual that we should have Arctic weather.' 'Just think how much more clement it is than Igloolik,' he had added cheerfully. The short afternoon ended in early darkness.

Tomorrow, I kept telling myself as I helped Lisa with her cross-stitch sampler, tomorrow we will be in our own little apartment. Tomorrow we would enroll both children in the local school . . . tomorrow . . .

But when *tomorrow* dawned Tristan's flushed cheeks betrayed a high fever. Hubert went to the Same Institute. When he returned at noon I exploded.

'When can we move into our own place? Tristan is really sick and I could make him so much more comfortable if I could unpack and . . .'

Hubert went up to Moose and felt his forehead. 'Any other

symptoms?' he asked.

'Some of his scratches seem to be infected and he won't take a shower and I'm afraid to use a washcloth to sponge him down for fear of spreading the infection. Now what about an apartment . . .?' I asked, my voice trailing off as I saw Hubert turn to the window.

'There *is* no apartment!' Hubert replied bluntly.

'But they knew we were coming . . .' I looked at the rough bunks, the naked light bulb, the radiator hung with the clothes I had washed in the little hand sink.

'Look, this is not Greenland. There we were treated like royalty. Here we are dealing with a native organization and there are different expectations.' Hubert had started speaking gruffly but now his voice softened, 'I've made inquiries on my own and there is a very acute housing shortage in this town.'

'How are the arrangements for the film?' I asked, fighting down my disappointment.

'Nothing . . . There are no arrangements . . .' Then he added in an effort at lightheartedness, 'At least they did remember who I was.'

By evening Moose was feeling better and we went to the dining room for supper. Below the Fjel Stua, the lights of the village twinkled and the car lights traced patterns on the road that ran north and south. Moose watched the lights in the valley, then with great feeling exclaimed, 'Look, how beauty-full!'

He seemed to feel that, this night, it was his turn to cheer us up. With his rare gift of mime, he did some of his best imitations until we were the merriest table in the dining room. Back in our own room he took up an imaginary microphone and did a most creditable impersonation of Elvis Presley. We laughed with an abandon that assuaged our disappointments; we laughed till our sides ached.

Then suddenly his energy flagged. The balloon of his joviality, inflated for our benefit, collapsed. It was an exhausted boy that I helped on with his pyjamas, noticing as I did so that there were a number of big white pimples on his legs. At night his fever shot up and we had to wake him to give him aspirins and sponge him down. Tomorrow, I decided, I must take him to a doctor. It proved not to be that easy.

The next day Hubert enrolled Lisa at the local school.

Dressed in Eskimo amouts, in Canada

Tristan's first birthday party

Playing the guitar

Tristan at about three years old

Just before leaving Canada for Greenland; from the left:
Nadine, Hubert, Tristan, Suzanne, Lisa, Hedy.

Sunflower days!

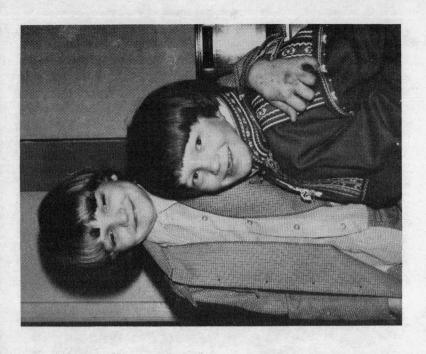

Tristan with neighbours in Norway

At a birthday party in Greenland. This was Tristan's favourite photograph at the end of his life.

Tristan, a few days before his death.

Despite her initial pessimism, Lisa discovered that the Petersons had a daughter her age and the two girls became friends. Hubert was away all morning, and when he returned at noon it was only to inform me that the doctor was out of town and that the nurse had said to keep Tristan in bed and to give him aspirins to bring down the fever. That was all.

I sat at the table by the window as the gray light of autumnal Arctic light faded, and wrote to Nadine and Hedy in boarding school, to my mother in Africa, to Grampa in Holland. Tristan slept fitfully. I prayed.

Several days later the doctor returned. I took Tristan, still feverish, to the hospital waiting room. How often had we sat on the wooden benches of hospital waiting rooms! Finally, it was our turn. To my immense relief, the doctor spoke fluent English. I explained about Tristan's condition, his skin problem, our long car trip, the increased itching and finally the last days with the fever and the pustules.

How thin Tristan looked in the well-lit room. Pustules covered his arms and legs.

'Impetigo,' the doctor concluded, 'but I want to get a swab and examine it under the microscope, and I'll send it to the lab in Alta as well.'

As a young teacher, in Labrador, I had watched, with ill-concealed distaste, as the nurse had swabbed gentian violet on the cases of impetigo among my students. The children who spent their summers on the islands where fresh water was scarce often came back with scalps encrusted with impetigo. It had been commonly assumed that it was a result of poor hygiene and neglect. Once established it was highly infectious.

In Greenland Tristan had come home with a spot of impetigo when it was going round the school, and Lisa had also had a spot but we had treated them three times a day with a clear cream and had good results. If this was impetigo, it was the worst case I had ever seen or heard of.

'Yes, just as I thought,' the doctor declared, turning away from his microscope, 'I'll send it out to the lab in the hospital just to be certain, but it must be treated right away. I'll teach you how to change the dressings at night, but for a while you must bring him in here to the hospital every morning.'

It took an hour and a half to remove every scab and to put medication on every pustule. Moose endured stoically. Then his arms and legs were encased in what looked like long sausage casings made of gauze.

'Keep his fingernails short and try to keep him from scratching. This medicine should help with the itching,' the doctor said at parting.

Every day I washed all Tristan's clothing separately, and carefully looked Lisa over in the shower, but neither she, nor Hubert, nor I developed any signs of impetigo, then or later.

On the third day, as the doctor was changing the dressing I noticed that the infection had spread to Tristan's chest. In fact, it was everywhere but in the genital area. The doctor was called away to an emergency. Before leaving, he brought in an efficient gray-haired nurse, gave her hurried instructions and rushed off.

She took a look at Tristan, and gave me a withering glance. I smiled back. As she dressed Tristan's arms, her face clouded and she cast scathing looks at me. By the time she had done his chest, she was pouring out a stream of indignant comments that even my ignorance of Norwegian did not hinder me from understanding. Women like this were not fit to be mothers. They should be jailed, or better still shot! Such child neglect should be reported to the police. Her gentleness to my son was counterbalanced by her vehemence towards me. Even Tristan was getting the drift of her remarks. Above her head, he was giving me winks as though to reassure me and share in the joke.

When the doctor returned, the elderly nurse fairly blew up in indignation. Unsmiling, he explained the situation to her. There was silence; then, eyes downcast, she turned to me and apologized. The doctor explained to her that I spoke no Norwegian. As she left, biting her lip, Tristan reached out and caught her sleeve.

'Thank you,' he said with a warm smile.

She turned and gave him a careful hug before hurrying out.

'I'm sorry,' the doctor said, getting back to work on Tristan's back.

'It's all right. I might have thought the same thing; he is so thin and the sores are so bad.'

A week and a half later Hubert was sitting at the table by the window. Tristan slept. All around the room were pyjamas and sheets drying. It looked and smelled like a laundry. Lisa was playing with Gunhild Peterson in another part of the Fjel Stua.

'We could move into some apartments that are set aside for the military,' Hubert began tentatively, 'They are expensive by local standards, but we could afford it. The fridge and stove are included.'

'But . . .?' I asked, sensing his hesitancy.

'It would isolate us from the Sames. They all think it is not fair that the military keep the apartments for themselves. At the Institute, they told me that many Sames would not come into the military compound.'

'Well, that's that,' I said. 'We came here to make a film about the Same people, didn't we?'

'I felt I had to let *you* make the choice. It's not easy for you and the children,' Hubert said.

'We've put up with worse!'

I had influenced Hubert to leave the Arctic for the sake of Tristan's health. It had been hard for me to accept that the most sophisticated hospitals and the most advanced medical technologies held no cure for his particular condition. I was determined not to make the same mistake again.

There came a day when the doctor said, 'It's clearing up. Here is the medicine. You have watched me do it so often, you can take over now. Come back to see me in a week.'

Tristan and I stepped out of the hospital into the low angled sunlight in holiday mood.

'You're getting better, Moose!' I exulted, as we began walking back to the Fjel Stua. 'Moose . . .?'

He had turned his face away. Without words, I felt the struggle inside him, the long-sustained effort not to give in to scratching, the pain, the loneliness . . . perhaps even a childish despair.

I squatted down beside him, 'I know it hasn't been easy for you. Don't think dad and I haven't noticed how brave you are. You must miss the farm, your friends, the Dances, Sweet's Corners School, Mrs Hopwood . . .'

Tears were rolling down his gaunt cheeks. I took his hand and held it. He looked away. After a while he asked in a hollow voice, 'Why did we have to come here?'

We started walking down the hill, Tristan's hand firmly in mine. 'Moose, each of us can give a different answer to that question.' I spoke slowly, sifting my words for truth. 'I am here because I want to be here as a Bahá'í, and because I had long ago decided that I would follow my husband to the ends of the earth.' That sounded somehow grandiose, but Kautokeino certainly did feel like the *end of the earth*.

I explained to Tristan the idea of the film about the Same Reindeer herders, the difficulties his dad was facing, and the suspicious and wary reactions he was encountering everywhere.

'Dad is having a hard time?' Moose queried. 'Poor dad!' he added, after some thought.

'I'm sorry that it's so hard for you here, dad,' Moose said, reaching out his hand over the supper table that night.

'Thanks, son,' said Hubert in a choked voice, as he took his son's hand. Then after a minute, recovering some of his old gaiety, he added, 'But now you are getting better and I have contacted a family, the Hettas, who might be willing to cooperate in making the film, things are turning for the better. Tomorrow is Saturday and I'm going to take you to Enontekio in Finland. We all need a change of scene.'

'From Kautokeino to Enontekio,' Lisa said, looking at the map. 'It sounds like the title of a book!'

About twenty kilometers out of Kautokeino, I noticed a few houses scattered along the banks of the Siebe River. One tall gaunt structure, once white but weathered to colorlessness, struck me as particularly lonely looking.

Well, at least I don't have to live *there*, I thought to myself as we drove by. That house really looks like 'the house at the end of the world', that in all the Polish and Russian fairy tales is reached only after crossing seven mountains, seven rivers and seven valleys.

'Lisa, do you think we have crossed seven mountains, seven rivers and seven valleys, like all the characters we read about in the fairy tales?' I asked, turning to the back seat.

Lisa half closed the book she was reading and looked off into space for some time before answering, 'I think it was more like nine.'

In Finland we bought a couple of puzzles for Lisa, and for Tristan some more cars for his matchbox collection.

Weeks passed. The Hettas had agreed to be filmed in their annual cycle of activities and migrations with their herd. Hubert was busy researching and, whenever possible, filming.

On the day that additional film was expected to arrive at the Alta airport we decided to take the day off and drive the children to the only fair-sized town due north of us. Alta, a harbor town on the Arctic Ocean, remained open to shipping year round thanks to the warming influence of the Gulf Stream.

Winter was coming. As we started back from the airport which lay at the edge of the gray cold-looking sea, the wind picked up and great white flakes began to fall.

The children had watched with much interest the descent from the high plateau on which Kautokeino is situated. We had driven down beside steep gorges and we had even disembarked, the better to look at the canyon carved from gray rock and visible from an overhang near the road. So now as we started back they were fully aware of the precipitous slopes that lay on either side of the narrow road.

Soon we were in a whirling mass of white and visibility was nil. The stretch of two hundred and fifty kilometers from Alta to Kautokeino had no other towns. Hubert slowed to a crawl. We saw another car that had gone off the road and into the gorge below.

'Well kids, let's start praying,' Hubert suggested.

'*Is there any remover of difficulties save God . . .*' Tristan began. Over and over as we crawled along, blindly feeling for the asphalt with our tires, we repeated the prayer.

'Does God really hear prayers?' asked a frightened voice from the back seat.

'He always hears, "*He is the prayer-hearing, prayer-answering God,*"' I answered emphatically.

'Let's say some more, then,' said the same little voice.

It was past midnight when we arrived back at the Fjel Stua with the storm still swirling snow with wild abandon.

'You children must be prayed out,' I said to the two in the back seat who had been saying the *Remover of Difficulties* for two and a half hours.

Lisa hugged dad and said, 'Thanks for getting us home safe!'

I looked around for Tristan. He had gone back outside and I found him standing looking out into the whirlwind of snow and shouting into the wind.

'Thanks, God!'

Was it then that Tristan began talking to God?

Chapter Thirteen

ONE evening after the children had gone to bed, I sat embroidering under the single bulb. Hubert was filming a Samic Conference and had been away all day. Lisa was on the last book of the box we had brought with us from Canada. There was so little for her to do! The room was not even big enough to start her on the jigsaw puzzles we had bought in Finland. Tristan tossed and scratched in his sleep. He was much better but pustules kept breaking out over his body. And his weight was dropping. If only I could get a place with a bathtub!

I looked out the window. On the hillside above us I could see the lights of the Same Institute. In the tiny little house attached to it there were never any lights! Hubert had already inquired about it but he had been told that it belonged to the Pinsevenner, or Pentecostals, who used it when their missionaries traveled through the area.

'God, my God, please help us . . .' I said, pressing my face against the cool window pane, 'or if it is not your will to change the physical conditions, then please give me the strength to put up with them.' That night I had a vivid dream that we were happily living in the Pinsevenner house. On waking I told Hubert about the dream.

'Why don't you ask them again? What do we have to lose?'

'I asked them before and they said "No". There is another lead, but it is very uncertain. The head butcher at the Reindeer slaughter house is building himself a modern new house on the ridge. When that is finished, his old house will be available for rent. It is out of town about seventeen kilometers. We must have driven by it on the way to Enontekio.'

It was then that I knew that by some fateful irony the bleak house that I had been so happy *not to have to live in* was the one that would be available for rent. What is God trying to teach me, I wondered. I was being thrown back against my old repugnance of squalor. Yet, I had always prided myself on detachment. Was this situation 'calling my bluff' in spiritual terms?

When we arrived at the settlement of Siebe, seventeen kilometers south of Kautokeino, the weatherbeaten house (Norwegian Gothic, I called it) looked even more forlorn that I had remembered. It was a basic two-story built right after the war when no insulation was available. Only in the kitchen and the living room did the heaters win the fight against the intruding cold; the rest of the house was as cold as outdoors. But for all its failings it was available for rent.

That same afternoon we called the Pinsevenner. They agreed to rent us their little house next to the Same Institute for a month. On Lisa's birthday, 2 November, we moved out of our room in the Fjel Stua where we had spent six weeks. Lisa was so happy she said she didn't want any other presents. We had a little party for her and her best friend Gunhild! I even baked a cake in the bright immaculate kitchen.

The Pinsevenner house was tiny; no, rather it was miniature. Everything was there but very compact. For Tristan the bathtub was most important, the laundry facilities were a delight, a separate bedroom was a relief. How pleasant to eat on neat blue and white plates instead of chipped odds and ends; and to bake in an oven; and to have more than one pot and one burner when preparing meals!

Hubert started to bring people over for tea and cake in the mornings and afternoons. Moose began to play games again after supper. Lisa started to work on an enormous jigsaw puzzle which took up a whole coffee table.

Tristan's resentment of his sister flared up after our move. It was as if it had been stifled by lack of space, in the same way that a fire is banked by diminishing the available oxygen. Lisa was learning Norwegian rapidly, her circle of friends had that absorbing intimacy so typical of eight-year-old girls, her leisure reading provided her with a ready escape into fantasy worlds; most of all, it was that enormous jigsaw puzzle that symbolized for Tristan all that was inaccessible to him.

At first there were small acts of sabotage, a few puzzle pieces thrown behind the couch. Then they became more blatant. The sky edge so painstakingly put together by the three of us the night before would be in pieces on the floor at breakfast time.

Hubert stopped working on the puzzle and set up Tristan's Lego train tracks. He made mountains, and even a tunnel, for the train to go through.

At times Lisa and Tristan played games together: parchesi and crazy eights, and old maid. His sister was quicker at counting, faster at perceiving what had to be done. Being a sensitive child she would help him and, often, let him win. All that was but salt in the wound of his pride. One day in an eruption of frustration and anger Tristan threw the whole enormous, nearly completed puzzle on the floor. For days afterwards I would find the scattered pieces all over the house; for years the pain and injustice of that action rankled Lisa.

One Saturday when Hubert was out filming and I was doing the laundry an arrestingly beautiful woman walked into our house without knocking or introduction.

'I heard about you,' she announced in an educated western-American accent, 'but it took me some time to locate you – Welcome!'

To say 'Do come in!' seemed rather pointless, for she was in and was removing a silver-fox hat with two pendant bushy tails. I stood, as mesmerized as the children, while out poured masses of waist length black wavy hair touched at one temple with a thin streak of silver. Before any of us regained our faculty of speech, we learned that our visitor had lived for a number of years in the area, and that she was working for a doctorate in socio-linguistics from Yale. Her name was Myrdene Anderson.

At this point Hubert returned home and we asked Myrdene to stay for dinner. As the evening progressed she took off layer after layer of an eclectic collection of garments she was wearing. Her own house was much colder, she explained. Eventually she was barefoot in trousers, blouse and a wool-mesh shawl that somehow seemed to hold everything together.

During dinner she held us enthralled by stories of her experiences as maid with a Same family, a job she had under-taken to learn the Samic language which she now spoke fluently. After dinner she helped Lisa with the dishes thus winning her eternal friendship and allegiance. We all played games, and since the evening had become stormy she curled up on the couch and stayed the night. So walked into our life a friend and source of information that proved enduring and invaluable. So, too, ended the first period of acute aloneness.

There were many short trips that year to Finland and Sweden and parts of Norway. For Tristan, it meant meeting new people and responding to new situations. We all participated in the excitement of the unfolding film ideas. The single film became two, one tracing the yearly patterns of a herding family, the other concentrating on the artists and artisans of the Same tradition.

There were many long dreary miles to be covered. When it was dark Lisa could no longer read; then real and imagined injustices upset the equilibrium of the back-seat passengers. To the games of twenty questions, synonyms, homonyms and rhyming games we always played Hubert added the welcome distraction of his *Road-Stretcher Stories*. When there was still a half hour of driving left and all other games and stories had been exhausted, the children would say, 'I bet the Road Stretcher has been at work!'

The notorious Road Stretcher was an all-time 'baddy', who would stretch the road so that it was even longer than marked on the map. The hero of these stories had clean cut features, was resolute and full of determination and brilliant insights that would make even the famed Canadian Mounties pale. After endless intrigues filled with local color, the Road Shrinker (as the Canadian hero was called) would 'get his man' and (here Hubert showed his true genius) would always manage to shrink the road back to its proper length, just as we drove into our destination.

In early December we moved into the bleak house on the Siebe River. Immediately, as if as an antidote to the physical isolation of the place, we were inundated by visitors. Ola and Gail arrived from Jokkmokk, bringing with them a new Bahá'í, Sixten. They set to work helping Hubert construct furniture for the nearly empty house.

Myrdene appeared with her knapsack full of reindeer legs from which we were soon making a thick soup. Tristan was in his glory, running back and forth with nails and hammers from one group to the other. By the time I had baked biscuits to go with the stew a rough deal table had been constructed in the dining room and one bench was ready.

Supper in our new home was so full of laughter and good

cheer that the lonely weeks seemed but an illusion. All our visitors stayed overnight and slept on newly constructed couches made of boards on cement blocks.

The next day bookshelves were made from bricks and boards and the last bench finished. Ola and Hubert even managed to construct a toy garage for Tristan's car collection.

In those days I was the early riser, so I would light the stove and warm the children's clothes by the fire. By the time they cascaded down the stairs the porridge was made and their clothes warm. After they left to wait for the bus by the side of the road, there was a quiet time to say prayers, to sit over coffee with Hubert and to do the housework. Tristan got home around eleven. We always had tea together and talked. It was our very own private time together. I did not know how much it meant to him to have all my undivided attention, until I saw the patent disappointment on his face when a chance visitor disturbed us.

Over tea and crackers, we talked of all sorts of things. He missed Canada . . . his school . . . his room . . . Mrs Hopwood . . .

Shyly he talked of Joannie, groping to find words to convey the feeling. 'When I think of her . . . it is an all warm feeling . . . and I feel like crying . . . Do you know, mom?'

'Yes, Moose, some people call it being in love.'

He thought about it, 'But I love you and dad and . . .' he hesitated, 'and Lisa . . . but it's different!'

'There are many kinds of love.'

'But do you *know* what I *mean*?' Moose reached out his hand for mine and I held it thinking how thick his knuckles had become and how gnarled his hands now felt.

'Moose, I understand. There is often pain in love.'

His eyes looked at me puzzled.

I smiled at him, 'It hurts a bit and yet it is a wonderful feeling.'

'Yes, yes, that's what it's like . . . hurty and wonderful!'

Another time he could not wait till we had our tea to ask, 'Do you think Joannie likes me?'

'Yes, I know she does,' I answered. 'But it is different for her; she is a young woman and you are a boy. When you grow up you will love someone who will love you in the same way.'

Not long after a letter came from Joannie. It was a beautiful, gentle letter letting him know that she was getting married and inviting him to attend her wedding if he would be back in Canada by then. She described her husband-to-be and said that she had told him all about Tristan, and that he, too, looked forward to meeting him.

On the delicate features, joy and pain chased each other until tears decided the issue. I let silence do its healing. At last Tristan shook his head and said, 'I can't understand it. I am so happy that she is happy . . . So why am I so sad?'

At times we talked of prosaic things, like how soap is made. Moose kept asking for more and more details. Finally, I leaned back and asked, 'What do you really want to know, Moose?'

'I know this sounds stupid,' he said glancing around to make sure we were not overheard. 'Is it ever made from people?'

My breath caught and I stared at him. At first he was merely relieved that I had not laughed or even smiled. Then his face grew troubled when he saw that I was upset. It had taken me a minute to piece together what must have been going on in his head. I recalled that all of us had been watching a rebroadcast of *The Ascent of Man* series. At one point Bronowski had picked up a handful of ashes outside the crematorium of Auschwitz. After the program someone had quoted a line from a book in which one of the characters had complained that every time he picked up a bar of soap he thought of his grandmother. During this conversation Tristan had been playing with his cars. I had not thought that he was even listening.

'During the war terrible things happened . . .' I began, taking a deep breath, 'many thousands of people were killed and burned. You remember we said that you need lye to make soap? Well, lye can be made from ashes. Some soap was made from the ashes of those burned people.'

'How terrible!' Tristan breathed.

'My two aunts were burned in one of those camps.'

He got up, put his arm around me and diplomatically changed the subject.

There were times that we talked about God. His favorite prayer was still 'Blessed is the Spot'.

'Is God really everywhere?'

'Yes.'

A thoughtful silence, 'How can He do it?'

'Do what?'

'Be everywhere?'

'If you stop thinking about God as a person it is easier to understand. Think of the wind. It can be in many different places. Or air . . . air is everywhere.'

'Can God see me?'

'Yes, and He can hear what we say, and . . .' I said, looking into his gray-blue eyes, 'He knows what we think and feel.'

'Really?' a long exhaled breath, then loudly, 'Hello, God, how are you today?'

Hubert and Lisa came home at two and we had a meal together. Tristan and I had by then finished our lessons in reading, phonics and math after our morning tea. So, after lunch, it was Lisa's turn. In Siebe with no friends living close by it was easy to concentrate on studies. I had never taught so receptive a mind. From Christmas to June we sped through Grades II and III and could easily have tackled Grade IV, but we did not have the books.

As soon as she had finished the cartons of books we had brought, her reading took a more sophisticated turn. I was reading *The Hobbit* at the time. I was so intrigued by the scene in which Bilbo gets the ring from the Golem that I read it aloud to the children.

Tristan immediately began to mimic the Golem. Writhing on the ground he spoke with most Golem-like sibilance.

'What have we got in our pocketses, my preciouss?'

The Golem Act became one of Tristan's *pièces de résistance*.

Just before Christmas we drove to Alta to pick up Nadine and Hedy. Years later they confessed how shocked they had been to see an unfamiliar shaggy bearded man in muskrat hat approach them with open arms. Our odd attire, for we had adopted the Same reindeer shoes with upturned toes and wore them stuffed with senef grass, struck them as incongruous compared with the parents they had last seen.

But their greatest surprise was to come when they got to the house. Dressed in their ladylike wool coats and matching hats and gloves they were finding the Arctic cold biting, so we sent them right into the house while Hubert and I stayed behind and pulled their luggage and our groceries from the car to the house on a sled.

When they entered they saw a beautiful witchy lady stirring

long bones in a steaming cauldron on the stove. She was barefoot and dressed in an odd assortment of clothes held in place, it appeared, by a black wool shawl. They stood rooted to the spot until Tristan and Lisa spied them and engulfed them in hugs and kisses.

The days were so short at the Christmas season that it was easy to oversleep and miss the brief half hour of daylight. Since twenty-three hours out of every twenty-four were pitch dark, it seemed to make little difference if we or the children stayed up past midnight. There was no school bus to catch during the holidays. Our sleep and waking patterns gyrated wildly.

Ola's gold earring was not in evidence the next time he came to see us. 'To some it gives the wrong impression,' he explained. Soon it became evident that he was Tristan's new role-model. Ola was very reticent by nature, but Moose soon had him singing for us in his soft tuneful voice. He sang Moose's favorites, like 'Moonshadow' and 'Country Roads' and, as his confidence increased, his own compositions. On Tristan's face the emotions stirred by the music passed like clouds over a clear sky.

Ola liked to cook and to make bread. This opened a whole new outlet for Tristan. Like most Swedes, Ola had difficulties pronouncing the 'j' sounds. He asked us always to correct him. So in the kitchen one could hear, 'Moose, have you heard the yoke about the Swede and the Norwegian?'

A shy whisper would be heard, 'Ola it's "J" . . . Joke.'

'O.K. . . . there is this joke about . . .'

Ola never followed a recipe, so his creations were always different and unpredictable. One day he called from the kitchen, 'Suzanne, what should I do with this extra joke?'

Peals of laughter from Tristan brought me to the kitchen. Tristan's laughter was always contagious, so we found ourselves standing around the table where a puzzled but laughing Ola held a half egg-shell with a yolk.

'Ola tells yolks but he cooks with jokes,' Tristan blurted out doubling up with laughter.

The family had long ago realized that Tristan's sense of humor, though infectious, was often tangential. He never laughed at anyone but always at some detail that captured his sense of the ridiculous.

Ola was relieved of his spare yolk and baked a very acceptable cake with Moose's assistance. From then on Tristan often concocted cakes. From his various attempts he gleaned a concept of basic ingredients. A recipe was something he never could and never would follow.

Our most famous visitor was non-human. Rhuna Bena was a red-haired herding dog that had adopted Myrdene during her period of being a 'maid' for a Same family. Herding dogs are indispensable during fall and spring migrations. There are slack periods during the winter, when the reindeer stay in their winter grazing grounds, and in the summer, after calving. Rhuna Bena chose to spend these times with his beloved Myrdene. He was a dog of remarkable abilities and intelligence. His owners, though they prized him highly, took no exception to his spending his 'holidays' with someone who fed him well and cared for him.

So it was that we met Rhuna during his winter break. Our first impressions were not felicitous. The dog gave the distinct impression of being embarrassed.

'That's only because he doesn't know English,' Myrdene explained. 'Watch him when other Sames come to visit.'

We did not have long to wait. Soon a neighboring family came in with their children and their dog. I watched Rhuna carefully. He sat under the table like a well-behaved dog and followed the conversation in Samic and gave the impression of being fully at ease.

When Myrdene asked if we could board Rhuna for three weeks we did so hesitantly for he did not seem to be comfortable with us. When we made this observation to Myrdene she laughed.

'As soon as he learns English he'll be fine!'

She explained it all in Samic to the dog and left. Moose took it upon himself to teach the dog English. On the floor he spent a lot of time explaining commands in his best 'speech therapy' style. The dog was a model pupil. Very soon the dog reacted appropriately to English commands and would stand by the door if anyone mentioned 'walk'.

Tristan was his particular 'reindeer'. The boy and the dog played ball outside and went sliding on a sealskin by the river. All was well unless Tristan wanted to go on the road. Rhuna would not allow it. Tristan would have to resort to subterfuge by keeping the dog in the house when he wanted to visit the neighbors.

On Myrdene's return, Rhuna was fluent in English and remained so. In later years, Rhuna's fame spread and dog breeders from Sweden and Finland brought females to be bred to the dog, whose intelligence and herding skills had become legendary throughout Lapland.

Many months later, as we were driving through Finland, we picked up some hitchhikers. They told us stories about their travels. Once they had been hiking across the 'vida' and had been picked up by a Same family in whose tent they were invited to spend the night. At this point it became clear to us that our hitchhikers were unsavory characters; it turned out that they had planned to help themselves to a few items from the tent and to make off while the others slept.

They whispered their plans in English, knowing that no one would understand. As it was, there was only a herding dog nearby. But the dog had sat looking at them while they talked. When they arose at night to execute their plan, he had barked and awakened everyone.

'That darn dog had spoiled it all!'

'Was it red-haired?' I asked.

'Why yes, it was golden red, not black like most of the Same dogs.'

'Rhuna Bena!' chorused the children.

'You've heard of it?' they asked, incredulous.

'I taught it English!' Tristan declared with pride.

The hitchhikers got off soon after. I often wondered how that story would grow in the retelling.

There were many trips that winter associated with Hubert's film. Once our travels took us to the most northern part of Norway, Hammerfest, where we stayed with a Bahá'í. Travel during the dark period is tedious. This particular trip was illuminated by the most breathtaking display of northern lights that we had ever seen. For over two hours green, blue, white and deep rose aurora borealis played like a visible musical score orchestrated on the expanse of the heavens.

'Thanks, God, that was terrific!' I heard Tristan whisper in awe.

We were cold, tired and hungry by the time we found the house of our fellow Bahá'í. Though we had never met before it felt like coming to the home of an old friend. We were still talking in the hall when I heard Tristan from the living room.

'At last,' said Tristan, looking appreciatively at the pictures, the rugs and tasteful decorations, 'a real house!'

It was then I realized how painful *he* found our bleak existence in Siebe.

'Do you think we could hear some music?' he asked later in the evening.

'Why of course!' our hostess answered. 'I may not have the sort of music you like though.'

'Do you have "Country Roads"?'

'That's John Denver, isn't it? No, I'm sorry I don't have it.'

'Well, Mozart will be fine, then,' Tristan answered with resignation.

Chapter Fourteen

'MARKENAD, we're going to the Markenad!' the children chanted as we drove off to Jokkmokk in February.

For centuries the nomadic Same peoples had congregated in that town for a 'market' week in winter. Despite the bitter cold the town and environs were bursting with visitors. The central square of the town was packed with stalls at which one could buy fur pelts or fur hats and coats sold by a bearded bear of a man, or leather items hung out on lines in front of a tent, or silver jewelry and belt buckles to adorn the traditional Samic costumes.

At strategic spots braziers were burning so one could stop to warm one's hands. Several stalls sold warm mugs of hot chocolate, reindeer sausage and other local delicacies. Steam rose from the cocoa and from the sausages and from the mouths of the holiday throng talking in more than half a dozen different languages, but the laughter was interlingual. The words and laughter hung in little puffs of steam like Arctic bunting that added to the crisp festive mood.

Every noontide a procession of harnessed reindeer would wend its way among the stalls. Each day a lucky child was chosen to ride in a sled pulled by draft reindeer. The procession looked for all the world like the illustration for Hans Christian Andersen's tale of 'The Snow Queen'. Pinsevenner walked through the market singing hymns and playing on tambourines.

The small local Bahá'í group in the area had for several years erected a tent near the center of the market. It was a large army-type tent. Inside it was strewn with evergreen boughs which were in turn covered by reindeer skins. A samovar was kept going all day, and those who were cold could come in to warm up and have a cup of steaming tea. Bahá'í literature was placed for perusal on an outside table.

We took turns playing host at the samovar. Tristan took delight in handing around the mugs of tea, and quickly learned enough Swedish to ask 'Milk?' 'Sugar?', 'More?'

When not on duty at the samovar he was off on his own. One day we saw him in the Pinsevenner parade behind the tambourines. He spent a long time with the English-speaking Lebanese vendor of trinkets. A huge red-bearded hawker of raffle tickets was another chum, though how they conversed was a mystery to us.

After Markenad Hubert and an ethnographer friend, Hugh Beach, spent several weeks filming the preparations for the spring migration and then the migration itself. Left on our own, the children and I became even more integrated into the life of the other four families in Siebe.

June came and the swollen Siebe river cracked its ice cover. Rafts of ice began to move down grinding and crushing. I liked to sit on the banks watching the movement of the ice floes. Over the meadows turning green and adorned with the first shy flowers Tristan came to where I sat. I had not realized that I might be depressed until I felt his hand on my back and saw the concern on his face. 'Dad says, why don't you come up now?'

'I'll come up soon, but I like sitting here watching the river break up. It makes me think of various life experiences that grind down and smooth out our edges.'

As I did not move but kept staring at the ice pans that were overlapping and swirling down the river, he said the one thing he knew would rouse me, 'Mom, come up now; we need you.' Then he walked slowly up the rise to the weathered house that stood out stark against the sky. Something in the composition of figure and house made me think of Wyeth's painting 'Christina's World'. I unfastened my eyes from the silver ice and the gray froth of the river and followed my son up the hill.

'We're going on a trip to the Lofoten Islands!' Hubert announced. 'Here, let me show you where they are on the map. Right here on the north-west coast! They are really remarkable islands in many ways . . . geographically they are unlike the mainland because they escaped glaciation during the last ice age.'

The children, veterans of so many journeys, looked casually

at the map. 'When are Nadine and Hedy coming back?' Lisa wanted to know.

'We'll be back in time to meet them in Alta,' Hubert assured her.

The landscape we drove through was breathtaking. On the high passes of the mountainous coastal area we were in the depths of winter, amid high drifts of snow. As we descended the vegetation showed the gradations of spring, from the pale chartreuse green of bushes with their feet still in banks of slush to the tender green of the deciduous woods, and still farther down to the intrusion of dark evergreens merging with the emerald grasses near the blue sea's shore. At the widely spaced farm—fishing villages were neatly prepared gardens with their tender seedlings protected by long half-circles of plastic mini-greenhouses.

On the second day of our drive as we came over a high ridge between two hills we spied a resort hotel nestled on the hillside overlooking a bright blue bay. On the wide balcony of the hotel we could see the guests reclining in deckchairs wearing sunglasses and heavy sweaters. Although we were driving through snow, the hotel midway down the slope was in woods that were turning verdant.

'Oh, dad!' breathed Tristan from the back seat.

'Could we stop there, dad?' Lisa asked, hope and realism fighting in her voice for it was still early afternoon.

'It makes me think of Vevey,' I said softly.

There was a whoop from the children as Hubert turned off the road. 'Now don't get excited,' he warned, 'they may not have room for us.'

But they did have room. Tristan, sporting a pair of sunglasses and holding a glass of ginger ale, was soon mingling with the other guests on the sun deck. Shy Lisa joined a game of monopoly that was in progress in the lounge. Hubert and I went for a walk in the woods. On our return we sat on the sun deck in the late afternoon sun.

'Perhaps Tristan should get involved in some way with the hotel industry when he grows up,' I mused aloud. 'Look how he enjoys mingling with all sorts of people.'

At first we had thought that the farm would be an ideal place for Tristan. He would be able to have a sense of accomplishment in working with plants and animals and contribute economically. As time passed it became ever more obvious that he would never be physically strong. His frame was slight and his extreme thinness prevented the development of proper musculature. He had areas of strength; for instance, he was good at arm wrestling and at yoga (he could sit cross-legged and then lift himself up completely off the floor with his arms). But he was not a child that enjoyed rough sports, even a game of kick-ball became too much for him if there were more than two participants. We were faced by a basically sedentary personality whose great and abiding pleasure in life was interacting with adults. Long after the horizontal rays of the sun had lost their warmth we sat talking of Tristan's future.

I thought of his inability to grasp 'number facts'. Would he be able to handle money? 'He certainly keeps track of his allowance both in Canadian and Norwegian currency. Often he is the only one who has money left at the end of the week and he lends it out to his sisters and charges interest!' I commented.

'We must teach him to use a calculator when we get back. He seems to have a lot of practical good sense. I believe he could be able to function in society with extra help.' Hubert reasoned.

'Do you think he will grow?' At eight Lisa was taller and heavier than her brother who was almost twelve. It was Tristan who looked more the eight-year-old and this stood him in good stead, for that discrepancy decreased expectations and made his slow and careful speech more acceptable, whereas his interest in people and social graces by contrast appeared precocious.

The Lofotens and the Bahá'ís we met there had a charm all their own. There was something of scaled-down Alpine scenery about the pointy peaks of the mountains.

Never before had I been in a Bahá'í community that was so permeated by the memory and posthumous influence of a pioneer as on those islands. Loyce Lawrence was a beautiful and charming American who had come to the islands when she was middle-aged. Numerous stories were related to us about her arrival on the islands with her red station wagon. It must have been lonely and difficult for her in the beginning. Everyone who had known her had been touched by her love and deep interest in them.

Though we would have liked to extend our visit we had to return to meet Hedy and Nadine in Alta in mid-June. On our last day there, while we waited for the boat ferry to unload, Helen D. asked us in for a cup of tea. Her house was near the harbor and had that air of slightly faded elegance that is so common and charming in Europe and so rare and valued in Canada. The large portraits of prominent members of the family looked down from their heavy frames as we drank our tea.

This was not to be an afternoon of polite chit-chat. Our hostess broached the subject of suffering and death. Her dearest friend, Loyce Lawrence, had died of cancer and in great pain. Though her suffering had been acute, it had been uncomplaining. Yet Helen's heart had been left with an ache of unresolved questions.

'Why would God inflict such pain on so good a person? Loyce had been so unfailingly kind, so selfless! She was as close to a saint as anyone I know. Why did she have to suffer so terribly?' Helen asked.

Lisa sat eating her cake and trying not to get any crumbs on the enormous picture book she held on her knees. At first Tristan had walked around the rooms looking at the enormous portraits. As our hostess had begun to speak he sat mesmerized. His sensitive features reflected the changes in mood as the narration unfolded. At the last words he rose and put his arms around Helen's shoulder.

'Now she is with God!' he said comfortingly.

Helen's voice caught in a dry stifled sob. 'I don't know any more. Loyce never doubted, her belief was never shaken and when she died there was such a peaceful look on her face!'

'Why are we on this earth?' I asked, hoping to shed light on the question from a different direction.

'I thought I knew. I though that it was to serve God and to worship Him,' came the thoughtful subdued answer. Then with such feeling that her voice rose she continued, '. . . serve God . . . How Loyce served God! She came here all alone, not knowing anyone, to a foreign country. This is a very closed society; it did not welcome her with open arms! I was her first friend and the first to become a Bahá'í . . . I loved her . . . and then to see her in such great pain!'

'God never gives us more than we can bear,' came a voice from above the picture book. Unnerved by the silence following her remark Lisa added, 'Isn't that what you always tell us, mommy?'

'Well, He has given me more than I can understand. There are other people who lead selfish lives and they die quietly in their sleep!'

The phone rang. The boat would be leaving in half an hour.

'Life's problems don't have easy answers and there are no ready-made solutions. But we must have faith that there *are* answers, and we can work to find them for ourselves,' Hubert suggested as we were leaving.

'You are dear children,' Helen said, hugging Lisa and Tristan as they were leaving. They returned her embrace warmly.

As we walked downhill to the harbor Tristan took my hand. His eyes were still glowing dark and bright.

'Mom, you believe don't you . . .?' I read the rest of the question.

'Yes, Moose, I not only believe that there is life after we die, I am as certain of it as I am that your hand is in mine.' Here I gave his hand a squeeze. 'In the other worlds of God, Loyce Lawrence may be even now praying for her dear friend, Helen.'

'Then why . . .' and he glanced back at the aging house we had just left.

'Each one of us must find our own certainty. I can't make you sure. I can only share my feelings and thoughts with you. Everyone must chase away their own shadows of fear or resentment. No one is spared that struggle.'

'Are you ever afraid, mom?'

'Yes, Moose, each one of us is afraid sometimes.'

'Even daddy?'

'Even daddy,' I assured him. 'But we can all do something about it. Loving God is like turning on the light. Did you ever notice how scary a dark room can be?' Solemnly he nodded his head as he was very particular about leaving his bedroom door ajar. 'All we have to do is turn to God and that is like turning on the light. Darkness disappears when there is light, for light is stronger than the dark.'

For a while we walked in silence. 'You told me love is

stronger than hate,' Tristan remarked.

'Yes, they both work the same way,' I assented.

The balmy weather and the endless daylight brought with it the bane of Tristan's existence: flies and mosquitoes. Unless a strong wind blew he kept indoors. The wind freed him from self-imposed confinement to the house. Each morning, his first concern was with the weather. When a wind blew he would step outside on the front steps and stand into the wind face uptilted, fair hair blown back and he would talk to the wind.

'O Holy Wind!' was one of the favorite songs that Rabbi Carlbach sang. 'A good friend is one who talks to the wind about you . . .' went the lyrics.

'Do you ever talk to the wind about me?' Tristan had once asked me.

'Yes, I often say to the wind, "Holy wind, don't blow out my little candles." Especially when Nadine and Hedy were away at school I would often wake up at night and speak to the wind about them.' Tristan smiled and seemed satisfied.

When the wind blew he would join the neighbors on the farm next door and help feed the ducks and the geese, or go for walks, or accompany us on gathering expeditions for fresh birch leaves or heather blossoms, which under Myrdene's tutelage we boiled for wool dyeing.

As soon as the wind dropped, the fierce Arctic insects came out in force and Tristan scuttled back indoors, where, armed with a fly swatter, he felt better able to protect himself.

His sensitive skin never completely recovered from the impetigo. Every few days a new pustule would develop somewhere on his body and would have to be tended and treated. The lesions healed, but for a long time the skin remained thin and sensitive.

From inclination, and later from necessity, Tristan was fastidious about his appearance. Daily he changed every item of clothing, even his pyjamas. Very early he developed a certain style of dress which he maintained. Wide wale corduroy that became soft after washing was his preference for trousers, and soft brushed cotton for shirts. Wool and, by this time, even acrylics and any synthetic fibres irritated his skin. Winter and summer he dressed the same way. Eventually for warmth he had to rely on cotton sweaters or extra shirts. Parkas and felt-lined boots in winter were his only additions.

That summer my mother wrote from Zaïre, urging me to meet her in Poland. I had not been back since we left in the summer of 1939. It was arranged that I would fly to Poland and then rendezvous with the family at the Bahá'í International Conference in Helsinki, Finland.

Chapter Fifteen

'HEDY, tell me what you remember about Tristan that summer in Siebe?' We were driving along a lovely country road in Nova Scotia. Often it is easier to talk when one is driving because as the scenery unfolds so does the inner screen of memory.

'Do you remember what a beautiful clear skin Tristan had before?' Hedy began. 'When Nadine and I had our teenage pimples, Tristan would look at them with disgust. He always said that *he would never have yucky old pimples*. Then that year when he was covered with pustules and raw spots, I would find him looking at himself in the mirror. It was so hard for him to accept that those yucky looking spots were on *him*.'

We were both silent for a while. For both of us the images of Lapland, for the moment, replaced the cultivated orchards of the valley through which we were driving. I saw Siebe, under the Arctic sun that didn't set on us that summer, the river curling silver and glistening at the back of the house. Across some meadows stood our neighbor's house. In my mind's eye I saw Moose slip out of the house and follow the narrow path through the meadows.

As if Hedy were already at our neighbor's house spinning and weaving with Brit Ellen, the young daughter of the family, she said, 'Moose loved to visit the neighbors! He was there every day and they loved him. It was as if he illumined something in everyone. He was so much *himself* that everyone felt comfortable with him around. But it was something else as well. It was as though he could see what was special about everyone.'

The road continued to unwind as did our memories.

'You know that they had another daughter? There was something wrong with her, I don't know what,' Hedy continued.

'No, actually I didn't even know she existed until Moose asked about her when we were visiting there,' I admitted.

'Well, Moose had a special understanding with that girl. He would always make a point of speaking with her.'

'How did they communicate?' I pursued.

'He spoke Norwegian. You know that slow way he had of enunciating everything. He was a real communicator!'

I remembered that before going out Tristan had often gone up to Hubert and had asked how to say a certain sentence in Norwegian, and had gone around repeating it till he had it right. Apparently he had built up a repertoire of phrases.

'It's interesting that at first the Same people had struck us as blunt, suspicious and even manipulative. At the end we did not see any of those qualities; they were simply our friends and neighbors.'

'Moose had a lot to do with that, I think,' Hedy commented.

'He was disarming,' I agreed.

'But it was at Helsinki that he really shone!' Hedy went on.

'Tell me about that and about your trip down because I was in Poland then.'

'On the trip down he was awful, just plain bad.' Hedy said.

'None of us understood how uncomfortable he found it to sit still for long periods of time,' I said, trying to make allowances.

'But at the conference! When we first arrived and he saw that huge lobby and the marble stairway and all the Bahá'ís arriving he just lit up. Then we lost him. Of course we didn't worry because he loves to be with Bahá'ís and we knew he would be all right. After that people started coming up to me and looking at my name tag and saying, "Are you *Tristan's* sister?" They were all misty eyed when they said, "He is *so* loving. . ." and "We think he is the *most beautiful* person!"'

'What did he do?' I wanted to know.

'Apparently, after not seeing many Bahá'ís for so long he got very excited as more and more people kept arriving. He stood by the entrance and greeted them. When colored friends came from the States he went up to them and touched their skin and told them how beautiful they were, and how happy he was that they had come. Mom, they were so moved when they told me about it, and something more – they were glowing. It was as if Moose had given them something.'

I had returned from Poland and joined the family during the second day of the conference. Tristan had indeed glowed when I observed him from a distance moving among the friends. Eyes alight, he saluted old friends, held a hand, patted a shoulder, put his arm around someone or hugged a departing friend.

If we wanted to find anyone, we had only to give the word to Tristan and he would find him or her and bring about a reunion. He scorned the children's classes and fidgeted after three minutes of listening to any speaker, but he fed on the presence of the friends.

How many tearful goodbyes there were at the end of the Helsinki Conference! Finally, as we got under way for our return drive to Siebe I glanced back at Tristan. He was sitting eyes closed, ashen and exhausted. There was not even an ember of his previous animation.

It was not many days after our return that Tristan burst into the house announcing, 'Bahá'í friends have come!' All his glow was back. A New Zealand couple with their son were the first of a line of Bahá'í friends, new and old, who took time after the Helsinki Conference to travel to our remote area of Lapland.

Our Same neighbors were quick to come for a visit and survey the new arrivals. With each new set of visitors the universality of the Bahá'í Faith became more clearly illustrated.

The last of our long line of international visitors were the most exotic, and for our Same neighbors the most impressive. The family consisted of a grandmother, father, mother and two teenage daughters, and they were North American Indian.

This was to be a festive occasion and we sent around invitations to every household in our little settlement. They came as usual, dressed in their colorful Same costumes, but on this afternoon they were not the only ones in costume, for our Indian visitors also wore their buckskin clothing adorned with bead work.

Our visitors explained their Indian beliefs, as a Norwegian Bahá'í translated. The traditional dances and songs enthralled our Same friends. They ended their presentation by recounting how they had become Bahá'ís and explaining that this was a religion that stressed *Unity in Diversity*. The customary distrust of the Sames melted before the heartfelt candor. It was a wonderful afternoon and evening and the women of the community had many questions about beadwork and craft techniques, while the young people spent time in the kitchen discussing beliefs.

Once more Tristan was in his element, running errands, introducing newcomers, radiating with happiness. The oldest daughter was raven-haired and very beautiful. In the evening, before leaving, we noticed that she took Tristan aside and put something on his arm, then gave him a kiss. After we had waved them goodbye, Moose's sisters insisted on seeing what it was she had given him. Reluctantly he raised his shirt sleeve and there on his skinny wrist was a thickly beaded bracelet; a red rose on a yellow background. He kept it ever after in his drawer of treasures.

The long day ended; darkness, at first for a short time then rapidly increasing in length, claimed the night period. The summer hay had been dried and stored in the barn. The reindeer would soon be getting ready to make their fall migration to their inland winter grazing grounds.

It was less than a year ago that we had first arrived. No longer was the paintless house a sight of lonely desolation; it was home. It was the place of joyous memories, surrounded by close neighbors who came late at night to see us off on our return journey to Canada. After the transport truck left with our belongings we went down the well-worn path across the meadows to have tea and cakes, to be loaded down with gifts and mementos of their friendship. Was this the same insular community we had been warned against, these dearly loved friends now waving to us with tears in their eyes?

Over the familiar vida we drove north to Alta. The children and I would be returning to Canada in time to start the school year. But first we would stop off in Holland to see Grampa who was seriously ill. Hubert would join us later in the fall after he had filmed the beginning of the fall reindeer migration.

After arriving in Holland we went to see Grampa. He looked well and talked of coming to see us next summer in Canada. The children looked at him with love but were embarrassed to answer for they had been told that there would be no next summer. The cancer had advanced too far for that.

'Grampa was itchy,' Tristan remarked in the hall.

'Yes,' said Aunt Alice taking his hand, 'that's why I brought him another change of pyjamas and a special salve that helps a bit.'

Tristan frowned and stopped to scratch himself.

'He looks skinny,' Lisa remarked.

'He's the same cheerful Grampa I always remember,' Nadine affirmed optimistically. 'I bet that if he sets his mind to it, he can get better and come to visit us next summer.'

Hedy stopped and looked searchingly at Uncle Hans. He had raised his eyebrows but had shaken his head slowly.

'You never know,' Nadine went on undaunted, 'Miracles and will power can do wonderful things.'

That evening, as I tucked the children in we talked of Grampa.

'I love Grampa. I don't want him to die,' Lisa said.

'We all have to die. Dying is only the beginning of a new life in the other worlds of God,' I replied.

Someone slipped into bed behind me, and I could feel a little body pressing close.

'It's scary thinking of dying,' said a tremulous voice behind me.

'Is that why Grampa talks of coming to see us next summer?' asked Nadine.

'Maybe he doesn't want to admit it to himself just yet,' I suggested.

'Maybe he doesn't want to make us sad,' Hedy added.

'Death is sad because we feel we are losing someone we love very much. But we don't really lose them. We all meet again in the other worlds,' I explained.

'Gramma will be waiting for Grampa when he dies, and it'll be like a family reunion.'

'What if Grampa had married again? He would have two wives in the other worlds of God,' Lisa suggested.

'There is no sex in the other worlds, so it would be O.K.' Nadine said nonchalantly.

'How do you know?' queried Hedy.

'Simple . . . no bodies,' Nadine replied.

Moose asked, 'What is it, mom?'

'I would like to be able to tell Grampa how *much I love him* . . .'

'. . . and?' prompted Tristan.

'You know, I feel that Grampa was a real pioneer in dad's family,' I went on.

'How do you mean?' Nadine asked. 'He's not a Bahá'í.'

'Not a Bahá'í pioneer but a spiritual pioneer. There are families who live without showing any interest in the spiritual side of life . . .'

'Yes, lots of my friends' families are like that. They never talk about death, for instance . . . like we are now,' Hedy responded.

'Well, Grampa's family was like that too, and he was the first to break out of that pattern. He made it easier for his children to accept spiritual realities as important.'

'Go on,' Nadine prompted as I hesitated.

'Gramma, my mother, was like that as well. Everyone else was interested in social position and wealth, but she saw things differently. If it had not been for her and Grampa, dad and I might never have met. They helped us to be receptive to the Bahá'í Faith.'

'If you had not married dad, we would not be here . . .' Hedy concluded.

'So you see, I would like to thank him for being the spiritual pathfinder for the family!' I concluded.

By now all of us were snuggled into the same bed. For a time we all lay still thinking.

'Let's say a prayer,' suggested Tristan.

'What should we say?'

'What about a healing prayer?'

In the darkened room we sat up with the covers around us and prayed for Grampa. Tristan ended up with his favorite, 'Blessed is the Spot.'

Next day, when we went to the hospital Grampa was not coherent. The children left the room troubled. I stayed for a while holding his hand. There were moments that his eyes focused, and I could see recognition in their clear blue, but like clouds across a sky, a distracted look would move over his face. Though he spoke in English, it made no sense.

I walked with Hans down the long corridors of the hospital. 'It is important that he realizes that he is dying and can prepare,' I suggested.

'Yes, I have already called one of his Sufi friends,' Hans assented.

In the car, the children talked in the back seat.

'I don't like it.'

'What?'

'That Grampa is dying.'

'I wish he wouldn't.'

'He can't help it.'

'He's sick.'

'He was the best Grampa in the whole world!'

'Do you remember how he would always buy us bubble gum?'

'He always helped me color in my coloring books.'

'Do you remember how he would always get two of everything?'

'Yes, mom would ask him to get something, and he would buy two.'

'Every Saturday he brought a big barrel of Kentucky Fried Chicken!'

Aunt Alice turned around and said, 'That's funny; in Holland he always ordered chicken and apple mousse.'

'Apple sauce!'

'He sure liked chicken,' Lisa concluded in her deep voice.

Everyone laughed.

Chapter Sixteen

'HOW much farther?'

'I want to get *home*!'

On the ridge of Foley Mountain I stopped the car. Below us twinkled the lights of the picturesque village of Westport, with the dark mysterious waters of the Rideau Lake cupping the land.

In the silence Tristan's voice spoke with wonder, 'How beautiful!'

'You're crying,' Lisa said in accusation.

'Well, you threw up!' Hedy intervened.

'Crying is certainly less messy,' Nadine concluded.

'Home! Home!' Moose's voice was choked but exultant as we finally turned into the circular driveway. The children spilled out of the car in front of the dark and silent house.

On the front steps I saw the silhouette of Tristan, face uptilted to the moonlit sky, gazing out at the lake. He spread his arms to me, as I came up the steps, and hugged me.

'You are happy to be back,' I said softly above the symphony of the crickets all about us. How inadequate were the words in the face of his overwhelming emotion.

'It's too much . . .' he responded, his voice still choked. 'Home!'

'Mom, you've got to come in and see . . .' the girls' voices came insistently.

After the sheets and bedding were located and the beds made I went to tuck him in. He had moved back his bed so that he could have his head right next to the door. We looked out at the starlit sky.

'It's the same and it's not the same,' he said thoughtfully.

'That's because memory compresses all our experiences.' I could tell that he did not understand, so I went on, 'When we have one rose, we look at its beauty and we smell its fragrance

. . .'

'Like the Little Prince, who used to water his rose and put a jar over it at night,' Tristan mused.

'Yes, just like that. But if you take a thousand roses and crush their petals you can extract from them their "attar". Remember Gramma once brought us some attar of roses. The scent was overwhelming! Memory is like that, it is the extracted essence of all that has happened and it is stronger than any one experience. Tonight is one rose – the house welcomes you back, your room welcomes you back, your bed welcomes you back and, outside, the same stars you used to watch are winking at you.'

There was a silence, then Tristan began:

Blessed is the spot and the house and the place, and the city, and the heart, and the mountain, and the refuge and the cave, and the valley, and the island, and the meadow, where mention of God hath been made and His praise glorified.

Nadine was still awake after I had tucked in all the others. I went down to her basement room and sat on her bed.

'Did you notice how moved Moose was?' she asked me. 'We were all glad to get back to Canada and to the farm, but for him it was different, much more intense.'

'I was thinking about that too,' I answered. 'Could it be that just as a blind man develops a keener sense of hearing, Moose's limited intellectual powers have led him to greater development of feelings and intuition?'

'Do you remember how he called, "Home! Home!" I cried with him and for him because I had no idea how much he must have missed it.'

I went to the basement window and looked up at the stars. 'Moose loves to look at the stars when he says his prayers.'

'Mom, I know that I get mad at Moose sometimes, and a lot of times I think he gets too much attention from you and dad, but tonight I felt so glad to have such a sensitive, interesting brother.'

A week later at suppertime, Uncle Hans called from Holland. Grampa had just died. He had made his peace with death and had passed gently into the next phase of his existence. From the children's faces, I knew that they had guessed the news as soon as I hung up. They burst into tears and huddled up to each other, all except Lisa who sat immobile and dry-eyed.

'He has lived a good and productive life and up to the last moment he was a growing person. He developed those qualities that we have to learn in this life, love, kindness, unselfishness, understanding, generosity. I hope that when I die I will leave as many good and happy memories and as much love in the hearts of those that knew me as he has!'

We moved to the living room and said prayers for the departed. Tristan said 'Blessed is the Spot'. Lisa sat silent and remote.

After prayers Hedy turned and asked Lisa, 'Aren't you sad about Grampa dying?' Lisa looked up startled, and fled to her room.

Tristan's skin problems persisted. We took him to the local doctors and to dermatologists, all of whom diagnosed 'scabies' and prescribed a series of elaborate and unpleasant treatments. None worked. Finally Dr McKee recommended a dermatologist who once more pronounced that it was a rare form of Norwegian scabies. When that, too, proved to be a wrong diagnosis, we went back to palliative skin creams to ease the itching.

More and more often Tristan complained of stomachaches, many times he had diarrhea and had to stay home from school. When this went on too often, he checked into the hospital.

On one such hospital visit, Tristan was insistent that I meet his friend Tony. We went to the TV lounge where a tall pale boy was sitting.

'Tony,' Tristan said, going up to the boy and putting his arm around his shoulder, 'Mom, I want you to meet my friend Tony,' he said formally.

'Hello, Tony!' I responded.

'Hi! Pal,' the pale boy said to Tristan, then turning to me he said, 'Tristan is my *friend*.'

The way he said those words, weighing each one equally, I knew that he did not say them idly, that he was pronouncing a truth.

A nurse came to wheel Tony away in his wheelchair.

'Tony just had a heart operation,' Tristan explained, 'and he can't do anything too active, but we sit and talk and watch

TV.' Then he added, with a worried look, 'He might have to have another operation.'

After Tristan's discharge from hospital an intern explained the theory about the abdominal pains. Since the liver had been damaged and the kidneys were possibly under strain, there might at times be a build-up of pressure which would cause the otherwise mysterious pains. He told us to watch for blood in Tristan's stools.

We are a bookish family. Nadine and Lisa were confirmed bookworms. Hedy, although more extroverted, loved to read poetry and to look at art books. Tristan used to pore over a big tome of Bible stories illustrated by famous paintings. He would examine each in great detail, but the painting of the angel staying the hand of Abraham as he was about to sacrifice his son on the altar brought endless questions about sacrifice.

At night, when I tucked him in and looked at his face in repose, I could see that the artist *pain* was adding subtle lines to his face. A slight blue shadowing under the eyes, a fine line of tension down the cheek, a cross-hatching in the hollow under the high cheekbones, and the traces of pain were etched indelibly. When he was laughing, the inner radiance obscured those lines; in the shadowy light of the bedroom they were unmistakable.

His feet itched unmercifully. Like his hands they were beginning to thicken. At times as I passed by his room I would catch snatches of his conversations with God in which he would ask for an explanation. When a particularly nasty bout of itching assailed him, his voice grew irritated and querulous, impatiently demanding of God why the itching. What had he *done*?

'Tell me, God; tell me what I have done!' I once heard him shout in exasperation.

That evening I started teaching him the simple healing prayer.

Thy name is my healing, O my God, and remembrance of Thee is my remedy. Nearness to Thee is my hope, and love for Thee is my companion. Thy mercy to me is my healing and my succor in both this world and the world to come. Thou, verily, art the All-Bountiful, the All-Knowing, the All-Wise.

'How come "sucker"?' Tristan asked.

'In the prayer it's not the kind of candy you lick, but "help".'

I continued, 'Did you ever wonder why there is sickness in the world?'

Tristan sat up in bed, 'Yes,' he exclaimed. 'Why?'

I took out a well-worn book that I dearly loved, *The Divine Art of Living*, and read from it.

> I beseech God to ordain prosperity unto thee in this world, to confer favor upon thee in His supreme Kingdom, and to heal thee from the illness which hath befallen thee for some hidden reason which no one knows save God. Verily the will of God engages occasionally in some matter for which mankind is unable to find the reason. The causes and reasons shall appear. Trust in God and confide in Him and resign thyself to the Will of God. Verily Thy God is Affectionate, Compassionate and Merciful. He will look at thee with the glance of the eye of mercifulness, will guard thee with the eye of bounty, and will cause His mercy to descend upon thee.

There was such a long silence that I thought he had fallen asleep, but when I glanced over I saw his eyes bright and glowing, staring ahead.

'That could have been written for you by 'Abdu'l-Bahá. Your illness is one that no one knows the reason for. All the doctors try to help you, but they don't know how. It isn't because you have done anything bad. It is not a punishment for anything. Maybe it will make you turn to God and trust Him . . .'

'I ask Him sometimes . . . I ask Him *why*!' Moose said in a far-away voice.

'I ask Him too,' I admitted.

'You? But you're not itchy?' He sounded surprised.

'I ask about you . . . why you are sick.'

'Thanks, mom, thanks for asking about me,' but his body seemed to grow slack and I could sense a terrible sadness.

'Do you ever wonder how God answers our questions?'

'He never talks to me!' he said passionately and with a repressed resentment.

'As far as I know he speaks directly only to the prophets like Bahá'u'lláh, and Jesus and Moses.'

'So what's the use of talking to Him?' came the voice from the bed.

'We know He hears our prayers, and knows our thoughts. I

have found that He does answer, but you have got to know how to listen.'

'How?' The bright eyes from the bed were searching my face.

'First of all you have to be able to accept that "No" is also an answer. I love you but often when you ask for something I say "No" because it would not be good for you . . .'

'How *does* he answer?' Moose insisted.

'Often when I pray and tell God my problem and ask for help I will open a book, *The Gleanings* or the Bible, and start to read at random, and so often the passage I read holds the answer to my question.'

'What's another way?' Moose pressed.

I realized that since reading was so difficult for him, it would not be a method that he could use readily. So I pursued, 'Another thing I do after I pray to God is to say, "God I want to do Your will, but I don't know what it is. Please show me the way and let my heart and mind be ready to perceive the signs."'

'Then what happens?'

'Well, for example, when dad and I were trying to decide if we should go to Lapland, we prayed about it a long time. Then things began to happen that made it possible to go, and we took these as confirmation that we *should* go.'

'Is there any other way?' Tristan wanted to know.

'There is for me. I use this for very personal questions that I put to God. After praying, I stay very still and leave my heart and mind open. The answer often comes, not as a voice, not always as words, but as a kind of knowing. At times, but not often, it comes as a picture or a scene.'

Tristan reflected, 'You always said that after we pray we must be quiet and listen to the answer.'

I leaned over to kiss him goodnight and felt his forehead warm.

'Do you need an aspirin?'

'No, I'm O.K. – Goodnight, mom.'

'Goodnight, sweet Moose.'

Later in the week Tristan asked, 'Read me from that book again, mom.'

I read:

145

> For these thy prevailing diseases are not on account of sins, but
> they are to make thee detest this world and know that there is
> no rest and composure in this temporal life.

'What does that mean?'

'Your sickness is not punishment for something you did
wrong. Did you ever wonder about that?'

There was a long pause and then a sigh, 'I guess I did . . . I
wondered why God was mad at me. And it made me feel mad
at Him.'

'Then it goes on to say that illness is to make you love this
world less.'

'But it is so beautiful! . . .' We both looked out at the stars.
'You love this world don't you, mom?'

'Yes, I do,' I acknowledged. 'It is beautiful and it holds
people I love very much like you and Lisa and Nadine and
Hedy and dad . . .'

'. . . and Tony, my friend, and the Dances and Mrs
Hopwood, and . . .' Tristan added.

'But there are people I love who are in the other worlds of
God, like Grampa and my father. I know I will see them again
and be with them when I die.'

'Don't die yet, mom.' Tristan's voice sounded plaintive.

'I don't plan to. There is still so much I have to learn,' I
assured him.

'What things?' he was interested to know.

'To be kind, to be selfless, to be loving . . .'

'Oh, those, O.K.'

'If we learn those virtues we will find the other worlds of
God beautiful, wondrous.'

'What if we don't learn?' Tristan wanted to know.

''Abdu'l-Bahá tells us that if we don't learn, we are
handicapped in the other worlds of God.'

'Handicapped? How?'

'When you were a little baby growing inside me, you grew
legs. You didn't need legs because you were floating in water
inside me and I carried you everywhere I went, but you grew
legs because after you were born you would need them.'

Tristan chuckled.

'There are a lot of people who get along all right in life
without learning to be kind. In the other worlds of God, if they

don't know how to be kind, they will be like people without legs, handicapped.'

On our return from Norway we had decided to add a barn to our establishment and to start raising some animals. Chickens, turkeys, ducks and pigs, as well as numerous cats and a couple of dogs, made the barn their home. Much as we enjoyed all the animals, it was the Nubian goats that were the chief source of entertainment. Nubian goats, despite their haughty appearance (due mainly to their prominent roman noses and their long droopy silky ears), are very companionable. After school we would often go to the back of the land: adults, children, cats and goats.

Summer was a good time for Tristan. He tanned, his skin improved, and the itching grew less pronounced. We all worked in the mornings, and in the afternoons the family drove to the beach at Westport and we would swim while Tristan splashed in the shallows.

Summer wore on and it was Tristan's birthday. His sisters had decorated the dining room with streamers, although we had decided to have a quiet *en famille* celebration. It was one of those clear August days typical of the area, sun-drenched but with a wind that sent delicate lace patterns of clouds across the sky.

On the stairs as I came down that day, I found a note:

'Please send wind for Moose's B day. Thank you.'

From the time Tristan had learned to write he would leave little notes all over the house. At first they were on small scraps of paper. Coming down for breakfast, Hubert would find, I LOVE YOU written in a childish print by his place mat.

As his writing improved, so did the quantity and quality of the notes he wrote. Many were weather bulletins.

Tristan was the family authority on weather and the phases of the moon. Daily he listened to the weather forecast. The rest of the news held no interest for him, but everyone had to stop talking when the weather report came on. How he became interested in the phases of the moon I never learned, but at any time one could ask him when it would be full moon or new moon and, without effort, he would give the day and date.

At times, for our edification, he would give impromptu announcements: 'Ladies and Gentlemen, we are now approaching Ottawa. Please fasten your seat belts and refrain from smoking. The weather in Ottawa is clear and sunny, the temperature remaining steady at 20 degrees Celsius. Have a good time and thank you for flying Air Canada. This is your captain speaking.'

His greatest desire was always for a wind. Although the farm at Westport was on an elevation overlooking the lake and caught every breeze and therefore was not plagued by flies, he was neurotic about every small flying insect. When you entered the house you could count on Tristan's voice to call out, 'Shut the door! Don't let the flies in!'

So, on this important day, Tristan came down the light oak stairs looking pleased with the wind and pleased with himself and pleased with being thirteen. Since the wind held, we persuaded Tristan to walk to the back of the land. In the acres that we had named Green Mansions stood two old apple trees, one gold and one scarlet. Nadine climbed the trees and shook down a shower of apples. Tristan held my hand as the hail of apples fell. We brought them home in our knapsacks and made fresh cider for the birthday supper.

Not all the memories were golden. Nadine and Hedy were growing up, strong-willed and independent personalities. There were frequent clashes with parental authority. When this happened Moose suffered. It did not help to explain that this was fairly normal to the growing-up process. He suffered mutely, but with an intensity that was overwhelming.

At one point it became obvious that for the sake of our teenage daughters it would be better if we could have Hubert home all week and not just on weekends. Our dreams of self-subsistence on the farm had to give way to imperatives for family unity.

In the fall we began to look for a house in Ottawa. The one that we all agreed on was a completely renovated stately house from an era of gracious living. The renovators had improved the plumbing and the wiring but the lovely proportions of the high-ceilinged rooms were preserved, as were the oak floors, the second back staircase and the butler's pantry. Most important, it was right in the heart of Ottawa and all sorts of after-school activities would be within walking or bussing distance.

Hedy was to enroll at Glebe Collegiate, which had a more diversified program than the Rideau Regional High School and was not as exclusively academic as Lisgar High School which Nadine was attending.

Just before Christmas we moved. From the outset we were plagued with difficulties. The varathane on the floors was not dry, the heating did not work well, the pipes froze . . . With the coming of the new year, things seemed to look up. The heating system was repaired, the water in the kitchen began to flow again.

In January when all the children had started school and a degree of normalcy once more descended on our family, Hubert and I breathed a sigh of relief. Tristan was enrolled in a school with a very good special-ed. class. He was full of admiration for his teacher, Miss Allingham. During my visits to the school, I too was very impressed by this small curly-haired teacher, who exuded an air of no-nonsense authority, tempered by a keen perception of her students' needs and problems.

Lisa made an easy adjustment to her school. Only Hedy still felt uncomfortable in her environment. She had a girlfriend who called her often and the art teacher took a special interest in her; but, over all, she did not feel that she fitted in.

One ordinary morning as I was reaching for a pot to make breakfast porridge, something seemed to snap in my back. The pain was excruciating and I found that I could not straighten up. It was now my turn to enter that solitary land of pain. For the next six weeks I was to lie flat on one of the couches in the living room. I got to know the high ceilings well. In the dining room, the mountains of unopened boxes sat and collected dust. Nadine and Hedy managed the household tasks as well as they could.

Then Tristan fell ill. He burned with a fever that would not go down, and once more he was admitted to hospital. But again his stay there was inconclusive. His temperature cleared; there was another biopsy to compare with the one which had been performed when he was an infant.

A few days later Hedy returned from school to report, 'My counselor said that with my attitude towards school it would be better for me to drop out.'

'Hedy, what is it that you don't like about school?' I

inquired.

'There isn't anything that I *like* about it. I don't see the point,' she said flippantly. Then, earnestly, she asked, 'Mom, could I quit and get a job?'

To everyone's amazement she had a job that same day working for MacLean Hunter as a magazine salesperson traveling with a group across Canada.

'The first bird has flown the nest,' Hubert said as we sat at supper.

'I miss Hedy already,' Tristan said, looking down at his plate.

The house felt quiet without her ebullience.

Ottawa had always been our favorite city, and living at its heart made us appreciate it even more. Tristan would take our Norwegian 'spark'* and go sliding down the streets around our house. When I got better he and I would slide on our 'sparks' on the canal while the other members of the family skated.

On our street, in the area known as Sandy Hill, every house on the north side had been sandblasted, gutted, renovated and reverted to what it had been originally, a single-family home. On the south side of the street were the shabby versions of the same kind of house, each filled to overflowing with students and interesting characters who hoped that their convenient and inexpensive rooming house would not fall to the renovator's hammer.

As spring brought warmer weather, the boarders across the street overflowed onto balconies and front steps. In the evening, guitars were brought out and impromptu concerts and singsongs could be heard. As the end of the University year approached, there were a series of street parties with sidewalk dancing.

Tristan got to know everyone. If we had to call him for supper, his sisters had only to stand on the street and listen for music. They knew they would find him there.

One of our neighbors had a motorcycle and, to Tristan's great delight, took him for rides. But Tristan also had his own wheels. Hubert had bought the kind of bicycle that could be

---

* A chair-like sled on long metal runners. The person using the spark holds on to the handles at the back of the chair while pushing with one foot and standing on the runner with the other.

collapsed to fit into the trunk of a car. From the beginning Tristan had exhibited an amazing sense of direction. As the spring progressed into summer he went on longer and longer rides along the numerous bicycle paths that form a network along Ottawa's scenic canals and parks. If ever he became tired when he was far from home, he had only to phone. Hubert or I could pick him up and fold the bicycle into the trunk of the car.

In early spring, Tristan came home from school jubilant. His friend Tony was out of hospital and, wonder of wonders, he was attending the same school. Better still, he was in the same class as Tristan!

Other children who have a series of friends take friendship for granted. They feel that friendship is their due, and part and parcel of the human environment. For Tristan this was not so. His attitude to friendship was reverential. How many years had I seen him pine for a *friend*. Often he had made overtures to a possible candidate; often he had been repulsed or disappointed. Until he met Tony.

Tony, recuperated from his heart surgery, was bouncier than Tigger in *Winnie the Pooh*. Tony's mother took the two boys to museums, films and concerts. When Tony came to our house we were overwhelmed by his energy. He danced to loud music in Tristan's room, chased Lisa up the back stairs, pinching her bottom, and talked non-stop during supper.

Tristan looked fondly at him and tried gently to guide him to conform his behavior to the expectations of the household. Despite the difference in energy level and the contrast in personality, the two were obviously the best of friends. At parting, I gave Tony a big hug that earned me a look of gratitude from my son.

The family went to all the National Bahá'í Conventions in Eastern Canada. Invariably, Tristan bloomed. There were a few friends, such as Allan Raynor, that he always sought out. In those years they both looked so frail that when one saw them together one knew that they shared experiences in that same foreign land of pain. The love and understanding between them was palpable.

Hand of the Cause John Robarts was a beloved friend of Tristan. At one workshop session Mr Robarts had been speaking in a seminar room. Tristan had stood in the doorway listening to the closing comments. Then he had gone up to greet his friend in the audience. After John left he turned to those remaining in the room and with deep conviction pronounced, 'Now that is a REAL *Hand of the Cause.*'

At the concerts that so often marked the community invitational event of the Convention, Tristan was transported with delight by the music, the dancing and the singing. It was he who introduced me to Nancy Ward and Gordie Munro.

'How did you get to know all these people?' I wanted to know.

'I guess I'm just lucky,' Tristan said modestly.

Since his travels abroad Tristan had become patriotic to the core. A little Canadian flag always stood on his dresser. Living in the nation's capital, the issue of the first of July, Canada's birthday, was not to be taken lightly. He studied the schedule of events, and he and Tony planned their strategies. Hubert was persuaded to take them to some afternoon events and the whole family planned to attend the concert to be given in front of the Parliament buildings in the evening, culminating in a blazing fireworks display.

Tristan had always had an amazing sense of direction, but what happened on that first of July celebration made us realize how competent a city dweller he had become.

There were several thousand people sitting or reclining on the vast expanse of grass before the stage erected in front of the Peace Tower. For Tristan the afternoon had been a full one and he began to tire soon after the program began. The traffic was cut off for blocks all around the area and only buses were running. Tristan worked his way out of the crowd, took the bus home, and watched the rest of the performance on television.

Lisa, by contrast, wanted to buy an ice-cream cone and got lost for over an hour in the dense throng.

When the announcer mentioned that the fireworks would be starting in less than an hour, Tristan, more rested now, decided to return to the family. He took bus money from his piggy bank, caught the right bus and without apparent difficulties rejoined the family group (one of thousands sitting densely packed on the grass). He was there in time to see the truly spectacular display of fireworks, which he so particularly loved.

Chapter Seventeen

AFTER Hedy left we would get phone calls from her sporadically. At first she loved the work despite its pressures. As they went farther west her phone calls came later and later. It is surprisingly difficult to be warm and caring at three in the morning!

Then we heard that she had left the group and was living in a shack on Mystic Beach on Vancouver Island. Those were anxious times.

The dishwasher hummed with its load of supper dishes. In the living room Maxine, a high school friend of Nadine's, was playing a flute duet with Hubert. From the pantry, where I set out the cups and saucers for the evening's refreshments, I could see Tristan come down the stairs. His fastidiousness had prompted him to change his shirt and put on his 'good' shoes. His hair, grown lusterless and stiff of late, had been combed and plastered down with water. He stationed himself, as he did every Friday night, in a bay window giving on the street. We were expecting the first arrival for our weekly fireside discussion group.

'She's here!' called Tristan from his vantage point by the window.

The two flutes broke off in mid-melody. Nadine came galloping down the stairs and everyone spilled out of the house to stand by the special minibus where Cathy Best and her wheelchair were being lowered, by hydraulic lift, down to the sidewalk. It took all the hands available to get the wheelchair up the front steps and into the living room. As soon as the chair was wheeled into position by the fireplace, Tristan ambushed its occupant in a bear hug.

'Tristan!' Cathy exclaimed in her ringing voice. 'How are you, old pal?'

Cathy was one of Tristan's favorites. She had been born

blind and spastic, the first of two handicapped children. Her parents had placed her, on medical recommendation, in the Rideau Regional Centre (the same that so many years ago had been recommended to us as a solution for our son). Cathy had been lucky, for some perceptive workers had realized that despite her physical handicaps Cathy had a lively mind. She now lived in a group home with other handicapped adults, and attended high school, went swimming and, every Friday night, came to our firesides.

Others began to arrive – several students from the nearby University of Ottawa, a visiting Bahá'í from the Maritimes, friends from Lucerne and from the Gatineau, an older lady with a heavy accent, a scholarly librarian . . . the usual interesting assortment of people who came weekly to talk and to discuss the Bahá'í Faith.

On this evening there was a keynote talk about the journey of the soul as outlined with mystic beauty in Bahá'u'lláh's *The Seven Valleys*. Harry Hill had composed a song about the story of Laylí and Majnún that Bahá'u'lláh used to illustrate the ardor of the valley of search.

A young man, Majnún had searched everywhere for his beloved Laylí. His heart knew no peace. One night, unable to sleep, he set out to wander in the streets. In medieval Persia, such behavior was suspect and the night watchman began to chase after him. Majnún ran until he found himself cornered in a dead-end street. In despair, with his last ounce of strength he scaled the wall that in so many eastern cities encircles the house and garden of each dwelling. As he jumped off the wall, cursing his luck and the watchman, whom should he see in the garden below but Laylí, lamp in hand, searching in the garden for a ring she had dropped.

The song was beautiful and deeply moving. As the last chord of Harry's guitar reverberated we sat silent. Tristan's hand was in Cathy's as he stood protectively behind her. Both their faces were rapt, both glistened.

Some people began to recall how utter despair had led them unknowingly to their heart's desire. Harry, the composer of the song, sang once more the last line, in which Majnún realizes that he should have blessed the watchman even before finding his beloved Laylí.

Suddenly, there was a commotion at the door. I had not

heard the bell ring, but Nadine, who had been sitting on the stairs, was letting in some latecomer. I had only time to spot a ragged blanket poncho and then a familiar well-loved face, before I was on my feet calling, 'Hedy! Hedy!'

'The prodigal is back!' she said, as we hugged.

We all took turns hugging and exclaiming, while Tristan tried to fill Cathy in on what was happening.

Later, as we sat over refreshments in the dining room and Hedy was getting cleaned up in Nadine's room, Cathy remarked, 'I could just *see* how moved you were when your daughter came back.'

It always unnerved me when Cathy used the verb *to see*, but I knew that, perhaps more than most, she perceived the impact of Hedy's return, just as early in our friendship she had sensed my deep concern for her.

Over tea, by the flickering light of the candles on the table, the conversation turned back to the topic of adversities in our lives. One young man, a student at the university, expounded at length on the difficulties in his life. A beautiful blond girl with a long face told about the afflictions and injustices she felt she had sustained.

Cathy interjected with deep sympathy. Her sightless face turned towards the young man's voice. Her speech was clear but at times halting due to her spasticity.

'I have been so incredibly lucky in my life', she said without affectation, 'that I don't know if I can even properly sympathize.'

The young man started up, but on Cathy's face he saw no hint of sarcasm. We who knew her realized that she was without guile.

'Sometimes, I wonder how come I have been so lucky,' she continued, her voice full of wonder. 'I had wonderful parents, and all the people at the hospital were kind to me. One lady became my special friend. She took me for a holiday in a plane! Then she arranged for me to move into the house I live in now. Best of all, this same lady told me about the Bahá'í Faith. So when I moved to Ottawa I called up the Bahá'ís, and now look how many wonderful friends I have.'

Tears were unabashedly flowing down several cheeks. No one could trust himself to speak. It was Tristan who broke the charged silence, 'Cathy, why don't you sing "Paper Roses"?

Hedy has never heard you sing. Would you sing it for my sake?'

'Anything for you, Tristan my pal!' answered Cathy. Tilting back her head, she sang without affectation, in a clear strong voice.

Tristan returned from school earlier than the others. A minibus dropped him off at the corner of the street. He watched carefully for the lights to change, looked both ways, and crossed on the crosswalk. He was a careful child.

No matter what other activities occupied my day, I made a point of being home for his return. The few times I had been away I left a note, but his withdrawn face showed his disappointment even though his words were invariably a polite, 'It's all right; I understand, mom.'

I used to watch him from the upstairs bedroom window coming down the back lane. Often he would stop and look at the pigeons swooping onto the ledge of the apartment block on the corner. As he came by a big elm tree, he would pat its bark as if saying hello to a friend. If our neighbor's yapping dog were out in the yard, he always stopped to talk to it and to pet it.

On this day I noticed that his parka hood was pulled so far forward that his face was hidden. Head down, he passed under the wheeling pigeons, and only brushed carelessly against the elm tree. Instead of talking to the yappy dog he kicked at the snow by the fence.

I greeted him at the back door and took his parka to hang up. I was barely back from the cupboard and plugging in the electric kettle when the question exploded, 'Mom, am I retarded?'

My back was turned, my hand had reached out to get the canister of tea. I closed my eyes. Always I had known that such a question would inevitably arise. I turned and placed the teapot of fragrant Lapsang Souchong tea on the delft blue trivet and looked at my son. He was watching me intently, his thin torso leaning across the table.

'One of the boys on the bus said I was retarded.' A pause. 'Am I, mom?'

I poured the fragrant tea into our Finnish glasses (just like the ones in the Neo–Citran ad, Lisa had remarked). Then I pushed the sugar box closer to Tristan.

Please God help me to answer this . . . it is the hardest question I have ever been asked.

Across the table I could see that Tristan was stirring the sugar in his tea. The fine features of his face were taut. He lifted his eyes to mine, searching for an answer.

'What does "retarded" mean?' I asked.

'Dumb . . . stupid,' Tristan answered.

'Actually, it comes from the French word "tard", late. When someone is 'en retard' they are late. In English to retard means to slow down.'

Tristan stopped stirring and watched the tea leaves in his cup swirling around and settle to the bottom of the amber liquid.

'Do you remember when I told you about being sick as a little baby. At that time many of your brain cells were damaged, killed,' I pursued.

'But', interposed Tristan, remembering Mrs Hopwood's instruction in anatomy, 'we all have many more brain cells than we need.'

'Yes, that's perfectly true. But in some parts of your brain there are so many that aren't working that the others that are trying to do the work keep tripping over the damaged ones, so to speak, and that slows them down.'

'So I am retarded?' The clear eyes with their burden of pain looked straight in mine.

From some recess of memory came the words of a prayer,

The lamps of truth and purity, of loyalty and honor, have been put out.

Love demands truth, came my heart's answer. Unflinching, holding his gaze steadily, I answered, 'Your development has been slowed down, retarded. That is why you learned to walk later than some children, that is why you took speech therapy, that is why you have more trouble with reading than Lisa, for instance.' I saw him flinch, but his gaze held true. 'But', and here I reached for his cold gnarled hand, 'you are not stupid or dumb. You are a very perceptive and articulate person . . . You understand people and situations and you can express yourself well and say what you mean.'

A long slow breath was exhaled. It was as though he had

held it from the first impact of the wounding words. I sipped my tea, its strong, pungent, smoky flavor invading my senses. This was part of our after-school ritual: 'smoky tea'.

'Some people use the word incorrectly. They say "you're retarded", or use it as a noun, "you retard".' Each time I said the word Tristan flinched, but I felt it had to be done. 'When people call you that, they are doing it to hurt you. If you understand, it does not hurt quite so much.'

Two lines appeared between his eyes as he concentrated on trying to understand.

'Moose, when I call you "a rat", you know I'm mad at you, but you also know that you are *not* a rat. You know that I know you are not really a rat. When you get mad at me you call me "a big fat turkey".'

At this point Tristan understood, and threw his head back to give a wonderful imitation of the turkey sounds he had learned from the farm. When we had finished laughing, we had some more tea. Then his face clouded again.

'When that boy calls me "a retard" I'm going to call him "a big fat rat",' Tristan said, gritting his teeth.

'If you *want* to hurt his feelings that might work. But do you remember what we are taught to do as Bahá'ís?' I questioned.

Together we repeated, 'When someone poisons your life sweeten theirs.'

'Did He really do that?' Tristan asked, fresh from his inflicted wound.

'Bahá'u'lláh suffered terribly from the cruelty of others; his own brother poisoned Him.'

There was a long silence as I plugged in the kettle again.

'Mom, I'm sorry I call you a turkey sometimes,' Tristan said thoughtfully.

I knelt beside him, my arms around his skinny shoulders, my face against his damp cheek.

'Moose, that is different; we love each other. When people love each other it doesn't mean that they don't get angry at each other sometimes, and when they do they need some way to blow off steam. So I call you a rat and you call me a turkey. That does not hurt me as it would if (and here I named a very dignified gentleman in our Bahá'í community) came up and said, "Suzanne, you big fat turkey!"'

This really caught at Tristan's sense of the ridiculous and he laughed in peals of cleansing laughter.

He was still laughing when Lisa came home from school. This was his cue to go to his room and watch TV or, if the weather were fine, to go out on his spark or his bicycle. Lisa did not like tea nor did she enjoy talking that much, but she felt it was only fair to have equal time alone with mother.

After supper, when Tristan and Lisa had cleared the dishes, the chronic arguments broke out over whose turn it was to rinse and who had to do the stacking of the dishwasher. Voices rose and there were recriminations. We heard Tristan's voice announcing in clear tones, 'Well, I may be retarded, but I'm not dumb!'

Those of us who were left at the table looked at each other dumbfounded. My smile was wide but my eyes were filled with tears.

I may be retarded, but I'm not dumb became a family 'bon mot'.

In March Tristan was sick again, with high fever and nausea. Once more we were in the hospital. Patience, I kept reminding myself, patience is a great virtue. Since Tristan's doctor was not available we went through the same interminable waits in the waiting room, and then in the little cubicle. Endless questions were asked, and then when the doctor who asked them went off duty the new one taking over asked them all over again.

All the time the patient, burning with fever, lay limp in my arms. Tristan asked for a drink of water. One of the nurses pointed to a fountain but there were no cups. At last some kind office worker brought me a paper cup.

We had reached the hospital at two in the afternoon. By seven that evening a doctor handed me a slip of paper and said, 'It looks like a kidney infection. Here is a prescription. You won't find it easy to fill because the more common remedy involves penicillin. Since he is allergic to it . . . we must try a substitute.'

'Could you give me some now just to start him off? It's Sunday night and there are not likely to be many pharmacies open.'

'Sorry, our dispensary does not carry them,' he replied and was gone.

It was nine at night before we returned home and started to

phone all the pharmacies in the yellow pages of the phone book.

The medication helped, but it took well over a week. The high fever had made him delirious at times. When he was recovered he looked like a shadow. The first time he came downstairs he had to hold up his trousers; so gaunt had he grown that they slipped off his hips. His shirt hung on his shoulders as though on the crosspiece of a scarecrow. He went to his father and sat on his knee limply, resting his head on his father's chest.

Nadine and Lisa said all the right things.

'Moose, you're down! How wonderful!' 'Look at the sign we painted!'

There, across the mantelpiece a painted sign read, GLAD THAT YOU ARE BETTER MOOSE. He tried to smile but instead a tear appeared in the corner of his eye.

That evening I caught the scent of approaching spring in the air and with a start realized I had not been out of the house for ten days.

Tristan recovered slowly. As he got better he talked of going back to school and of seeing Tony again. At times he watched television. At other times he sat with me in my sewing nook amid the plants.

'Are there plants and flowers in the other worlds of God?' he asked.

'I remember reading about people who had died and been revived speaking of flowers and meadows,' I responded.

'If there are flowers, are there bees?' he asked anxiously.

More and more often Hubert and I talked of pioneering.

'What would you really like to do?' I asked when once more Hubert had railed against the prison of a desk job.

'I'd like to make films,' came the ready answer. Then he asked, 'What about you?'

'The place I was happiest, the country of my soul, is Labrador. From the standpoint of profession, well, I would like to teach again and eventually I would like to write, but most of all I would like to lead the life of a pioneer.'

We determined to pray that the opportunity for service as pioneers would present itself. How differently I see it now, I thought, remembering our first pioneering adventure. It is now my dearest longing and an honour of which I am unworthy.

Shortly after, Hubert met an old friend from New-foundland who mentioned in passing that a position was available with the Extension Service of Memorial University in Goose Bay, Labrador. It sounded as if there were a good chance that film work would be part of the job.

To give up a senior position with the Federal Government with all its monetary compensations and security struck some of our friends as madness. Some of the Bahá'ís understood.

Next, we went to see all of Tristan's doctors. They agreed that Tristan's condition was stable. Even when it deteriorated, they assured us, there would be nothing medically that could not be done as well in a small hospital as in a big one.

Nadine had previously decided to go to Memorial University in St. John's, Newfoundland, the city where she had been born. By moving to Labrador we would be, despite the distance, at least in the same province.

The house was sold and we moved into our condominium.

As soon as school was over we intended to drive to Newfoundland and take the boat up the coast to Goose Bay. Hubert's position with Memorial University began in July. And then Tristan developed another infection.

'Why don't we do a series of X-rays on him and see what is the cause of all these infections,' Dr McKee suggested.

Tristan was instructed not to eat anything the day before, and then in the morning at the hospital he would be given a drink of barium that could be followed on the X-ray monitor.

'It will take, at most, an hour,' the technician informed us, as Tristan with his usual compliant good nature lay down in the darkened room under the enormous suspended machine. I looked at my watch; it was nine o'clock.

Dr McKee came in. Several doctors were called in consultation. They studied the X-rays. Tristan was given more barium to drink.

At one-thirty Dr McKee told us that we could go. Tristan was limp from his extended fast so we went to the hospital cafeteria and I watched him pile up his tray.

Getting a second cup of coffee at the counter I bumped into Dr McKee.

'What did the tests show?' I asked bluntly.

'His kidneys are hardly functioning at all. It is a surprise to us as this did not show up on any other tests,' he explained, obviously puzzled.

'You know that we are moving to Labrador in four weeks. Will this necessitate a change in our plans?' I wanted to know.

'There is the possibility of dialysis, but I will have to consult with some of the other specialists and let you know,' he answered.

Tristan was eating his yoghurt when I got back to our table. 'What did he say?' he asked.

I looked at the long-suffering face, peaked and sallow, crowned by tousled hair. The demands of love struggled from beneath the debris of collapsed hopes. I took his hand, cold and coarse to my touch. There have never been lies between us; let there be none now, I resolved.

I forced my face into the semblance of a smile, 'Your kidneys are not working well,' I said.

'I thought it was my liver,' he said blandly, returning to his yoghurt.

'It's because your liver has not been able to do its share of the work, your kidneys have been overburdened, and now they are tired out.'

'I'll have to give them a rest,' he attempted to joke.

We got back to the apartment just in time for his favorite television program. I slipped out under pretext of getting some milk at the corner store. I wanted to phone Hubert from some soundproof place.

There was a long silence when I told him all the news. 'Hubert, are you still there?'

'Yes . . . I'm just thinking. What if he needs treatment in a larger center? Will he need dialysis?' Hubert asked.

'As I understand it, dialysis is not a long-term solution. Why don't I ask Hossain Danesh about it?' I suggested.

My hand was shaking as I dialed the number at the hospital. Everything around me had a heightened sense of reality ever since I had spoken to Dr McKee. I will never forget the texture of the wallpaper in the lobby where I made those phone calls, nor the random scratches on the metal near the coin return, nor the fact that someone had shaded in with a pencil the number nine on the dial.

Thank God, Dr Danesh was not with a patient and was able to take the call. After I had spilled out all the information I halted breathless.

'I'm sorry to unload all this on you, but as you know we are leaving in a few weeks and we need some help in coming to a decision . . .'

'How do you feel about prolonging Tristan's life?' Hossain asked.

'I have not been able to think of anything *but* that all afternoon.' I hesitated, trying to put into words the swirl of images and thoughts and emotions that crowded into mind and heart. 'He has had so much pain, so much illness. It is not as though it were only his kidneys that were malfunctioning, there is also his liver. I personally feel that to keep him alive by means of machines would not be right. I would like him to enjoy the rest of his life as much as possible and live it in dignity. When the time comes for him to die, I hope it can come naturally.'

'Believing in life after death makes that kind of decision easier,' Hossain commented. 'I'll try to find out what I can for you and, meantime, you and Hubert should talk about it.'

In the apartment Tristan was still watching television and eating an apple. Lisa was home from school and doing her homework at the desk.

'Dad will be home soon. Would you set the table, Moose?'

'What's for supper?'

'Your favorite, macaroni-and-cheese and a salad.'

After supper Hubert and I went for a walk. Minute unrelated details stand out in my mind: I scuffed my shoe on the gutter, Hubert's shoelace was unraveling at one end.

'I guess we always knew that Tristan would not live as long as an ordinary child,' Hubert began, tentatively.

This was the life of our child we were holding in our hands. In the Garden of the Provinces we sat and said some prayers. Cautiously we began to examine possibilities. We were willing to reverse our plans and stay in Ottawa. Was an existence on dialysis really what we wanted for Tristan? Was it what he would choose for himself? Should we put the decision to him? No, we both felt that it would be wrong and cruel to do that.

May God help us to make the right decision, we prayed. Then, having reached agreement, we walked back. Subsequent consultation with Tristan's doctors reinforced our decision. Dialysis was not a practical option.

Our apartment was within walking distance of Tristan's

school. One day he asked to bring Tony over for lunch. They bolted their food and Tristan took his friend on a guided tour of the building. They were not gone long before the phone rang. It was the security guard. My son's friend was climbing the cross beams over the underground parking, he informed me. I rushed down.

The swimming pool gave on a terrace, part of a raised garden. The garden ended in a well from which heavy metal beams formed a grid over the garage and parking area on a lower level. It was on these beams, some eight feet above the cement floor of the garage, that Tony was balancing himself. Below, Tristan was calmly trying to talk him down.

'Careful, Tony, just keep going straight. Don't look down! You're almost at the garden!' Then he turned to me and whispered, 'Mom, can you open the door from the garden to the lobby. It only opens from the inside!'

I was so grateful to get the two of them out of that scrape that I drove them back to school.

'Thanks, Tristan's mom, that was lots of fun. You sure live in a neat place,' Tony said as he jettisoned himself out of the car.

'I'm sorry, mom. I never would have asked him over if I had known he would get into so much trouble.'

'That's all right, son. You did a great job getting him down.'

'How did you know he was up there?' Tristan asked, mystified.

'The security guard called me.'

'Oh, no! Now I will be embarrassed to say "Hello" to him.'

'Moose, you know incidents like this make me realize that a wonderful son you are!' I leaned over and gave him a kiss.

When Tristan came home from school, he was triumphant. 'Tony really beat up a kid for me today!' he announced.

'How did it happen?' asked Lisa, looking up from the book she was reading.

'This big guy called me a sissy because he saw mom give me a kiss when she dropped me off at school this afternoon. But Tony just lifted him up. You know how big and strong Tony is!' Lisa and I nodded assent. 'Tony just lifted him up and shook him hard! I bet that kid will never tease me when Tony's around!'

Chapter Eighteen

THE drive from Ottawa to Newfoundland had the surreal elements of a nightmare. Tristan's itching was all but unbearable. Our efforts to break up our drive, with picnics by the St. Lawrence, met with his screaming objections. He refused to venture among the flies that often inhabit the seaweed garlands washed ashore by the river and the open sea.

To give him a break from the ordeal we detoured to Prince Edward Island where we rented a cottage by the sea. On windy days he consented to go to the beach and fly kites with Hubert and Lisa. At times like that we watched Tristan's face relax and come out of the grimace of discomfort that so often pervaded his features.

In Western Newfoundland we stopped for several days outside Corner Brook in some cabins near Marble Mountain. Bahá'ís from the area came to visit. Tristan once more became transformed into the gracious host offering our Bahá'í friends what hospitality the cabin could provide.

The morning we left the cabin I watched Tristan standing by the car, girding up his courage to get in once more. There was so much resignation, so much quiet courage in the uncomplaining sigh before he embarked. But I noticed that he gave the tire a kick to vent some of his frustration.

'Only a few hours today, son!' Hubert assured him. 'Nadine is meeting us in Lewisport, and we will have a day and a half with her before we catch the *Sir Robert Bond* for Labrador.'

There were effusive cries of 'Nadine! Nadine!', and then everyone was trying to hug her at the same time. All strain left Tristan's face at that moment as he clung to his sister.

How alike they are, I thought as I saw their two fair heads together. The same pale blue eyes and high cheek bones distinguished both faces.

Lewisport is a lovely harbor town. On the road that winds

along the water's edge stands a turn-of-the-century hotel next to the wharf where docks the *Sir Robert Bond* on its return from Labrador. We checked in, explaining the nature of our family reunion. The new owners were very understanding and gave us two rooms, on the top floor, overlooking the sea.

In the room that the two youngest were to share with their eldest sister we heard giggles followed by a long serious conversation.

'Nadine says that I should read a non-fiction book for every three fiction books I read,' Lisa confided later in the afternoon when Nadine was reading Moose a story in bed.

'That's a very good idea,' I concurred, looking at Lisa, the acknowledged bookworm of the family.

'She said that otherwise I won't ever be a well-read person!' Lisa continued.

'Being well-read is very different from just reading a lot,' I emphasized.

The late afternoon was cool and windy; in other words, perfect weather to take Tristan for a cookout. Driving north out of Lewisport, we found a beach with a good supply of driftwood and made a fire. Tristan told jokes and did imitations. As the wind picked up, we huddled closer together and sang songs. In the car on the way back we laughed at each other's marshmallow faces.

There was a good television play on that evening, so we sat on the beds and watched. It was about a ten-year-old girl with a serious heart condition from which she would soon die. Her parents were coming apart psychologically. The mother dragged her daughter from specialist to specialist, at home and abroad. The father rented extravagant props, including a real pagoda and actors, to stage a Chinese party for her birthday. By the end our children were in tears.

During the discussion of the play, I kept silent. Tristan went to bed early and Lisa and Hubert settled down to read, so I suggested to Nadine that we take a walk along the harbor front. Stacks of herring barrels for the European market lay by the shore, and from the sea came the familiar tang of salt and fish.

'What did you really think of the play we just saw?' I asked Nadine.

'It was well done,' Nadine answered.

'Don't you think that the reactions of the parents were . . . somehow exaggerated?' I pursued.

'Not really! After all, their child was going to die. They were terribly broken up about it.'

'Nadine, did you ever consider that our family is in the same situation?'

In the fading light I saw her stop and an incredulous look came on her face. 'You mean Tris?'

'Yes,' I said, continuing to walk. 'He may not have that long to live.'

There was a long silence between us, which Nadine broke, 'I guess I always knew Moose was sick. Ever since I can remember, Moose has always been sick. But mom, he's only fourteen . . . Is there something new about his condition?'

I told her about the last-minute discovery of the malfunctioning kidneys and about the difficult decision that we had had to make.

'I'm really glad that you told me all this, mom. It will be terrible if Moose dies . . . I love him so much. I can't imagine the family without him.'

Next day Nadine returned to St. John's and we boarded the *Sir Robert Bond* for our thirty-six-hour sea trip to Goose Bay.

In the rose light of early dawn we stood on deck as the ship edged towards the dock. For the last hundred and fifty miles we had been sailing west in the Melville inlet, which in other lands would have been called a fjord. The children had been excited by the big icebergs on the open sea and the whales at the mouth of the inlet. What did they think now, in this cold early dawn?

I looked at Lisa and Tristan shivering in their winter parkas at the railing of the upper deck. Did they see the majestic forests sweeping down from the Mealy Mountains to the mirror-still waters of the inlet, or did they see merely an old dock with some sad-looking warehouses?

As we drove the car from the ship we explained to the silent children in the back seat about the scattered enclaves of communities in the area. The American and Canadians had both had a military presence in the area and each left a legacy of buildings.

It was to Happy Valley, the town built by native Labradorians, that we were driving. Twenty years after meeting there,

Hubert and I still found it the sprawling frontier town that we remembered so vividly. There were a few additions, a new Vocational School, a new restaurant. 'Take me as I am,' the town seemed to say.

Tristan and Lisa were polite when we showed them our new house. Nadine on her first visit home was more outspoken. 'You live here in this, this . . . shack?'

It was indeed a small house. 'Typical Valley architecture,' Hubert was to say on many occasions.

While we painted and effected some minor changes in the house we were able to live in the home of friends who were away on holidays. The work was progressing well. One morning when Hubert had left for work at Memorial Extension and the children and I were sleeping in after having worked hard and late the night before, I awoke to hear the garbage truck coming down the street. When I looked out the window I realized that Hubert had forgotten to put out the cans. I jumped out of bed, pulled on a dressing gown, ran down and started pulling at the heavy garbage cans.

They were such heavy ungainly things! My frustration mounted as I tried to get them over the uneven path to the side of the road. Something in my back went 'Pop'. Doubled over with pain and unable to straighten up I limped back to the house. I was crying with frustration. 'The whole house to paint, and my back has to go!'

Some of the anger was directed at myself. If I had not been so irritated at Hubert for forgetting the garbage I would not have risked lifting the heavy garbage cans. I *knew* that I could not safely lift them!

The same familiar pills and the same instructions to lie down on a firm surface. The family was sympathetic. Hubert brought a foam mattress and installed it downstairs. He and the children went off to paint in the other house.

That afternoon I prayed, 'God, I have been so foolish. I have allowed my anger and impatience to jeopardize our whole move. My Lord! I know that You can transform even such a foolish action of mine into something that will turn out for the good. We have to move out of this house in two weeks, the other house is not even half ready. Please, please, turn this disaster into a means of doing Thy good pleasure.'

Ardently I prayed all that afternoon, fighting the drugging

effects of the valium. I knocked without cease at the door of God's mercy. I felt myself like a beggar with her bedroll squatting at the threshold of God's grace and assistance.

That evening I phoned Hedy. 'I have done something really stupid!' I confessed.

It was her turn to be comforting. 'It's O.K., mom, we're all allowed to do something foolish once in a while!'

'Do you think you could come to Labrador and help us get the house ready? I can't do anything but lie here on the mattress!'

Hedy responded with a question of her own: 'Could Robert come with me?' Robert was her French-Canadian boyfriend.

Hedy and Robert arrived a few days later in the full regalia of the flower-child generation. It looked out of place in Happy Valley.

But they set to work with a will, and soon it became apparent that Robert knew a lot about plastering. He and Hubert worked well together on the renovations. Over supper conversations we got to know him better and became good friends.

During the next month Hedy came under the spell of Labrador and decided to stay. It was hard for Robert to accept that she would not be leaving with him.

The sun was illuminating the dining area through the wall of windows Hubert had installed. A great angel-wing begonia was bending under a weight of heavy pink blooms behind Tristan, as we all sat after supper around the round table that had traveled with us to so many houses. It was our first meal in our new house.

'When did Nadine become a Bahá'í?' Tristan asked.

'I think it was soon after she turned fifteen,' Hubert answered absently.

'She became a Bahá'í youth,' Lisa insisted. 'You can't be a Bahá'í until you're twenty-one.'

There was a look of distress on Tristan's face.

'Moose, why, you have just had your birthday! Would you like to become a Bahá'í youth?' I asked.

His face cleared. 'Could I? Would it be all right?'

'Moose, my dearest Moose! Don't think I had forgotten. I was going to ask you at the next feast.'

That evening I heard him singing a little song to himself:

'I'm going to be a Bahá'í, I'm going to be a Bahá'í!'

When I came to tuck him in that night his face was radiant. 'You know, Moose, signing that card is only a formality. What is in your heart is what is really important. You have been a Bahá'í for a long time.'

'Really?' He sounded surprised.

'A Bahá'í means a follower of the light.'

'What light?' he asked, looking at the light bulb in the darkened room.

'The light of God,' I said, turning on the light. 'Is it easier to see with the light on or off?'

'On!'

'The light of God makes it easier to see what is right and wrong.'

'How does it turn on?' he asked.

'God sends His messengers, His teachers to mankind, Abraham, Moses, Jesus, Zoroaster, Buddha, Muhammad, the Báb, Bahá'u'lláh. They turn on the light for us. Without their teachings we wouldn't know what is wrong or right.'

'What about the sun?'

'What about it,' I wanted to know.

'Who turns that on? God?' Tristan asked.

The next morning he went to the window and called out, 'God's light bulb is on!'

Unexpectedly, I was offered the position of French teacher at the High School at the end of August. The next weeks were a blur of preparation. To her delight, Hedy had been accepted as a nursery school teacher at the Mother Goose Nursery. Tristan and Lisa went to the same school for the first time.

Fall is a glorious season in Labrador. The tamarisk needles turn golden and the wild cherries flame scarlet. The birch and the evergreen, the two most common trees, balance deep green and melting gold against each other, like cellos holding the balance of a melody that is taken up by the vibrant tones of the violins.

At the end of October, on a fine sunny day reminiscent of Indian summer, we set off for a picnic at Muskrat Falls. On the way I spied a lovely patch of redberries on a knoll not far from the road. I persuaded Hubert to stop. As Hubert and Lisa joined me in picking, Tristan became upset and then grew frantic, slapping at the few lethargic remnants of mosquitoes.

He became so hysterical that Hubert decided to drive him home.

Lisa and I picked for awhile in silence. The scene reminded us painfully of the frenzied objections Tristan had made, on our drive up to Labrador, to any picnic venture by the St. Lawrence. It became undeniably clear to us that Tristan would be unable to participate in most of the outdoor activities that enliven and focus many social and recreational events in this area. The question once more flashed through my mind how well advised were we to take Tristan from the city setting that he loved to this wilderness that for so many months was dominated by insects that were anathema to him.

Labrador is an important homefront goal, I told myself. We are the only Bahá'ís in the area at the moment. The Labrador city assembly has ceased to exist and there are in all only two or three other Bahá'ís in this vast region.

Hubert returned grim-faced. 'Well at least I know a bit more about why he panics so much at the sight of a fly!'

'Why?' Lisa and I wanted to know.

'Do you remember, in Ottawa, when he went to see the film *Superman*?'

'Yes, I went with him,' Lisa interjected.

'Apparently,' Hubert continued, 'there was a preview for a film called *The Swarm*!'

'Yes, it was an Alfred Hitchcock film,' Lisa confirmed.

'That preview was so terrifying for Tristan that he doesn't even want to talk about it,' Hubert concluded.

'That, alone, should not make him so scared of one or two flies.'

'But mom, don't you remember he always hated flies. He once sprayed Raid all over the barn at Westport,' Lisa reminded us.

'And he is itchy, anyway,' Hubert continued, 'so the fear of getting more itchy bites plus the memory of a scary preview all add up to one terrified little boy where bugs and flies are concerned.'

Later that fall, Tristan's temperature suddenly skyrocketed. He complained of aches in his sides and back. We phoned the hospital.

At the door of the hospital we were met by a nurse with a wheelchair and Dr Kevin Columbus, who had been at

Tristan's birthday party.

My eyes filled with tears of gratitude for not having to sit for hours in a waiting room, for not having to answer pages of interminable questions, while Tristan hung limp and feverish in my arms, and for having a doctor who spoke as a friend to my son. Flushed and glassy-eyed as he was, Tristan still tried to joke with Kevin.

I was allowed to stay until Tristan was installed in a bed. A large fan blew over a bowl of ice cubes towards him. In the hall Kevin stopped me and asked a few questions about Tristan. Wonder of wonders, he explained in great detail the treatment being undertaken and also spelled out the name of the new drug they were proposing to use, one that had proven successful with patients allergic to penicillin.

Flaring kidney infections were frequent that year. They did not last long, but recovery was a slow process. Like a ball whose bounce back gets progressively weaker, his periods of recuperation took longer and longer. We had to admit that he was no longer bouncing at all but merely rolling along.

It was the tenacity and determination in his spirit that was now exposed. Sheer will made him get up wearily every morning and go to school. There was no longer a skip in his step, and only the force of his determination propelled him through his days.

On one day a fat envelope came addressed to: Tristan Schuurman Esq.

Delightedly he tore it open. It was from the Bahá'í Community of St. John's, Newfoundland. At the Nineteen Day Feast at which his Bahá'í declaration card had been received, many had decided to write a personal welcome. Some had remembered him from a brief visit when the family had stopped over on the way from Greenland; others remembered him from Bahá'í conferences; some were new friends. I read him each letter several times; he looked at them with glowing eyes and held them reverently.

'Well, do you feel like a Bahá'í youth now?' I asked, laughing.

Too moved to answer, he merely nodded. Years later I was to find those letters among his few 'prized possessions'.

More and more there was pain for Tristan. When he was on the toilet he would often call out for me, his face contorted with pain. I could but sit opposite him and hold his hand and talk soothingly.

His face grew more gaunt and hollow-cheeked and the sore spots became more pronounced. Only his refusal to have his picture taken at school made us realize how aware he was of his appearance and how distasteful it was for him, who loved beauty, to be unlovely.

Nadine read an article in a scientific journal about a cure for chronic itching through the use of a sun lamp. She wrote to the Harvard Medical School, to the doctor who had pioneered the treatment. Hubert ordered the lamp and Nadine even kept Tristan company under the lamp when she was home on holidays from university. She got a tan; Tristan itched as before.

The 'special ed.' class of which Tristan was a part had a work-training program. Mrs Fulford, Tristan's teacher, was a person of warmth, maturity and experience. When Hubert went down to see her to explore possible areas of participation for Tristan, they came up with an inspired solution. Arrangements were made for Tristan to do his work experience program at the newly opened Paddon Memorial Home, a home for senior citizens, located a half block from his school.

Joy Headland who ran the home did so with a rare combination of competence and compassion. She did something else that was perhaps even more rare. She gave it touches of beauty, a painting here and there, a lovely fish aquarium, a display of stained glass and plants. Tristan's 'job' was to visit the elderly people for whom getting out to visit friends had become difficult or impossible. He soon developed a set of regulars and he would come home full of stories from the Paddon Home.

One day, after someone had inquired about Mrs Goudie, he simply sat shaking his head. Mrs Elizabeth Goudie, who was the well-known and well-loved matriarch of Happy Valley, was his greatest favorite and he often told us of jokes and stories they shared. On this occasion he just shook his head.

Finally, he looked up and said *sotto voce*, 'You know, mom, she does complain a lot. This hurts her, the other part aches!' He had spoken confidentially, almost as though he felt he was telling tales out of school.

'What do you say when she tells you all this?' I questioned.

'Mostly I just listen,' he said sadly. Then with a change of mood and assuming an impish expression that I remembered well from earlier years, but which seemed a travesty of humor worn on his pale gaunt face, he added, 'Well actually today I told her that she should think of all the good things she *has*, and to be grateful for them. I hope that wasn't a saucy thing to say?'

'You're just like Pollyanna!' Lisa exclaimed, looking up from the book she was reading.

'Oh, shut up!' Tristan snapped back at his sister, for whom he had little patience these days.

Next day Tristan was alight as he recounted the events at the Paddon Home, '. . . And Mrs Goudie took my hand and said that she always looked forward to my visits.'

'You see, she did not think that you were brazen' (I used the typically Labrador expression for saucy).

'No, she was really cheerful today, but there is this other lady who is just little, about my size, and she is blind and has no family. I always go and sit beside her. She talks to me a lot about her life.'

Our first year in Labrador we were the only Bahá'ís in Happy Valley. At our feasts Lisa was the recording secretary and did a fine job of keeping the minutes. On rare occasions we had a Bahá'í visitor who happened to be there in connection with work. For the children this was a real occasion, and for all of us it was a sharp reminder of how keenly we missed a Bahá'í community.

In early spring Nadine came home from university. On Sunday it is a family tradition to have waffles for brunch with berries and yoghurt. On this particular weekend Lisa and Nadine were setting the table, I was putting in the last waffle and Hubert was shaving in the bathroom. Only Tristan was still in bed. This seemed unusual, for he was not one to sleep in. I sat on his bed and kissed his face, strangely cool, especially his nose. I looked at him more carefully. He was perhaps paler than usual and his nose looked as if it had been dabbed with white powder.

'Are you getting up, darling Moose?' I asked tenderly.

'I want to, but I'm so tired,' he said languidly.

I looked away from the wan face to the window, where the birch branches were waving in the wind, and then to his immaculate dresser and to his clothes neatly folded on the chair. Pushing back a growing feeling of unease I said cheerily, 'Well, come to breakfast anyway. You don't have to get dressed; just put on your dressing gown.'

Scarcely had I returned to the kitchen when Nadine's urgent voice called me back.

'Mom, come quickly, it's Moose!'

He had been obviously on the way to the bathroom when 'He simply crumpled,' Nadine explained. Her eyes searched my face for reassurance.

'Let's get you back to your room, Moose. You are going to have breakfast in bed, my son!'

The phone was in the living room. Hubert went to sit with Tristan while I phoned the English doctor who had just arrived in Labrador and whom Kevin Columbus had recommended when he left.

'Dr Hawkes, I'm sorry to call you on a Sunday like this, but it's about Tristan. It does not seem like anything else he has had . . . no symptoms, no pain. He just says that he is terribly tired and he crumpled when he tried to go to the bathroom. His face looks perhaps a shade paler, and his nose . . . well, it looks white and it's cold and so are his hands.'

Within minutes the tall young doctor was leaning over Tristan, who gave him the same sweet slow smile that I remembered from his babyhood.

'You had better get him to the hospital right away,' Dr Hawkes advised.

'What is it?' I asked.

'I'm not sure and I'd rather not say until we have given him a thorough examination. I'll see you at the hospital.'

Hubert carried the limp body and laid it on my lap. Since he was only half-shaved Nadine drove through the gray landscape of early spring to the hospital.

Everything was ready for us when we arrived and Tristan was whisked immediately to an examining room. Very soon Dr Hawkes emerged.

'Tristan is bleeding internally. Do you know his blood type?'

'A positive.'

'Good, we have some of that on hand and we'll start calling up volunteer donors immediately. I'm going to set up the transfusion. Why don't you go home now and come back

175

early in the afternoon. I'll be able to tell you more then.'

In silence we drove home.

'I'm only glad that we are here and not in Ottawa,' I said finally.

'Why is that?' Nadine asked.

'Because it is so much simpler and more human in a small hospital . . . and we are told what is happening. When I took Tristan to the Children's Hospital in Ottawa an intern explained that as his liver functioned less efficiently pressure would build up. We now know that his kidneys don't work well either . . . anyway, he did warn me that internal bleeding was a possibility.'

In the afternoon we found Tristan in a private room with a red serum bag hanging by his bed. On the white hospital pillow he looked ephemeral. His hair looked like straw that had been left in the field all winter and had emerged from under a cover of snow, damp and bleached of color. His eyes flickered open and I saw the effort at a smile as he looked at his father.

'Well, son?' Hubert leaned over and kissed his face.

'They have me all hooked up!' he responded, with an almost imperceptible nod at the drip. 'Hard time getting a vein,' he said, looking at me.

How many times, in how many labs, clinics and hospitals had I held his hand while technicians, nurses and doctors had taken blood samples. Lately Tristan had named the technician in the hospital *Dr Dracula* because she was always 'after his blood'. There was no energy to spare on joking now.

'He was a very brave boy,' said the nurse who came to check the drip. 'The doctor would like to see you,' she added, turning to us.

Hubert went into the hall. Tristan closed his eyes.

' . . . Fresh blood is better,' Dr Hawkes was saying. 'One of the nurses gave her blood this morning and the donors have been coming in all afternoon. The trouble is that we don't know where he is bleeding or how to stop it.'

We walked farther down the hall. 'I have been on the radio-telephone consulting with Dr Gray, the internist in St. Anthony. Dr — the pediatrician will be arriving on her regular monthly visit tomorrow so we will consult with her.'

'Thank you.' It sounded so inadequate. 'We really

appreciate your coming to the house like that, this morning, and all that you have done since . . .'

'Hubert, why don't you take the car and go home? I'd like to stay with Tristan. I feel someone should be there with him. In a few hours, you or Nadine can come to spell me.'

'I'm thirsty,' Tristan whispered soon after I had seated myself by his bed. With a bent straw he negotiated the liquid and then sank back to the pillow.

I'm glad I stayed; he was too weak to ring the bell when he needed something.

Dr Gray – I remembered John Gray in St. Anthony. How many years ago was it? We had met at a party at the hospital. I had seen him smiling at me across the room. All that winter and spring we had hiked on the hills and barrens around St. Anthony, talked about books and listened to music together. And now he was at the other end of the radio-telephone trying to save my son's life.

With that heightened sense of reality that comes during times of peril I became conscious of the great interweaving that takes place in life. An enormous fabric stretched before me and I could see for an instant the threads of my own life crossing once more that of John Gray's in a pattern both intricate and breathtaking.

The effects of the transfusion were remarkable. Color returned and lethargy faded. By the time Hedy came in to relieve me Moose had asked to have his head raised and announced that he was hungry.

We took shifts next day (Nadine, Hedy, Hubert and I) so that Tristan had someone by him at all times. It was as if a giant brush had put a wash of gray over all the world, save for that one small hospital room. Here there was color and light. This was the only dot of reality. At home we did all the essential things like washing, eating a little, changing clothes, but none of those things mattered.

On the second day I asked for compassionate leave from school. Tristan's blood was flowing out as fast as it was being replaced. Already, his entire volume of blood had been replaced three times.

That evening, when I sat beside him saying prayers, Moose opened his eyes and wearily asked to go to the bathroom. Before, he had managed to walk to the bathroom, while I supported him and wheeled the drip stand. This time he could not even sit up and collapsed back on his pillow while from him flowed blood and feces.

The nurses who came were kind and infinitely gentle. As they settled him back on the clean pillow, tired tears glistened on his cheek. He lifted a limp hand. 'I'm so sorry', he said in a hollow voice, then stopped for an intake of breath, 'for all the work I give you!'

Marion, the English nurse, hurried away wet-cheeked.

Later at night, it happened again. This time he did not say anything, for he seemed scarcely conscious. As we changed the sheets his head rolled, and when his eyelids lifted only the whites of his eyes were visible.

He struggled for air and at every breath a rattling sound came from his throat.

Later still the pediatrician came in to look at Tristan. She asked a few questions and then sat by his bed observing. I would call this meditation, I thought to myself. I liked this doctor; one had the feeling that if one were quiet enough, one could hear her thinking.

'Don't give him anything to drink,' she said, rising from the chair. 'If he's thirsty, he can have an ice cube to suck.'

In the shivery morning hours I went home for a bath and change of clothes. Hubert had come to relieve Nadine. On my return to the hospital we went together to a little office used by doctors to fill out their reports and waited for Dr Hawkes. Absently I gazed at a spindly plant that struggled towards the light on a high window. Dr Hawkes came in. The three of us sat silent.

'How much longer can he be kept alive like this?' I asked.

'Not *much longer*, but I feel we have to keep trying,' he answered.

'I watched him last night . . . I wonder . . . I question continuing this procedure indefinitely,' I articulated with difficulty.

'How do you feel, Hubert?' Dr Hawkes asked.

Slowly, as if weighing every word, Hubert answered, 'I don't think he is ready to die just yet. I feel he needs more time.'

When I came back at noon Tristan looked better. 'I'm thirsty! They won't give me anything but ice cubes!' he exclaimed.

It was the ice cubes that saved his life. They allowed the hemorrhage spot to heal over. The internal bleeding stopped. However, he still needed transfusions. These became increasingly difficult for his veins kept collapsing. Eventually he was getting them through the veins in his legs.

'Look! I can't even itch my feet!' Tristan exclaimed that evening. By this time his sense of humor was reviving and he was able to laugh.

'I feel like a steak and onions!' he declared one day when I came in after school. Seeing my surprise, he added with a mischievous grin, 'And a beer!'

'We'll have to tell the blood donors to eat a good meal before they donate their blood. Their blood is making you hungry,' jested one of the nurses who was checking the drip.

Cards flooded in from his schoolmates. Many people came to visit. Marion, the English nurse, never tired of telling stories about her patient's courtesy and consideration. All the nurses joked with him and, since he was on a liquid diet, made him special eggnogs.

A lovely young teacher, Kathy Coutts, whom Tristan adored, came to the hospital and entertained him by singing and playing on her guitar. How many times did she play *Mull of Kintyre!* Tristan was rapt!

One day while Hubert and I were visiting, the military chaplain dropped in. Tristan greeted him like an old friend and turned to introduce us, 'Padre White, meet my mom and dad.'

'What a lucky chance to meet you like this,' Padre White exclaimed, 'because I am here to give Tristan an award!'

From behind his back he produced a tall trophy. At the top of a column stood the athletic figure of a young man holding a laurel wreath. At the base on the marble stand was inscribed: 'To Tristan, for example and courage. From Padre White and son Derreck, 1980.'

Padre White read aloud the inscription, turned to us and said, 'Tristan is an example to us all. The nurses all talk about his courtesy.'

'Thanks a lot,' came Tristan's hoarse choked voice as he was handed the trophy.

'Well, Tris, I hear you will be going home soon. Maybe I'll come and visit you at home some time. When you feel up to it

I'll give you a game of checkers. Remember, that's a date!'
Turning to us he added before going out, 'It's an honor
knowing your son.'

Silently Tristan handed me the trophy. I read the inscription
aloud.

'What does it mean?' Moose said, puzzled.

'It means you were brave.'

'I didn't do anything special,' he said, wondering.

On the pillow the faded gold of his head turned towards us.
The skin stretched over the delicate bone structure looked
almost transparent, but the eyes were dark with depths and
lights. For a long time we looked at each other.

Many sons bring home trophies for prowess in running,
rowing, or debating. You, my son, have brought home a
trophy of greater value than anything that strength of muscle
or rigid training could accomplish. This trophy recognizes the
strength of your *spirit*. I am so very proud of you, my son!

Did he read all that in my eyes? He turned away.

'It was very thoughtful of Padre White to do that. I didn't
thank him very well. The words got stuck . . . He used to
come every day to see me, and the other minister came too.'

'Rev. Buckle?'

'Yes, Rev. Buckle came every day. He would sit and talk.
He always knew what to say.'

Tristan was intensely interested in going to all the different
churches in the Valley. Every Sunday he would plan to visit
one or another. He always knew the hours for the services.
Since independent investigation of truth is a fundamental tenet
of the Bahá'í Faith we encouraged him.

For my son the sphere of belief was not something to be
taken lightly. Earlier that winter Hubert had brought Sister
Wilhelmina over for supper. She was a visiting lecturer for a
course on Shakespeare's tragedies. The tiny gray-haired nun
was a fascinating person, and we spent an engrossing evening
discussing spiritual matters. Tristan visited her several times at
the rectory, to which she invited him for tea. On one of his
visits, since it was the week before Good Friday, she had taken
him to the church and shown him the stations of the cross.

That night Tristan hardly touched his supper. At last, it all
spilled out: 'How could they be so cruel to Jesus? Those
branches on His head were making His forehead bleed! And

the cross was so heavy! He was nearly bent double with it!'
Tears stood brightly in his eyes.

'But it all happened thousands of years ago,' said ever-
sensible Lisa.

'Oh, you wouldn't understand!' Tristan exclaimed and
went to his room.

I had never seen Tristan so upset as the day before Good
Friday. His stooped frame was straight and he looked
somehow taller. His eyes, usually a pale blue-gray, looked
coal-black and flashed with righteous indignation. It was a
while before he could trust himself to speak. Pacing about the
room burning with an energy that amazed me, he blurted out
what had happened.

Their teacher, Mrs Fulford, had been explaining to the
special ed. class the meaning of Good Friday. Although
Tristan did not allude to it, I knew he had been deeply moved.
Then Mrs Fulford had been called away. While she was gone
some of the students began to mimic Jesus on the cross, using
a pointer as the crosspiece.

At this point of the story Tristan had to stop. His breathing
was heavy and his eyes flashed darkly.

'What did you do?' I asked softly.

'I yelled, "STOP – *How dare you make fun of Jesus!*" I was so
mad at those kids, I grabbed the stick and broke it on the desk.'
His breathing became calmer again. His shoulders assumed
their usual droop. There were angry tears in his voice when he
said, 'How could they do that, Mom? How could they? Even
Jim . . . Now Jim should know better.'

Jim was a fellow student with multiple physical handicaps. I
realized that intuitively Tristan knew that suffering can yield
the fruit of compassion.

'Then what happened?' I prompted.

'The kids were afraid of me and ran away. When Mrs
Fulford came back I had to tell her how I broke the pointer . . .
she understood . . . she said they didn't know any better . . .'

On Good Friday Tristan asked, 'Is He dead now?'

I looked at my watch. It was two-thirty. 'Come here,
Moose, and let me tell you about it.'

Lisa came to sit on one side, Tristan on the other. I told them
the story of the crucifixion and of the repentance of one of the
thieves.

When I came to Christ's words, *Forgive them, Father, for they know not what they do*, Tristan added quietly, 'Just like the kids at school . . . they didn't know what they did . . .'

Lisa was in the kitchen for awhile. She came back with a sponge soaked in vinegar, 'Taste that if you're thirsty!'

All of us screwed up our faces.

'How mean of the soldiers!' both children remarked.

'What about the sun turning dark?'

Then I told them about the execution of the Báb, and the extraordinary parallels in the two tales became apparent. I told them how the Báb had been suspended on the square in Tabriz, how the first volley from the muskets had merely severed the ropes that bound Him and had left Him unharmed. How, when the second time that He was tied up, the commander of the regiment refused to carry out the execution and another regiment had to be called in. As after the execution of Jesus, a terrible wind had come up and the sun was obscured. We sat close, my arms around both children. Silently we contemplated man's repeated cruelty to God's messengers.

When Tristan's strength had returned somewhat, Hubert took him along on a trip to Ottawa. At home we worried about them. Was Tristan's strength holding up? Late one evening Hubert phoned. Tristan had been homesick at first. There had been a joyful reunion with his friend Tony, but Tony was even bouncier than before and Tristan tired much more quickly.

At the airport I watched Hubert and Tristan disembark. Hubert was smiling. Moose walked with his usual splayfooted gait. Before he raised his eyes and saw us at the window I caught sight of his tired face, the lines of pain, the stamp of his patient endurance, the shadows under the cheekbones, the mauve shadows under the eyes. He must have been scratching his head, for his dry lackluster hair, no longer blond but rather pale and colorless, stuck out brittle and stiff all over his head. Then he spied us, and the tired face lit from within and the eyes unveiled their warmth. As I hugged him the slight shrinking on his part warned me that he was sore and that I must not hug too tightly.

With relief he went to his room for a good scratch. Later he confided that he didn't scratch on the plane because he was

182

embarrassed. He must have been itchy, indeed, for little beads of blood were on his ears and his bare feet were gouged with scratch marks.

'Would you like a hot bath?' I asked. This and a good slathering of cream seemed to bring temporary relief. As he drank his evening cup of tea I rubbed his feet.

'It's good to be home again, mom!'

Chapter Nineteen

THAT spring I had a dream: I was in the other worlds of God and one of the heavenly host was showing me around what looked like a celestial control center. There were big monitor screens on tables at which sat an angel, or heavenly being (I don't remember seeing any wings). Each screen monitored a person on earth who was that angel's particular responsibility. The singular thing about the screen was that it showed only good deeds, altruistic conduct, self-sacrifice and the like. Some of the angels were obviously bored sitting before totally blank screens. On some screens, however, there was so much activity that other heavenly beings, who were not busy, came to look and consult about the next course of action. The conversation I overheard went something like this:

'Look at that wonderful reaction!'

'Do you think they are ready for the next test?'

'They have just had a real dilly!'

'Well, it's "my soul" and I think it can handle it. After all, the more it learns the better. Are you forgetting that there is a time limit here?'

The next test would be sent down and several angels would gather at the console to watch the soul's response and progress.

'Beautiful! I knew it could do it!'

The dream had been so vivid! I had told it to all the family over breakfast, but at the time I did not heed it as some preparatory explanation for the year that was to follow. The year that began that fall was undoubtedly in the annals of our family the most difficult, and the most fraught with heartbreak.

The summer unfolded pleasantly enough. We had bought the abandoned boarded-up house next door. On closer inspection, Hubert had decided that the empty house had possibilities and contracted a carpenter to renovate it with him.

Lisa at twelve and a half was a very dependable and conscientious child who offered to be in charge of the household for six weeks, while I went to St. John's to take some summer courses in techniques of French teaching.

After my course was finished, Hubert brought her down to St. John's with him as a reward for a job well done. She had a little holiday in Newfoundland and returned home on the plane to be picked up by Nadine who was working in Goose Bay that summer.

Both Nadine and Hedy approached me that summer, with concerns about the older girls that Lisa was 'hanging around with'. Each had talked to her about it privately as it turned out.

Hedy especially counseled her sister on several occasions, for she had grown intensely aware that a choice of friends can make a great difference in a person's outlook.

Hedy had done so well in the nursery school program that she had been asked to run a new nursery school that was to open in Happy Valley that fall. Since this job occupied her only half the time, she planned to open a health-food store in the basement of the house Hubert was renovating.

It would be called the Labrador Tea Post. Labrador Tea was a plant with medicinal properties that grew plentifully around the area. The premises would be rough and unfinished so 'post', after the early 'trading posts', seemed appropriate.

In the fall we moved across to our new house. Hedy moved in with us as did Kim, a friend whom she had known in Ottawa and who came up to help her open the store.

In the upheaval of moving Tristan and Lisa did not get too much attention. Hedy and Hubert worked late into the night preparing the basement for the opening of the Labrador Tea Post.

Tristan's room was the first to emerge out of the chaos. His bed was always neatly made. His exercise bike stood in one corner, little used now as he scarce had the energy to get through the ordinary exertions of the day. In the other corner was the sun lamp, also abandoned as ineffective in controlling the itching. His dresser drawers were always neat and organized. On the dresser stood his trophy from Padre White, a little Canadian flag, a prayer book and *The Divine Art of*

Living, from which I read him every night. Two brass figures of a Dutch boy and girl had been gifts from Horace Dance, and in the baskets that the figures held Tristan kept his spare change. A picture of 'Abdu'l-Bahá smiled down on his bed. There was a new addition, a picture of Hand of the Cause John Robarts. Tristan had written John and, after much thought, had sent him a photograph of himself taken when he had been younger and his skin had been clear. His beloved Hand had written him a warm letter and had also sent a picture taken in younger years. It was this picture that Tristan had hung above his dresser.

It was Saturday and we were sitting over our morning coffee. Hedy was downstairs in the Labrador Tea Post. If it got too busy, we were ready to go down to help her. Kim was telling us the story of how, when she was a little girl walking home from Brownies, she had been hit by a car. She had suffered severe injuries that had left her with a partial paralysis of one arm. She wore boots with braces.

I questioned her about her relationship with the person who had caused the accident. It was someone whom she had known and who had been devastated by the harm she had done to the child. 'Did you ever think of calling her up and telling her how well you are doing? It might take such a terrible weight off her heart,' I had suggested.

During this time Tristan had been in his room with the door closed. We had been able to hear his voice, but recently his discourses with God had become a common occurrence. Now he came purposefully into the kitchen.

He stood in the middle of the kitchen floor and announced, 'Well, I'm ready – I don't know what God is waiting for!'

'Moose, what do you mean?' Kim questioned.

'I'm ready to die. Why doesn't God just let me die?'

There was silence. Deep scratch marks showed over his neck and hands. His ears had swollen red again from the merciless scratching and looked like the cauliflower ears of a pugilist.

With great force he stated, 'All I do is itch and scratch, itch and scratch. I can't take it any more. I told God – this is it – I want to die!'

Kim broke into tears, 'Moose, you mustn't say that . . . you mustn't talk like that.' She fled from the kitchen crying.

'Maybe God doesn't think you are quite ready yet,' I suggested.

'Well, He's wrong! I want to die!'

'Do you remember last spring when you almost died? Dad was sure you were not ready yet. By the way, do you want a cup of tea? There's some Earl Grey ready.'

'I guess I wasn't then . . . but I am now.'

'Do you want tea?'

'Yes, please.'

'What I like about you, Moose, is that you might want to die but you never forget to say "please".'

A smile fought for a second with a frown. Neither won, but he sat down and stirred sugar into his special mug, given him by Nadine.

'You know, mom,' he said in a low conspiratorial voice, 'I have thought of killing myself!'

I did not let a muscle of my face betray me, but I had to steady my hand as I raised my cup.

'But I don't have the guts!' he said, spitting out the last word with disgust.

We sat in silence.

'I know what Bahá'u'lláh says – that it is wrong, but mom, sometimes . . .' his voice overflowed with anguish. 'Sometimes, I can't stand it any more.'

For a long time we looked at each other. I forced back the impulse to hug him to my heart. 'Please God give me the words . . .' was my silent prayer.

'Did I ever tell you the story of Job?' I asked.

Tristan turned his head away.

'One day God and Satan were talking together. Satan said to God, "You know people only love You because You are good to them."

"That may be true of some of my servants," admitted God, "but there are some that truly love Me. Look at Job now, he is a true and faithful servant."

'But Satan only laughed, "Look how rich he is! Make him poor and he will curse You to Your face!"

'So God made a plague to come on the land and Job lost all his cattle and sheep. But still he praised and worshipped God.

'So God said to Satan, "Now are you satisfied?"

'"Well," said Satan, "he still has his wife and children to comfort him."

'So God sent a sickness and Job's wife and children all died. Although Job was very sad he still praised and worshipped God.

'So God said to Satan, "Now are you satisfied?"

'But Satan said, "Let the disasters touch his own skin and then You will see that he will not praise You any more!"'

At the sound of the word *skin* Tristan's face turned back from the window. His eyes hung heavily on me.

'So God sent terrible sores to cover Job's entire body. So smelly were the sores that no one would go near him. He sat on the garbage dump and scratched himself with broken pieces of plates and cups.'

I paused. On Tristan's mobile face I could see the mental images that the words created.

'No one would come near him?' he asked.

'No, he smelled so awful.'

'Did he still pray to God?' Tristan wanted to know.

'What do you think?'

Like sun and clouds the thoughts of Job's options passed over Tristan's face. In a very tired voice he finally said, 'He still loved God.'

How long is patience, I had often asked myself.

'Yes, as he sat on the garbage heap he still praised and glorified God.

'And God saw this and He turned to Satan and said, "Now are you satisfied?"'

'And what did Satan say?' Tristan wanted to know.

'Satan went away mad.

'And the Lord God raised up Job, His true and trusted servant, and He caused his sores to leave his body and the bad smell to leave him. Then He restored his wealth, his cattle and his sheep, and He got him another wife who bore him more children. Once again Job was content and prosperous.'

During the story Kim had returned to the kitchen. Tristan put his arm around her and said, 'I'm sorry I upset you, Kim.'

That night I helped him get ready for bed. His itching was so acute that he regularly made holes in his bottom sheets from the friction of his two feet rubbing against each other. He needed help with his buttons, for the pyjamas had been reinforced at the buttonholes where he had torn them while in a frenzy of scratching. The top part of his pyjama bottoms had worn out with rubbing and been replaced by new cotton flannelette and a soft elastic.

He moved the two little Dutch figures in brass. 'I wonder how Mr and Mrs Dance are doing!'

'Why don't you write them tomorrow,' I suggested.

'Mr Dance wrote that Tippy had died.'

'Do you think they'll get another dog?'

'I don't think so; Tippy was special.' He paused.

'At times he looks like a man not a boy. He is grappling with the most profound of adult problems,' I thought to myself.

'You know, mom, I wasn't kidding when I said I've thought of killing myself.'

'I didn't think you were kidding,' I said evenly.

I took his gnarled hands in mine and kissed them on the palms and on the backs.

'When you asked why your hands were ugly, I told you we cannot help if our body is not beautiful but we can help what our soul is like. We can make our soul beautiful.'

'How?'

'By being patient, kind and brave, by loving people and loving God. You have a beautiful soul, Moose. But if you do something stupid like taking your life, something you know is against God's commands, you would be endangering everything. You could end up with nothing . . . a miserable life *and* a darkened soul. We are only in this life for a short time. It seems long when you are hurting and itching but compared to forever, it is short. If you are firm in the love of God, if you fight your spiritual battles, your soul will be happy and free in the other worlds of God.'

'No more itching?'

'If you don't have a body, how can you itch?'

We said the healing prayer. I leaned over and kissed his forehead.

'I love you, Moose,' I whispered.

'I love you too, mom. At least I don't have to scratch on a garbage dump but have a nice clean bed to lie in,' he said with a glint of humor in his eye.

Our Bahá'í community had grown spectacularly that year. The first native Labradorian, Mary Michelin, moved back from the settlement of Paradise where she had been living. Another Bahá'í, Ken McFeeters, formerly of Labrador City, was attending the Vocational Institute for the year. What joy it was to have a group of friends to work with and plan with.

It became our custom to have all the Bahá'ís over every Sunday for brunch and a study class. As the year went on friends of the Bahá'ís came as well. In May Ivy Turner and then her boarder, Jerry Sillet, joined the Cause of Bahá'u'lláh. Our hopes were kindled that we might be able to form an assembly. This hope rose when a young woman, Dorothy King, from Saskatoon offered to come to Happy Valley as another Bahá'í to swell our group's numbers.

For Tristan a Bahá'í community was as water is to a fish. He was in his element and glowed with pleasure at each reunion. This community held for him a special gift, that of friendship. Ken was a young man in his twenties, very sensitive and a real scholar of the Bahá'í Writings. He became Tristan's special friend and confidant, and the two spent much time talking together.

Sometimes, watching them, I was reminded of the line from Gray's 'Elegy Written in a Country Churchyard':

He gave to Misery all he had, a tear, He gained from Heaven ['twas all he wished] a friend.

To our great delight at Christmastime Nadine came home. Tristan and Nadine always had a relationship marked by special understanding. During the holidays she read to him and massaged his feet and even held his hand when he was racked with pain in the bathroom. One evening I was rubbing his feet with Tiger Balm, a preparation that Hedy carried in her store. The room was filled with its pungent aroma. Soaking his feet in a bowl of steaming water and then rubbing them with Tiger Balm seemed to ease the gnawing itch.

Jim Henson's 'Emmet Otter's Jugband Christmas' was on that evening on television. It was a great favorite of Tristan's who made sure to watch it every Christmas. His sister Hedy sat beside him, and when Hedy Otter came on the screen Tristan snuggled up to Hedy in delight. When mother Otter sang 'We're closer now than ever before . . .' Tristan took my hand and mouthed the words as if he were singing the song for me: 'Love is teaching us how . . .'

We all looked in delight to see that, at least briefly, the pall of pain seemed to have lifted from Tristan's face and the old glint of humor and lightheartedness had returned. We made spiced hot apple cider and popcorn.

Hubert tried to find ways to broaden the scope of Tristan's activities. During the Christmas holidays, he set up an elaborate platform for the electric train set that had grown considerably over the years. From the dentist, a family friend, Tristan received another engine, and now on expanded tracks he could operate two electric trains so that they could go over bridges and under tunnels. The plaintive sound of a train whistle punctuated many a lonely winter afternoon.

In the fall of our second year in Labrador Tristan had announced that he no longer wanted to go to the same school as his sister. As a modified system of denominational schools existed in the Province of Newfoundland we applied to another school in Goose Bay. He was placed in a class for the trainable retarded. From the beginning it was not a happy solution. The children in his class had so many more problems than Tristan that he could not identify with them or relate to them as friends. One Indian girl was a constant affront to his sensibilities, for she came to school dirty and often soiled herself. It was no use explaining about cultural background. Tristan was fastidious. He spent a great deal of time wandering over to other classes and to the library. The school wanted conformity to its rules.

One day Tristan brought a note home from school saying that he was suspended! Neither he nor I knew how to handle the emotions that welled up within us. My talk with the teacher and principal showed me that there was in the system no room for latitude. Tristan transferred back to Peacock Academy. His first day back with Mrs Fulford and in the old familiar setting was such a relief to him that he came home and admitted, 'I made the wrong decision about changing schools. It was stupid of me!'

'That's all right, Moose. We are all allowed to make mistakes, and luckily this was one that was easily righted.'

At Peacock Academy there were no rules so rigid that they could not be bent to accommodate a given child. He was even allowed into the staff room, to make himself a cup of tea at recess.

One of the teachers met Hubert at the Hudson's Bay Store and told him that one day she saw Tristan holding a tea bag under running water. In response to her question, he explained that he had heard that all the caffein was released in the first minute of contact with the water. 'I'm getting rid of all the caffein!' sagely he had informed her. Then he had popped the damp bag in his cup and poured boiling water over it.

Mrs Fulford was away for a long period of sick leave. The lovely young substitute teacher, Cindy Wass, bore a strong resemblance to Tristan's old love, Joannie. Eventually Mrs Fulford returned and Tristan developed another 'great' love among the teachers, Kathy Coutts.

Everyone in the family agreed that Tristan had good taste. Everyone of his 'loves' had not only a lithe physical beauty, but also a quiet charm and a glow that was not only wholesome but reflected a lively sense of fun. All were intelligent, talented young women. Kathy Coutts and Cindy Wass were also actresses in the Mokami Players, a very active theater group in Goose Bay.

Yet despite all these contacts with people, Tristan's world was shrinking. More and more of his time was spent by the wood stove in the scaled-down rocking chair that his friend Ken had made for him. Tristan had given Ken the nickname Kenshee. It worried him that our dear family friend Frank Peters did not yet have a special name. 'He should be called Fonzie, because he has curly hair like Fonzie Bear on the Muppets,' but that name did not stick.

The long winter seemed to stretch out indefinitely. Then for the Intercalary days of Há Tristan received a gift that brought with it an element of anticipation that made the long days of winter pass less drearily. Grandmother sent Tristan a cheque for five hundred dollars. For days the cheque simply sat in the center of the table, too magical to be believed. How to spend it?

Grandmother had made a suggestion that Tristan might want to go to the Bahá'í Conference being held in Montreal that year. When the money was banked, it was on that plan of action that Tristan decided. Hubert and Tristan would go to the conference and stay in a luxury hotel. Now *there* was something to look forward to!

One day, sitting in his small rocker by the wood stove, Tristan spoke longingly of the family outings, the cookouts with singing and poetry reading. Hedy, ever ready to respond, arranged a poetry evening and invited several of her friends to bring their favorite poems. It was an inspired evening with poetry throbbing through the air with a pulse of emotion and a flow of music in the words. One of the last poems to be read that evening was William Blake's, 'The Tiger':

> Tiger! Tiger! burning bright
> In the forests of the night;
> What immortal hand or eye
> Could frame thy fearful symmetry?
>
> In what distant deeps or skies
> Burnt the fire of thine eyes?
> On what wings dare he aspire?
> What the hand dare seize the fire?
>
> And what shoulder, and what art,
> Could twist the sinews of thy heart?
> And when thy heart began to beat,
> What dread hand? and what dread feet?
>
> What the hammer? what the chain?
> In what furnace was thy brain?
> What the anvil? what dread grasp
> Dare its deadly terrors clasp?
>
> When the stars threw down their spears,
> And watered heaven with their tears,
> Did He smile his work to see?
> Did He who made the Lamb make thee?
>
> Tiger! Tiger! burning bright
> In the forests of the night;
> What immortal hand or eye
> Dare frame thy fearful symmetry?

Tristan asked to have the poem read again.

'How beautiful!' he exclaimed, lost in wonder. 'What does it mean?'

Over the next few days he memorized most of the verses.

'Tiger! Tiger! burning bright . . .' It was a delight to watch his face; he took such visible delight in the cadence of the words.

One week in March was particularly mild and Hedy exclaimed, 'Why don't we take Tristan on a winter cook-out?'

'A cookout!' Tristan exclaimed with a faraway look. Over his face seemed to pass memories of past boil-ups in Lapland, of the singing, of happy times with the family. He smiled, 'Yes, a cookout would be nice . . . and there would be no bugs.'

'We'll find a good spot not too far from the road. It will be like old times!' Hedy exclaimed and hugged Tristan perhaps too forcefully, for the pain returned to his face. Often I noticed that pressure, even on the upper part of his body, brought discomfort.

He rose stiffly from his rocking chair by the fire and opened the wood stove door to look inside. Then he went to the wood pile to get another log.

'Dad, come here! I can't seem to lift it!' he said, looking at the piece of wood with surprise. 'I guess I'm getting like an old man,' he added with a laugh that tried to be lighthearted.

'It's O.K., son,' Hubert said tenderly, 'I'll put it on the fire for you. You just let me know when we need one. You be the stove watcher and I'll be your stoker!'

Hedy chose a good spot for a cookout. It was not far from a side road and the ski-doos had packed the snow to a good consistency for walking so we could reach a grove of sheltering trees without wading through deep snow.

The morning was sunny and bright. Frank Peters came with us and he and Hedy went ahead to cut some dry wood and start the fire. Hubert and I walked slowly beside Tristan. The fifty yards seemed an interminable distance for him as he took one slow and painful step after another.

'Frank is like the tinwoodsman in *The Wizard of Oz*,' Tristan observed when Frank emerged from the trees with his axe over his shoulder. It troubled Tristan that Frank still did not have a nickname. 'What about Fonzie the Woodsman as a name for Frank?' he suggested.

The weather, with the unpredictability of all northern climes, turned overcast as we unloaded our knapsacks. We roasted pieces of caribou on sticks on the fire and held our enamel mugs with hot cocoa in our hands to warm them.

Great snowflakes began drifting down. Frank put more branches on the fire and we drew closer to the blaze to keep warm.

'Hedy, why don't you sing, "He's Got the Whole World in His Hands"?' Tristan suggested.

We had sung several verses, when Tristan's voice took the lead, 'He's got my sister Lisa in His hands. He's got the whole world in His hands!' Lisa had scorned our invitation to come on the cookout. Now we all joined Tristan in this verse of his favorite song.

Faster and faster flew the huge snowflakes. A wind came up. We bundled Tristan up in a quilt and pulled him on the toboggan the short distance back to the car. 'No matter how the weather turned out, it was a great idea to have a cookout!' Hubert had exclaimed when we were back at the house and warming ourselves by the stove. 'It is important to break the monotony of life with special events!'

But as time went on there were fewer and fewer special events for Tristan. He had always greatly enjoyed theatrical performances, but even these were hard for him to sit through without itching. The production of *Cinderella* by the hospital staff was something he was determined to see.

One of the nurses told me that she had been very nervous on opening night, but when she saw Tristan in the audience beaming at her and heard his infectious laughter, she realized that the play was going well and she began to enjoy herself.

Some people who live in isolated northern areas become 'bushed' and never want to go back to the outside world. Tristan never had this problem. He never experienced reluctance in leaving for a trip to a big city. So when it came time for him to take out his five hundred dollars and go to Montreal to the Bahá'í Conference, it was in high good spirits and great anticipation that he waved us goodbye and boarded the plane with his father.

Hubert was to tell us later how delighted Tristan had been to be once more in a luxury hotel. The metro rides had been a bit scary, especially the long descents by escalator, but he had held on tightly to his father's hand. At times the two blocks from the metro to the hotel had been too much and they had taken a taxi. Hubert had realized that it was no longer possible to stay the whole day, and he had learned to look for signs of fatigue. When Tristan had that wilted look they returned to the hotel for a bath, a rest and some quiet television.

How was he at the conference, I wanted to know. Hubert's face shone with that same reflected radiance that Tristan's face must have had. 'He was right in his element, going up to old friends, talking to people. He just beamed!'

The Tristan that arrived back was 'wrung out'. I who saw him every day received a shock after a week's absence. Suddenly I saw the stooped walk of an old man, the sunken cheeks, and eyes outlined in bruise blue. Stamped on his face, however, was a determined endurance. I kissed him gently at the airport, making sure that I did not press him to me. To Hubert I gave a long strong hug.

'I think Tristan can't wait to get back to his cozy home,' Hubert said.

By spring growing tensions with Lisa had become unbearable to everyone in the family. When exactly, we were to ask ourselves so often, had the metamorphosis begun? For a metamorphosis it was, so startling, so unsettling, so devastating that surprise was quickly followed by concern and then by acute distress. At school the teachers could not understand it. Lisa, who had been an excellent student and a model of deportment, began to lose interest in her work, grew sullen and uncooperative, began to miss classes and eventually barely made it through the year. Family counseling, though helpful, had not brought a solution. I was desperate to understand why the lovely daughter I had known for twelve years had become transformed into a hostile stranger.

My mind kept trying to climb out of the dilemma by getting a foothold of understanding, but kept falling back as though it had slid off the glass walls of total incomprehensibility. I chased ideas in circles. Compared to the growing-up problems that Nadine and Hedy had experienced, there was the totally different dimension of being blocked out, shut out of any stream of communication with Lisa.

'*I will lift up mine eyes unto the hills from whence cometh my strength. My strength cometh from God the Lord of the Heavens and of the earth.*' The familiar words rose up in my memory like a cork bobbing up to the surface of consciousness. If there is seemingly no rational solution, there must be a spiritual one. What is the source of help for us as Bahá'ís beside individual prayer and family consultation? If only we lived in an area where there was a Local Spiritual Assembly.

The closest Spiritual Assembly was in St. John's, Newfoundland, over a thousand miles away. Once more we had a family consultation and all agreed that we would go to consult the St. John's Spiritual Assembly as soon as school was over.

There is something disarming about early spring in Labrador. At last the air turned balmy. I walked to the river's edge noticing the cracker-berry flowers like little white stars on the background of the dead brown leaves beneath the trees. I brought back a branch of blooming pin-cherry. Hubert was having a cracker and cheese in the sun-drenched kitchen when I returned. The house was silent save for the sound of Tristan scratching in his room.

Suddenly there was a snap, as if someone had cracked a small dry branch over his knee, followed by a sharp cry of pain. Tristan emerged from his room. On his pain-etched face was a grimace of anguish. His left arm hung loose at his side as if the sleeve were empty.

His words came with effort, 'I was just scratching myself in the back, when it went "snap".'

'We'd better get you to the hospital,' Hubert said decisively.

Yes, the arm was broken. Luckily the visiting bone specialist, Dr Jones, from St. Anthony was in Goose Bay on his monthly visit. Dr Hawkes and Dr Jones spent a long time with Tristan and looked carefully at his X-rays. Finally, Dr Hawkes called me into his office while Dr Jones set Tristan's arm.

'How could he just break like that? Are his bones so brittle now?' I could not contain my questions any more.

'We were concerned that he might be developing a bone disease,' Dr Hawkes explained, 'but we are reasonably sure that it was a simple break.' He smiled reassuringly, 'Tristan was very anxious to know if he could still go on the boat to St.

John's. It would do him good to go on holiday. Just take reasonable care . . . I know you will.'

Tristan was glad to get home after the morning spent in the hospital. He made straight for the bathroom, meeting Lisa as she came into the kitchen. She bumped into his bandaged arm and he cried out in pain.

'Oh, don't be such a sissy!' she threw after her brother as he disappeared into the bathroom.

'He has a broken arm,' I explained, trying to keep my voice level.

'Well, excuse *me*!' Lisa said in mock sarcasm. Then turning to me she asked sharply, 'When is he going to die, anyway?'

My heart froze. I looked at my daughter's face. There was no malice there, only a hard anger. Fighting for control over my voice I managed to reply, 'I don't know . . . God only knows the appointed hour for any of us.'

At that point Tristan called out from the bathroom. He must have trouble with his zipper with only one hand available I speculated. But it was pain that had made him call out and he clutched my hand, as his face drained of all color and I could feel from the force of his grasp that he was racked with a spasm. When I got back to the kitchen my purse was lying open on the table. The back door swung on its hinges. Lisa had gone out. Outside I saw two great black ravens sitting on the neatly stacked woodpile. I could hear Tristan getting into bed.

Heavily I sat down at the table. 'God, O my God!' I heard myself say out loud, 'Please, please help this servant of yours.'

'Mom?' came Tristan's voice from the bedroom.

'It's all right, Moose, I'm just talking to God.'

'Oh!' He sounded reassured.

Tears flowed down. I picked up the prayer book that Hubert had left on the kitchen table.

O My Lord! Thou knowest that the people are encircled with pain and calamities and environed with hardships and trouble. Every trial doth attack man and every dire adversity doth assail him like unto the assault of a serpent. There is no shelter and asylum for him except under the wing of Thy protection, preservation, guard and custody.

The soothing words fell like balm on my bruised soul. I rose from the table. Outside the tender green of the unfolding leaves looked almost too delicate for so harsh a land. A chipmunk scuttled by the woodpile and the two ravens flew off cawing loudly.

In his bed Tristan slept peacefully. He slept all afternoon.

Chapter Twenty

WE arrived in St. John's in dense fog. Does this reflect our inner reality as well, I wondered?

Always, when we returned from an isolated area, reentry into the warmth and love of a Bahá'í community was overwhelming. It was like being on a spiritual subsistence diet for a long time and suddenly being given a rich banquet.

Tristan reacted expansively. He was like a plant that had been given barely enough water, and then suddenly immersed in life-giving moisture. His face brightened, he became more animated, his eyes shone.

Hubert and I met with the Spiritual Assembly. Lisa met with the Spiritual Assembly. Together we had a consultation. The Assembly stressed that there were rights and responsibilities for both children and parents and both had to be observed.

During this period of consultation we had a phone call from Hedy in Happy Valley. A very good friend, Patricia De Villeneuve, had called from Ontario inviting Lisa to spend the summer with her family. Lisa was delighted to accept and the Assembly concurred that it might prove to be a good cooling-off period for the stresses that beset the family.

Across from the Rochesters, with whom we were staying, lived another Bahá'í, Lynn Soerenson, whom Tristan loved to visit. Two Bahá'ís on one street! Tristan could not believe his good fortune.

One day, when Tristan had gone to see Lynn, Elizabeth and I were talking in her study when we heard music.

'I didn't think John was home,' I remarked, referring to her son who often played the piano.

'That's not John,' Elizabeth said in hushed tones.

The music seemed to ripple and cascade, to foam and tinkle, to grow soft and tender and then to rise in crescendo. It most resembled Débussy but sounded more modern.

At a sign from Elizabeth we tiptoed to the living room. Sitting at the piano, head thrown back and eyes closed, was Tristan. As cadenzas flowed from his fingers they seemed, in reflected emotions, to pass over his face. He was rapt, as if transported by the music he was making.

He became aware of us and stopped.

'Please go on playing,' Elizabeth urged.

'I'm sorry I disturbed you,' Tristan apologized. 'I didn't think there was anybody home.'

For a time after we returned to the study we sat in silence. The music began again. There was a constraint about it; it was self-conscious.

Hubert had resigned from his position with Memorial University to free-lance as a film-maker. On our return to Happy Valley in July he had barely time to get packed before leaving for his first assignment working on a Bahá'í film.

At the airport I waved Hubert off, knowing that for the next year we would be seeing each other only sporadically between filming in various locations as distant as British Columbia, Guadeloupe and Europe. I was happy for him that he would, at last, be doing what he loved to do most, make film.

Returning to the house I was aware of a sense of quiet. Tristan still slept. On his neat dresser I saw the photograph taken in Greenland that he had found the other day while looking through albums. Taken at his eighth birthday party, it showed a golden-haired boy in a pensive pose, chin resting on slender well-shaped hand. He had studied it carefully.

I sat motionless on the bed and observed Tristan's sleeping form. Once, long ago, I had received a dozen red roses. They had been so dear to me that I kept the petals long after their red velvet had turned brown and crumpled. That same shade of wilted rose-petal-brown formed wide blotches under the closed eyes of Tristan's sallow face. Yet the line of the jaw was as delicate as before. Near the ear was a trace of golden fuzz! He will be seventeen next month. The nose retained its finely chiseled shape but had been so white lately and so covered with raw sores and crusty spots among the craters of his skin. The cheeks were sunken and the one exposed ear was thickened like the ear of a boxer. The once-blond hair, now dry and brittle, still reminded me of the pale gold of moonlight.

A hand gropes over the covers. My heart turns. The hand is so gnarled and thickened at the joints, the skin so cracked and coarse, and the fingers so permanently bent and bumpy! I understand why he studied the photograph . . . it is hard to reconcile present reality with the charm of the golden child in the photograph.

The bruise-brown eyelids flutter open and the blue-gray eyes engage mine. In that instant, the glint of the eyes and the smile perform a miracle that makes the face appear lively and lovely.

'Dad gone?'

'I just came back from the airport. He told me to give you a kiss goodbye.' I leaned over gently to plant a kiss on his forehead.

'I wanted to get up,' he said, sitting up painfully, 'but I just sleep and sleep.' He followed my gaze to the Greenland photograph. 'Did I *really* look like that?'

'Yes, you were a lovely-looking little boy.'

He sighed a deep unselfconscious sigh. 'I'm so ugly,' he stated matter-of-factly as, with difficulty, he put his legs over the side of the bed.

'The real you, the spirit part of you is beautiful,' I stressed.

Once more I was struck by how much like a survivor of a concentration camp he looked. He dressed while I handed him the items he needed. There was no musculature on his arms or legs, the bones were visible clearly through the dry scratched skin. His knees were rounded knobs and his chest and waist were ravaged by scratching. All over his body were raw spots and some that were in different stages of scabbing. Each of his movements was slow and deliberate. I handed him his well-washed cotton clothes and helped with the buttons that his gnarled hands could no longer manage.

Over breakfast Tristan asked directly, 'How do you know my soul is not ugly?'

'Our souls mirror our actions,' I explained. 'What are ugly actions?'

'Hurting people, lying, hating, killing . . .' Tristan enumerated.

'Yes, and some less obvious ones like backbiting or seeing the bad rather than the good in people. Now what are some good actions?'

'Being kind and loving, doing things for others, making them happy . . .'

'Which do you try to do the most?' I asked him.

'But sometimes I got so mad at Lisa!' His hands clenched and I could see through the thin skin the jaw muscles tighten, 'I hated it when she was mean to you and dad!'

'Is that why you locked yourself in the bathroom so often?' I asked.

'I was afraid that I'd *do* something!' he confessed.

'But you didn't . . . and you were polite to her on the boat, and at the airport you kissed her as she left. When you want to do something ugly but do something kind instead, that is a victory for you. There is no victory if it is not hard.'

He thought about it, 'I won't be ugly in the other worlds of God?'

'I can't guarantee it!' I said in a mock-officious tone, 'but I would guess that you would be a luminous soul.'

'What's that?'

'Shiny!'

'Is Grampa a lum . . ., a shiny soul?' he wanted to know.

'He was a good person, Grampa was! The nice thing is knowing he will be waiting when one of us dies. He will be there to help us through the transition from this world to the next. That is really all that happens in death, we "switch worlds"!'

'How do you know, mom?'

'Bahá'u'lláh says that if we knew even a little about how wonderful the other worlds are for the sanctified (the good) soul – why we would all want to die right away!'

'Does he really say that?'

'I'll read it to you,'

The mysteries of man's physical death . . . still remain unread . . . Were they to be revealed, they would evoke such fear and sorrow that some would perish, *while others would be so filled with gladness as to wish for death, and beseech, with unceasing longing, the one true God – exalted be His glory – to hasten their end.*

We sat thinking, the words of power ringing in our ears.

13 August 1981, was Tristan's seventeenth birthday. On that day he was 'at home' to his friends. All day various people kept dropping in with cards and good wishes and stayed for

the tea and cake that Hedy kept serving. There were birthday wishes for him on the radio, and as part of the evening sports broadcast it was announced that Tristan Schuurman of Happy Valley had won the checkers tournament against Padre White.

In the evening, a messenger sent by Padre White brought a silver cup that the Padre had won in a checkers championship while stationed on Cyprus. The messenger had been instructed, by Padre White, to say that since Tristan was the new champion, it was he who should have the trophy.

Tristan looked at me knowingly. We had always played games straight. He knew his own capacities and limitations well.

'Accept graciously,' I whispered to him.

This he did, praising Padre White's thoughtfulness and kindness.

Dr Hawkes dropped in and some of the people from the Paddon Home. Hedy and I looked at each other, impressed by the wide range of Tristan's friends. There were old and young, professionals and people of the land, Innuit and Indian, Labrador settlers and Newfoundlanders, recent arrivals from England, like Dr Hawkes, and mainland Canadians. The many layers and strata of Happy Valley–Goose Bay society were represented at Tristan's birthday. We realized that we knew only part of Tristan's life and only guessed at the extent it touched the lives of others.

During the summer Tristan had gone regularly to the Paddon Home. Besides the many residents he visited he also became good friends with the cook, Mrs Baggs. She invited him over to her house on her days off. He enjoyed that.

Another friend was Ivy Turner. One day the two of them went to see a matinée together. During the film Ivy was called out. She was informed her son had committed suicide. We drove to the home of the friend who was trying to comfort her. We found Ivy, dazed and still incredulous. I looked at Tristan and realized that we must get him home right away. His pallor was alarming. His eyes stared out of dark shadows. After some prayers for the departed we bundled Tristan into the car and drove home.

He lay gasping for air and fighting for breath. It was the result of shock but frightening nonetheless. Hedy called the doctor while I tried to soothe and talk to him. Dr Hawkes was away, but Dr Playfair (who, Tristan claimed, had the gentlest hands of any doctor he knew) came over. In time, Tristan calmed down and fell into an exhausted sleep.

In the kitchen Hedy made us all tea and crackers with rowanberry jelly, which was a particular favorite of Dr Playfair. We talked to him about Tristan's aspiration to take a cooking course at the Vocational Institute. Dr Playfair saw no objections to this provided that Tristan did not have to lift anything heavy, for he had very little strength in his arms. Part-time attendance seemed more realistic as Tristan slept every afternoon.

The next day Tristan wanted to talk of the suicide. He knew the whole family, including the beautiful young Indian widow and the two small children. The only thing we could do was to pray for his soul, and this we did. Often in the days that followed I could hear Tristan on the phone comforting Ivy and assuring her of our prayers.

School would soon be starting. Lisa phoned and asked if she could attend high school in Ontario. Patricia and Allen, with whom she was staying, had a son, Peter, the same age as she and the two could attend the same high school. We agreed.

With a certificate from Dr Playfair there were no obstacles to Tristan attending the Vocational School, where our good friend Dave Lough was principal, yet September edged on and he did not feel well enough to begin. He liked to get out of the house and to go shopping with me but he hated it when small children stared at him. Yet more and more people did stop and look at the emaciated boy with the crushed rose-petal skin and the slow painful movements of an old man.

One day while we were in the car, we saw, coming out of the hotel, a man who had the same close curly hair of our friend Frank Peters. Unlike Frank's, it was snow white.

'Just like a sheep!' exclaimed Tristan with some of the old twinkle in his eye. 'We should call Frank "Sheepy". He needs a nickname you know!'

'What about "Baran"?' I asked. 'It means ram, or male sheep, in Polish.'

'Perfect!' Tristan was delighted. 'He's always spinning wool, too. Why don't we give him a naming party when he gets back from the coast?'

That evening Tristan and I drew up an official letter

bestowing the new name on Frank.

'I hope he likes his name!' Tristan mused as I tucked him in that night.

'People like nicknames because it means that those who give them the names care for them. It is a sign of affection. You wouldn't be called the Moose, if we didn't love you.'

Soon after school began, on one of those luminescent fall days that flood the soul with beauty and waft back some of the warmth of the summer past, Dorothy King arrived from Saskatoon with her two-year-old daughter, Mary Willow, and their Siamese cat, Pekoe. They came to live with us until they could find other accommodation. Once more the house was full of life.

Tristan had always loved small children. Observing him with bright-eyed Mary Willow I noticed that he was like a grandfather to her. He would help her with a puzzle if she sat beside him at the table while he had a cup of tea. As a great concession, he would play for her his favorite children's records. As he grew more fond of her, he would teach her to pronounce words like 'yellow' with the patience and clear enunciation of well-remembered speech-therapy lessons. But as his pains increased he grew easily irritated by the noise and commotion that a two-year-old was bound to make, and he would go off to his room stooped and muttering to himself like an old man.

That year, at the end of the summer, our house was bursting at the seams with visitors. A call came from the airport that another respondent to Hedy's liberal invitations had just arrived. On this occasion she was at home, so she herself was able to drive to the airport and pick up Carlos, a Mexican student whom she had met earlier that summer at the North–South Youth Conference in Montreal. He arrived at the house wearing a red serape with knapsack and sleeping bag on his back. I noticed the sleeping bag immediately and with relief as my supply of linen was running low.

The whole household plus several friends were in the kitchen when Hedy brought in Carlos and introduced him all around. Tristan went up to him immediately and gave him an effusive hug. One thing about Moose, I thought to myself, he always responds differently to people. He can be warmly welcoming or formally polite, and on rare occasions he will even put on his disappearing act.

Several frosts had already taken their toll of the mosquito population. More important, a strong wind was blowing. So Tristan was planning to come to at least part of this particular cookout. Our new Mexican arrival was outfitted with a warm sweater and windbreaker, and the group got into three cars and drove to a place where the wide Hamilton River had flung sand beaches along its banks.

We were a group of friends who often went out together, so everyone had accustomed areas of responsibility. Frank chopped the wood with his ever-sharp axe; Hedy made stacks of kindling. Others cleared the site and brought over boughs to sit on. One girl kept the dogs busy throwing sticks for them in the water. My job was looking after the food. Someone else was responsible for seeing that the coffee in the well-blackened kettle did not boil over. One of our visitors was Harry Hill from Ottawa who had brought along his guitar. I suspect it was for the music that would follow the baked beans and salad that Tristan had made the concession of accompanying us on this cookout.

Around the fire that night we sang all the old favorites. Carlos taught us some Mexican songs. Then the wind dropped and a few dilatory mosquitoes emerged, Frank offered to drive Tristan home.

Tristan had a bad night. Secretly, I blamed the wieners and baked beans for his stomach pains. Many times that night he called out for me, and I would sit beside him holding his hand till the pains passed. I worried that we would wake those who were sleeping on the living-room floor.

Next morning I rose late. For the first time I felt weary of all the people in the house. On his last visit home Hubert had joked that the house was like an inn and he never knew whom he would find there when he came home. I had regarded him with surprise that after all these years he would feel that way. Yet, that morning I felt ill-equipped to deal with the logistics of feeding ten or more people. I could hear Mary Willow in the kitchen talking to Hedy.

'Let me make you some coffee, mom?' Hedy said after her morning hug.

'Thanks, dear, I need it. Moose was up a lot last night!'

'I bet it was the hot-dogs!' Hedy said with the conviction of a dedicated vegetarian.

I looked glumly in the fridge, thinking of the menu for the day. If I make brunch now, I calculated, and two of our visitors go out for supper, that leaves eight to feed tonight. There was a casserole of lasagna in the fridge. Hmm . . . a bit skimpy for eight, but with garlic bread and a big salad it would just do! How lucky that I had made a triple batch the day before.

Dorothy came in sleepily and then Carlos. I began to beat the eggs for the waffles. I was not the only one who was moving in slow motion that morning, I noticed. Even Hedy, usually so bright and chirpy on waking, was lingering over her coffee.

Then Tristan walked in pale, with blue shadows under his eyes but neatly dressed and with his unruly hair plastered down with water. He greeted everyone warmly, especially Carlos.

'Hedy, keep an eye on the waffles for me!' I called, as I went to my room to get dressed.

When I returned I saw Carlos taking out the dish of lasagna and putting it in the oven. I shook my head in disbelief.

'We are going to have breakfast in just a minute,' I said, trying to sound bright and cheerful.

Suddenly, it was all too much for me. I felt a stranger in my own house. Hedy sprang up to set the table in the dining room.

I returned to my room to say a few prayers and to regain equilibrium.

The lasagna was just emerging from the oven right onto the surface of the kitchen table as I walked in. 'I think it needs a trivet!' I suggested, keeping my voice level and even.

Dorothy rushed up with a pot holder but I could see the discolored mark which the hot dish had already made on the table.

'Breakfast is ready in the dining room,' I announced, taking in the waffles and the yoghurt. Hedy followed with the stewed blueberries.

'You're upset, mom,' she whispered.

'I'm boiling mad,' I whispered back. 'That's tonight's *supper* he's eating. Why couldn't he wait five minutes and eat breakfast with everyone else . . . Look, you start without me.

Everything is getting on top of me. I'm going to walk by the river and cool off.'

The Hamilton River, where it flows by Happy Valley, is a peaceful river. Elsewhere it hurls itself through gorges and cascades down the enormous chutes that produce six thousand megawatts of electricity. Even at Muskrat Falls it boils and fumes; but behind the house it flows serenely, swirling around the wooded island, dropping elliptical sandbanks on the opposite shore.

I always saved the most comforting thought till the last. Across the river, past the thick stands of forest on the opposite bank, beyond the Mealy Mountains (bruise-blue, like the circles under Tristan's eyes), there is not a human being for miles and miles. Only wilderness, only the hush of the moss-carpeted forest. I never knew why the thought was like a lullaby to me . . . only wilderness . . . only wilderness.

I returned to the house. Carlos looked up at me from his dish of lasagna as I walked in. 'I'm so sorry,' he said. 'I'm a diabetic and when I got up I knew I had to eat something. I'm sorry that I upset you.'

But why a whole casserole of lasagna for breakfast, I thought, despite the calm I had regained at the river's edge. Tristan got up and stood beside Carlos, his arm protectively around his shoulder. There was an imperative in his look. I obeyed.

'Carlos, it was a misunderstanding. You did not know that on weekends we all eat breakfast together. If you are finished, why don't you join us in the dining room for a dessert of waffles and blueberries,' I invited.

I saw Tristan bend down his head to Carlos. As he looked at Tristan's loving, smiling face the look of embarrassment and strain left his own.

During the rest of the visit Tristan took it upon himself to be Carlos's special protector. As we got to know Carlos better we realized how much he needed one.

When Carlos was leaving I experienced a short inner struggle; then I gave him a big parting hug. Tristan and Carlos stood for a long time clasping each other in a bear-hug, then they looked deep in each other's eyes and Carlos nodded. To Hedy he left his red serape. Whenever I see it I blush with shame to remember the brink of pettiness to which one can be driven by a dish of lasagna.

After school, when I came home Tristan had the water boiling for tea. Over our traditional cup of Lapsang Souchong we would discuss the day. 'How was school today?' he would ask, looking at my face as though he could read more there than in my words. He asked about the teachers and the progress of specific students. I would share with him the funny incidents and the exasperating ones. With him as the listener I would spin theories and explore new insights. While I prepared supper he watched his favorite programs on television; if supper were late, he would put on his favorite records or tapes.

One day I came into the dining room to get a serving dish. Tristan was listening to his tapes of Rabbi Schlomo Carlbach. His face in repose looked more shadowed and sunken, I thought to myself. As the music changed to a faster tempo I saw Tristan slowly raise himself from his chair. Before, this had been the cue for us all to join hands and start dancing to the lively hora rhythm. How many times had Tristan put his arm around my waist and coaxed everyone else to join in the dance. I stood silently watching him now, as with great effort he lifted his arms above his head. Eyes closed, head flung back, and face reflecting the intoxication of the mystic rhythm, he snapped his fingers to the beat.

At least three times a week Tristan visited the Paddon Memorial Home. I picked him up on my way home from school. One day he was at the far end of the long hall when I walked in. I watched him progress slowly towards me. Each step was a deliberate victory over pain. I waved in encouragement. Beside me one of the nursing aides muttered, 'Bless his heart, he is in a worse way than some of them he visits!'

Mrs Baggs, the cook, came out of the kitchen and looked at Tristan as he made his labored progress. 'We think the world of Tristan here at the home,' she said, dabbing at her cheek with her apron.

At last he reached us. He smiled at his friend Mrs Baggs. It was a wan wintry smile, and it seemed that it required so much effort that he could not have done both, walk and smile. Mrs Baggs, her cheek once more moist, said, bending down, 'I'll carry you out to the car, m' dear.' She scooped him up to her ample bosom and preceded me to the car. Following behind, I could see Tristan's face contorted with pain. Gently she placed him in the front seat. Then, to hide her emotion, she took off her cook's hat and placed it on his head at a rakish angle. 'There you are, luv!'

'Thank you, Mrs Baggs. We'll be seeing you!' I called after her as she hurried away dabbing at her eyes.

In the car I looked over at Tristan. His face was ashen and tilted back against the backrest, the bruise-brown eyelids covered his eyes.

'Did it hurt?' I asked in a low voice.

'I wanted to scream!' the words struggled out slowly. 'But I didn't want to hurt her feelings.'

I started up the motor. 'Are you O.K. now?' I asked.

'Let's go home . . . she wanted to help . . . it's just that . . .'

'I'll make sure no one tries to lift you any more, Moose,' I assured him. 'I know you have been sensitive even to a hug lately.'

'I'm sorry, mom.' His voice seemed to come from far away.

As we drew up to the house I once more blessed Hubert for having built a ramp to the back door. He had observed what a painfully long time it took Tristan to get up the five or six steps to the back deck, and on his last visit home he had constructed a long easy ramp with a young birch tree that he had cut by the river bank as a railing. Valley architecture, he had called it jokingly as we stood around admiring the rustic effect.

It took Tristan forever to shuffle up the ramp. He went straight to bed and we had trouble rousing him for supper.

Chapter Twenty-One

AT times Tristan was so stiff that merely getting in and out of the bathtub was painful and difficult. I would call Hedy to help and, together, we would ease him into the steaming water that brought temporary relief to the itching.

'You know, mom, I feel like a rotten apple . . . rotten to the very core!' he said with a tone of wonder in his voice.

'Funny, you don't *look* like an apple!' I responded, trying to pass it off as a joke. No, no, I must not do this, I told myself. It is cowardly to joke about someone else's pain because I can't bear to see it. So I added seriously, 'What do you mean, Moose?'

'Everything in me feels rotten. You know what a rotten apple looks like . . . not one part is good any more.'

'How does that make you feel?' I asked gently.

'I'm ready to die . . . I told God . . . Whenever You're ready, God . . .'

'You need to get away, mom,' Hedy told me one Saturday. I went with Frank to pick red berries. On the way home we talked of Tristan's impending death. What a relief it was to have a friend who did not say, 'You mustn't talk about such things!' who did not feel uncomfortable with the subject of death. What a gift friendship is, I thought, as I returned home with a bucket of bright red berries and my heart lightened and swept clear of apprehensions.

One evening Tristan was in more pain than usual. 'Can I get in bed with you?' he asked. I read to him from *The Voyage of the Dawn Treader* by C.S. Lewis. He moved about in discomfort, but the story was gripping and helped keep his mind off the pain.

I stopped reading and massaged his feet and we talked about the symbolism used in the Narnia series. 'Why do you think the boy turns into a dragon?' That was easy for Tristan, but when we began to discuss the Lion he found it harder. At last I suggested that the Manifestations of God also return again and again. Then it was as if a light had dawned and we talked of all the other Narnia books, and he remembered that the Lion had been shorn and killed by the evil witch but had arisen from the dead! His eyes shone with excitement. 'Just like Jesus, just like the Báb and Bahá'u'lláh!' he had exclaimed.

September gave way to October. No longer was there talk of Tristan going to the Vocational Institute. He slept sixteen hours out of every twenty-four.

Dr Playfair came with another doctor, who would replace him in the next week when he went on vacation. After the examination the new doctor turned to me with eyes so full of compassion that I recoiled. 'No, no, it can't be true!' I thought. I felt as though a sudden cold chill had passed down the length of my back. I stiffened and set my shoulders.

Next day Dr Playfair came again. Tristan was in bed. After he had examined him he joined us in the kitchen for tea and a cracker with rowanberry jelly. Hedy told him about Tristan's comment that he felt 'like a rotten apple'.

'He may have many physical problems,' Dr Playfair commented, 'but there is certainly nothing wrong with his perceptions. All the systems *are* breaking down.'

Hedy continued, 'Tristan always says he doesn't know what God is waiting for . . . he's ready to die.'

'And how do you feel about it?' Dr Playfair asked, looking at me and at Hedy.

We looked at each other. 'I think he is ready . . . he has suffered so much!'

'Well, if he feels like that . . . there is no reason why we shouldn't try to make him more comfortable.' Dr Playfair began to rummage in his black bag. He took out a small glass vial which he broke and, taking a spoon, went back to Tristan's room.

'What did you give him?' I asked.

'Morphine,' he said, looking at me steadily.

I realized dimly that this was the beginning of the end. This step was irreversible. So often when I had gone to Dr Hawkes, at my wits' end to try to alleviate Tristan's pain, he had patiently explained that since any medication must be metabolized by the liver and kidneys it was impossible at that stage to give him anything that would not aggravate those two weak links. I had retained the mental image of the Chinese drawing of a serpent biting its own tail.

Dr Playfair left. Frank was in the living room spinning. Both Hedy and I picked up our knitting.

To our surprise Tristan emerged from his room. His eyes were shining and his manner was more animated than it had been for years. He sat down beside us and began to talk rapidly. The lines of oppressive suffering smoothed and lifted. It was as if, gradually, veils of pain were being removed, one by one. Each exposed the image of that dear face at an earlier time. Hedy and I put down our knitting and sat mesmerized. Frank's spinning-wheel stopped turning. Now the unnaturally animated voice began to tell jokes. Our eyes filled with tears, though we laughed for his sake. But, like an overwound toy, Tristan began to run down. He asked Hedy to sing 'He's Got the Whole World in His Hands'. She began valiantly, but her voice quavered and broke on the familiar words.

Already the lines of pain were returning, one by one, to overlay his features. His over-bright eyes hooded over with brown-purple lids. We guided him back to bed.

That night Hubert phoned from the Toronto airport. Incredulous, he recounted that he had missed his plane to Guadeloupe. In all his life this had never happened before; he usually erred on the side of generous time allowances. When he heard about Tristan's condition there was a long silence.

'It was providential that I missed that plane. I'll come home as soon as I can get a flight,' he said.

Lisa also phoned that evening to ask after her brother. There must still be a strong intuitive bond between the two, I thought. She asked if she could come home for a visit. Remembering the tensions and eruptions before her departure I discouraged her. I could not handle it right now, with Tristan so sick, I explained.

Those nights Tristan woke often and would call out for me. I would sit beside him on the bed stroking his forehead. Sometimes I would sing the old Ukrainian lullaby I had learned from my grandfather. It had a soothing effect. Often we said healing prayers. 'It's O.K. now,' Tristan would say at last.

I learned to fall back to sleep immediately. When he called for me again in an hour or so I would be wide awake instantly. One evening I was so tired that I suggested to Tristan that he try not to call me in the night but endeavour to sleep right through.

The next morning after the first good rest in weeks I said, 'Well, see, Moose! That was a great sleep we had last night!'

Dark eyes looked at me, 'I'm glad you slept well, mom.'

I swallowed. 'Didn't you?' I asked.

There was no answer and he had turned away.

I took a deep breath; I could only learn from his unselfishness. 'Thanks so much for letting me have a good sleep. But from now on, you can call me any time you need.'

The dark eyes turned back to mine. There was a flicker of light in them. 'Thanks, mom,' he said.

So we kept the dark vigils of the night together. Sometimes he would awake from a nightmare and his heart would be pounding when I came to him, more often it was the pain that was too much to bear alone in the dark.

At school, I tried to teach my lessons competently. The other teachers tactfully did not ask too many questions. My body felt so weary that I no longer operated on any normal reserves of energy but on some gray force that would maintain momentum for as long as it was needed.

Dr Hawkes returned from England. Tristan was delighted to see him and asked about his wife and children who were still away. 'Who cooks for you and irons your shirts now?' he asked with concern.

'Mom, don't you think you should have Dr Hawkes over for supper; you know what hospital food is like!' Tristan suggested. Then he added, 'And mom, ask Frank too. We still haven't given him his new nickname yet.'

Sunday night at supper we were not a very merry group. Tristan did not feel well enough to get up. Before returning to the hospital Dr Hawkes went in to see him. 'I see you have a clean shirt on!' Tristan remarked appreciatively. 'Did you wash it yourself?' There was the echo of his teasing humor in the remark.

'I'll be by tomorrow,' Roger Hawkes assured me before leaving.

'Now, mom!' Tristan urged when I came into his room

after the table had been cleared. 'Do it now!' There was an urgent insistence in his voice.

'What do you mean, Moose, my dear?'

'The nickname for Frank!'

'Don't you think we should wait till you are better and can join us for supper, and we can have a real party?'

From the bed in the darkened room two eyes glowed at me. The silence was eloquent. I went to my room to get the scroll we had drawn up.

'Frank, Tristan wants to officially confer a signal honor on you. Could you come to his room?' Dorothy and Hedy came too and stood in the doorway to watch.

'Frankie,' Tristan said fondly (he was the only one who ever called him Frankie), 'we have a special name to give you.'

Frank took the scroll and the little ram. He stooped over the boy and kissed his forehead. Then he walked into the light of the dining room to read the scroll. There was much laughter as the scroll was passed around and I explained how the idea for the name had been born.

'There! I'm glad,' Tristan sighed when I returned to his room. 'Is he pleased?'

'Yes, you can see he is!'

On Monday Dr Hawkes asked if we wanted to have Tristan in hospital. Hedy and I answered simultaneously, 'No, we want to look after him at home.'

'There is nothing that can be done for him medically and he is comfortable here,' Dr Hawkes acknowledged. 'I'll have a public health nurse call once a day. Here is a prescription.'

Bronfman's Cocktail, I read. I remembered that it was the medicine given to children dying of leukemia.

The druggist looked down kindly, 'If there is anything we can do, Mrs Schuurman, even if it is in the middle of the night, just call us!' I bowed my head. Suddenly the fluorescent lights of the pharmacy made me feel very cold, very exposed.

'Tomorrow, what day is tomorrow?' Tristan wanted to know when I got back.

'Tuesday, Moose.'

'I've got to go to the Paddon Home, I promised . . .'

'Moose, you're sick; they'll understand,' Hedy interposed.

'But . . . I promised . . . they'll be expecting me . . .'

'Let's see how you feel tomorrow,' I suggested.

The next day it was evident, even to Tristan, that there was no question of going to the Paddon Home. 'You'll phone them for me? You'll explain? I don't want them to think that I'd forgotten or didn't care,' Tristan reminded us.

On Wednesday morning I left for school reluctantly. Hedy assured me she would stay by his bedside. 'You've been up all night with him anyway, it will do you good to have a change of scene!' Mid-morning the secretary called me from my classroom. Hedy's voice was urgent. 'You'd better come home, mom. Tristan is asking for you. I've called Dr Hawkes.'

I drove from school in the gray October noon. The familiar hills loomed across the river. They had their first sprinkling of fine snow . . . like icing sugar.

I thought Tristan was asleep when I came into his room, but his eyelids flickered open showing eyes blue-gray and clear.

'Mom,' he said, gratefully, 'you're here!' Over the covers a gnarled hand groped for mine.

'I'm not going back to school. I'll stay with you now,' I assured him, but he seemed to have drifted off again. I stood by the window looking out at the birch tree waving in the wind.

'Moose always loved the wind . . .' Hedy said, coming up behind me and slipping her arm around my shoulder. 'Oh! Mom!'

'You are being a wonderful sister, Hedy. I'm proud of you!' I assured her.

Visitors started dropping in. By an unspoken agreement Hedy served them tea and cookies in the kitchen while I sat with Tristan. The beloved pale face hardly stirred on the pillow. When he surfaced to awareness I held his hand and stroked his face. There were hours for prayers.

Hubert called; he was coming on the 'red-eye special' from Halifax. The number of flights from mainland Canada to Labrador had been cut back after the summer. I promised to arrange for him to be met at the airport.

At night I put a foam mattress beside Tristan's bed and stretched out on it. It was so close that I would be able to hear even the change in his breathing. In the middle of the night he awoke. He seemed more alert than he had been all day.

'Mom!' he said, 'Mom, I love you so much!'

'I love you too, Moose. You are a wonderful son!' I answered.

'And I love dad, very much,' Tristan continued. 'And I love Hedy and Nadine.' There was a pause, 'And I love Lisa . . . *you know I really love Lisa!*'

'Yes, Moose, I know that in your heart you do.'

'And I love Gramma and Grampa . . . yes . . .' His breathing was labored, and he stopped to gasp for air.

'It's all right, Moose, my dear, rest now,' I whispered tenderly. But he was driven to complete his litany of love.

'And I love my teachers, Mrs Fulford and Mrs Hopwood, and I love Mrs Allingham and I love my friend Tony and Kenshee, and Frankie . . . Baran.' Again there was a gasp for air. Then he enumerated all his dear friends in Happy Valley and Goose Bay.

He stopped for a while, his chest heaving. When he began again he named people he had not seen for years, friends from Lapland and Greenland, Bahá'í friends from all across Canada. It was a torrent of . . . 'and I love the Daintys, and the Bressees and Horace Dance and Mrs Dance.' Panting for air he paused. Then with an internal effort to overcome the annoyance he had of late felt at the noise of the two-year-old, 'I love Mary Willow!' he pronounced decisively.

His eyes opened wide and he looked out into the room. My arms were cradling his head, so I did not catch their look. Enunciating clearly, he said with a sense of grateful relief, 'I'm so glad that I'm a Bahá'í . . . because . . .' The last word faded away. There was a slight spasm and he went limp. I cradled his head for some time, still listening to his shallow breathing.

The gray morning tinted the sky and still I sat beside his bed praying.

A high wind whipped at the bare branches outside. I thought of Rabbi Carlbach's song, 'O Holy Wind', and prayed . . . 'O Holy Wind be gentle with this flickering candle . . . O Holy Wind!'

Then I took paper and wrote to my mother in Zaïre:

'On the bed Tristan lies dying. His breathing draws on the wellsprings of life. So painfully, with so much travail is that breath inhaled, convulsing the whole chest, and, after an agonizing pause that lasts and lasts, exhaled with a rattle through the pale dry lips half-glued with mucous. How beautiful his face is, calm and withdrawn. The fine lines of his nose and cheekbones and the pale moonlight colour of his hair move me.

'He is at home and we orbit around him, around his center of stillness, but as he withdraws farther and farther into that unconscious world where the spirit waits in the antechamber of the other worlds, we draw closer together, pulled in by the gravity of his being and of his passing from being.'

When the public health nurse came she listened to Tristan's breathing. Hedy and I watched her at his bed, holding each other around the waist. 'He breathes like a person who will not live long,' she said gently. 'You will want to change his position every so often, to make him more comfortable. Remember that hearing is the last faculty to go.'

Hedy thanked her for coming and accompanied her to the door. 'Strange,' she said rejoining me, 'it isn't what a person says . . . That nurse, by her very presence, brought peace and acceptance.'

Visitors came all through the day. Heroically, Hedy served tea and cakes. A thoughtful friend brought a casserole for supper. Suddenly I felt impelled to talk to Tristan, remembering the sense of incompleteness I had felt when I had not had the opportunity to tell Grampa how much I had valued him and loved him.

Sitting on a low stool beside his bed, I began to talk softly to him. 'Tristan, my dearest son. Don't be afraid. This time is like being in a waiting room. This is an in-between time. Everyone is a little scared of the unknown. We are all here close to you and in the other worlds are Grampa and Gramma who love you and who will be there to greet you and to help you.'

A gentle tap on the door and Hedy let in Kevin Columbus, the doctor Tristan had so liked. She said that she had recognized him outside battling the wind when she went out in the car on an errand. He had just come into town and was leaving again to go north. Kevin, she felt, was someone Tristan would have liked to visit him.

'How are you, old pal?' Kevin said softly, touching the pale forehead.

Then as we went out into the kitchen, Hedy, ever hospitable, served up some soup. 'Kevin, make mom eat something.

Come on, mom, it's warm and it will keep you going.'

When I returned to the room there was an expectant air. I knew Tristan had heard me. Again I sat down beside him. I kissed his sunken cheeks. 'Tristan, my son, thank you for being the most wonderful son a mother could ever wish for! I have so often thanked God for sending you as a trust to our family.

'Moose, my dearest Moose, we will always be held to each other by bonds of love. And love is stronger than death. My love will always be warm around you. I will pray for you always and I hope that you will remember us in your prayers from the other worlds of God.

'So many times I was sad and you cheered me up, or downhearted and you lifted my spirits. You have enriched me; now I can't ever be poor, for you are my jewel.'

On and on poured out words of love . . . not thought out or weighed out or interrupted.

When the gray light turned to violet Dr Hawkes came in. As he examined Tristan's wasted body it was seized by a convulsion. A slight trickle of foam appeared on his lips. Hedy looked on amazed and asked what had happened. My first thought was how thoughtful to have a convulsion at the moment the doctor was there; otherwise we would have been so perplexed.

Frank came and offered to pick up Hubert at the airport as his flight arrived in the small hours of the morning. Peggy and Dave Lough came with their two boys. Dave read from *The Prophet* by Kahlil Gibran. Mary Willow came in to give Moose her customary kiss. 'Good–night, Moose,' she said unconcerned by his apparent lack of response, then she turned and said clearly, 'YELLOW, see I can say that now!'

Our lights stayed on after the last visitor had departed. 'Let not this house fall into darkness.' Hedy decided to sleep on the couch upstairs so she could greet Hubert when he arrived. We said some prayers together in Tristan's room before she fell asleep exhausted.

For awhile I wandered about the house, noting that the kitchen looked neat and tidy despite the flow of visitors. Outside the moon rode through dark clouds. Sporadic shafts of moonlight made daggers of light on the dark waters of the river. On the distant shore the spruce trees stood close guard by the water's edge, and beyond the tops of the Mealy Mountains glowed white with new-fallen snow.

There was a warm feeling of coming home when I returned to Tristan's room. As always, when I had hurried home from school to have tea with him, so now his room exuded a welcome.

'Your father will be home in about three hours. He's coming home to see you.' Then, picking up a prayer book, I said, 'Here's a prayer for your soul's joy.' The lovely words of the prayer seemed to fill the room with golden images:

> From the sweet-scented streams of Thine eternity give me to drink, O my God, and of the fruits of the tree of Thy being enable me to taste, O my Hope! From the crystal springs of Thy love suffer me to quaff, O my Glory, and beneath the shadow of Thine everlasting providence let me abide, O my Light! . . .

The cadence of the prayer calmed and soothed. Then as if from a long habit of tucking in for the night, I smoothed the unrumpled sheets, kissed his forehead and from memory recited his favorite evening prayer:

> How can I choose to sleep, O God, my God, when the eyes of them that long for Thee are wakeful because of their separation from Thee; and how can I lie down to rest whilst the souls of Thy lovers are sore vexed in their remoteness from Thy presence?
>
> I have committed, O my Lord, my spirit and my entire being into the right hand of Thy might and Thy protection, and I lay my head on my pillow through Thy power, and lift it up according to Thy will and Thy good pleasure . . .

On the pillow the tousled head lay motionless. Hot tears fell on the prayer book. There would be no lifting up of that head from the pillow.

Slowly the hours passed. 'If I could wrap you up in my heart's warmth, my son!'

In my lonely childhood I had developed the habit of saying over to myself the names of God. Now I began again . . . 'I call on Thee My God, my Beloved, my Heart's Desire, the Wise, the All-Bountiful, the All-Knowing, the Answerer of the cry of the needy, the All-Powerful, the Ever-Forgiving, the Most Praised, (what was the one I liked so much. Oh yes) the

Prayer-Hearing the Prayer-Answering God, (outside black darkness enveloped the world) O Thou Breaker of the Morn, O Thou Who slayest the Lovers, O Thou Who art gracious to the evil-doers.'

How many mothers in the long pages of the world's history have sat by their dying sons? The pain is in the unnaturalness, that the parent should outlive the child. Grief over death is different if it comes after a long and fruitful life.

Does sacrifice always entail giving up what is dearest? Tremulously as if laying a sacrifice on the stone altar of the Old Testament Jehovah, I whispered my offering, 'The Lord hath given, the Lord hath taken away; blessed be the name of the Lord!'

In the silence of the night I could hear a car approaching. Tristan had always been able to distinguish by the sound of the motor who was coming to visit, footsteps on the back deck always revealed the identity of a caller. We used to call him 'the bionic ear'!

My watch showed 2.50. I could hear Hubert's voice thanking Frank, then the door slamming in the hollow echoing darkness. I glanced at Tristan; he lay as he had for the last twenty-four hours, immobile. Then I hurried to greet my husband.

'How is he?' Hubert asked as he hugged me.

'Still alive.'

Taking off his coat as he went, Hubert strode into Tristan's room.

'Son, I'm here! It's your dad!' The shrunken body lay unmoving. 'Let's say some prayers,' Hubert suggested.

After, Hubert knelt down and with one hand around his head he kissed his son's pale forehead saying, 'I love you very much, my son!'

For a second longer the body lay still, then it was seized by a massive convulsion. A thin line of bloody froth came to the lips. Then he was absolutely still, not even a shallow breath disturbed his deep sleep now.

No tears now – no tears.

He was gone! The frail shell that contained his spirit lay so very still . . . and empty.

'Well, you are free at last, Moose, free of itching and of pain. I hope you're happy . . . we will miss you so very much.'

'We'd better tell Hedy,' Hubert said, rousing himself.

Soon Hedy was beside us, crying, kissing his face, disbelief still in her sleep-glazed eyes.

'You know, I just didn't realize . . . I always thought that if he tried harder . . . ate the right things . . . it was so silly . . . but I somehow thought it was up to him . . . that if he only made the effort . . . he'd be all right. Moose, Moose, I'm so sorry, I never let myself realize how sick you were.'

'Hedy, you were always a wonderful, loving, caring sister.'

'But I could have done more for him . . .'

'You can help me now – its the last thing we can do for this poor body he left behind.'

'I'll help you, mom.'

'We must wash him and lay him out.'

'I'll get a bowl of warm water and some towels.'

Never had I done this before, but somehow I knew that the dead should be cleansed and laid out. In the back of my mind I knew that I had a new set of pyjamas and a dressing gown I was planning to give to Tristan. In the back of the cupboard I remembered having put a new white sheet.

Gently we washed him. So evanescent a form!

Long ago I had made a small pillow from the down of ducks we had raised on the farm. In rose pink ticking I had covered it and made a case from cut-out lace. I had tried to give it to my mother but she had looked at it strangely, 'Don't give it to me – it is not practical. You will find a use for it!'

The faded golden hair combed down neatly, now rested on that rose pillow. Yes that was 'right'. But the new sheet looked cold, I fought down the desire to put on the quilt.

I could hear Hubert phoning his brother in Holland.

Tristan was laid out. 'Should we light a candle by his head?'

'I don't think he would have liked that.'

'Well, Moose, my brother, I wish you well in your new world! Does he still hear and know we are here?' Hedy asked.

'I don't know for sure, dear, but in all my reading about people who have been pronounced clinically dead and have been revived, they speak of being out of the body and floating near the ceiling and of being able to hear and see all that is going on around them.'

Hedy looked up to the ceiling, 'Moose, I hope you are satisfied with how we dressed you and . . .' She burst into tears and we held each other close.

We had tea around the dining room table and planned all that had to be done. It was as if my sleepless days and nights had put me outside the orb of practical concerns. I knew arrangements had to be made but I sat back and let others make them. At last Hubert suggested that we get at least a couple of hours sleep.

Once more I went to Tristan's room. It was no longer inhabited by that welcoming warmth. I kissed the brow – cold now, quite cold. It did not *feel* like Tristan any more. 'You are moving out, my dear, I'm not surprised.'

My head shook in disbelief. Dead, dead. Will it take you time to get used to your new state? I read the prayer for the dead once more . . . 'Cause them to enter the garden of happiness . . .'

In the bright light of the kitchen I could not miss the signs of exhaustion on Hubert's face. In bed we talked in the warmth of each other's arms, affirming life with love.

At six-thirty we were up again. I phoned Lisa. She answered on the second ring. 'Tristan's dead,' she said when she heard my voice.

'Yes,' I admitted.

'Why didn't you let me come home earlier?'

'I didn't know how long it would be.'

'I knew.'

'I'm sorry, Lisa. Do you want to come home? I can send you a ticket today.'

'Will I be in time for the funeral?'

'No. The funeral will have to be today unless we want him to go to the morgue.'

'Don't let them take him there!'

'If he stays at home he must be buried within twenty-four hours.' We talked some more but distantly.

I prayed that someone would be able to console her; grieving had never been easy for Lisa.

Nadine was at sea. She had decided to take a year off from her university studies and was working as a fisheries inspector on foreign fishing boats. In the summer when I had driven her to the airport after a visit home she had said, 'If anything ever happens to Moose while I'm at sea don't try to contact me on the boat. I would rather you left a message on land. It would be hard to handle something like that alone among strangers . . . and they would all know.' I remembered that now and phoned the fisheries office. Her boat was expected in a few days.

Dr Hawkes came. 'Tristan was such a thoughtful person,' he recollected. 'He was so concerned if I ate well or had my laundry done while my wife was away!'

Frank came before going to work. A look across the table and no explanations were needed. Wonderful to have such friends, I thought.

Rev. Buckle came. Hubert asked if Tristan could be buried in the cemetery. I could feel beams of compassion coming from him.

Hubert went next door to our neighbor, who was a carpenter, to ask if he could put together a simple coffin.

I escaped to Tristan's room. It was quiet there. I leaned against the closed door. The room felt different, as though someone were packing and most of the belongings were already out.

On the walls hung the familiar posters. There was the picture of 'Abdu'l-Bahá smiling benignly, the trophy on the dresser, beside it stood the bottle of Bronfman's Cocktail with its accompanying spoon on a white plate. In the bed lay a still form covered by a white sheet, the face alabaster on the rose and ivory lace.

Outside the door I heard Hubert and Hedy organizing friends to dig the grave.

'The Loughs can bring a shovel,' someone said.

'It should not be hard to dig in that sandy soil.'

Hubert steered me to our bedroom: 'You go and lie down while we dig.'

'Don't worry about a thing,' Hedy called before going out with a shovel, 'everybody is bringing something tonight.' The door opened again and Hedy called out, 'And, Oh, mom! I called your principal and he said he would let the school out a bit early so the teachers could go to the funeral.'

Mary Willow must have been spirited away somewhere, for suddenly the house was silent.

I lay in the darkened bedroom. What was reality? This heightened sense of awareness or all the activity around me? My eyes closed. There was a blue space all around, clear and lucid. Then a voice called in delight, 'Look, mom!' It was like the call of a child who first learns to swim or dive and can't get over the wonder of it, and calls the parent to witness the new ability.

Then I became aware of Tristan (not his form or likeness, but *him*) floating free in that blue space, free and unencumbered. 'Look, mom, I'm free, I'm free!' Somersaults, a swooping dive – delight.

Somewhere a door banged. I got up and went into his room. It was empty. No one was home. He had moved out. Only an unfamiliar form lay on the bed. I heard a voice behind me. A well-meaning friend had come over to keep me company.

My mother had not worn mourning after my father's death, I recalled as I reached for a dress. I put on my best, a simple black wool, and earrings and a pendant that Tristan had liked. Would I ever wear perfume again? It was Tristan who had always commented, 'You smell so nice, mom!'

Our neighbor brought in the simple coffin he had made. The scent of fresh wood came with it. They laid it beside the bed. Irresolutely we stood around.

'No, it looks too hard,' I heard myself say.

Hubert looked at me questioningly.

'Wait, I'll get a light blanket to put down first.'

The men laid the slight form on the folded blanket. Hedy and I placed the pillow under his head and covered him with the sheet.

'Wait.' It was Hedy who spoke now. 'You remember the message Padre White had phoned in this morning to be read at his graveside? He asked that the silver chalice that he had sent Moose on his birthday be buried with him.'

Delicate and chaste was the shape of the trophy cup. Hubert fastened it down in the coffin so it would not rattle around.

'I have heard of knights of old being buried with silver chalices.'

'Sir Tristan of the Round Table was who he was named after!'

'He was a true, loyal and valiant knight.'

The first nail they hammered into the coffin lid went through my very heart. The pain of each succeeding nail transfixed me. Hedy stood beside me, bearing me up as each nail made me flinch anew. Oh, the finality of those hammer blows. The sound was obscene. I walked away to the kitchen window. The river flowed silver through the overcast day. Behind me the hammer continued to pound.

How many nails are they putting in? Are they afraid he will raise the lid with his skinny little arms? Watch it, I told myself, you are getting irrational. But the harsh sound was tilting my reality, it was cracking the solid image.

At last it stopped. Once more it was a quiet house but with a nailed down coffin in one of the rooms.

Hedy was speaking, 'It was so hard! At the hospital I had to go up to the desk and ask for a death certificate. The lady didn't hear me the first time, and when I said it louder everyone in the waiting room turned around to look at me.' Tears were flowing down her cheeks. 'And I thought to myself, what am I doing asking for a piece of paper that says my brother is dead!'

'My dear, my dear.' It was my turn to comfort her. 'I appreciate it so much that you did this difficult thing. We could not have managed all this without you. I have been completely useless today.' We stood hugging each other.

Friends began to arrive. Some brought flowers, some brought plates of sandwiches.

Frank was asked to read the twenty-third psalm. Hubert and Hedy read from the Bahá'í Writings on death. Others read prayers. Rev. Buckle said some appropriate words.

The coffin was loaded onto Dave Lough's truck. But although we were to lead the procession of cars to the cemetery, halfway there I remembered something and we had to turn back. It made us laugh to see the startled looks on the faces of the passengers of the cars following us. We spilled out of the car and back into the house to look for the message that Padre White had phoned in and asked to be read at the graveside.

The cemetery is on the shore of the same majestic Hamilton River. I had never been there before, but driving by it daily on my way to school it had always struck me as a *comfortable* graveyard. Some of the alders had been cut back and the underbrush cleared, but the willows and the pin-cherries and some spruce were left standing in clumps. Among the graves, in the sandy soil, grew patches of blueberries, reindeer moss and crimson redberries. There was no attempt at uniformity and the graves were placed this way and that. Not far from the water's edge I saw the newly dug hole. Rev. Buckle said the ancient traditional graveside words, they sounded in my ears like the deep voice of slowly tolling bells. Hubert read the prayer for the dead and asked anyone who wanted to contribute a thought or a prayer to do so. Dave Lough read from *The Prophet*, Tony Williamson read a poem by e. e. cummings that he said for him epitomized Tristan.

> i thank you god for this amazing
> day: for the leaping greenly spirits of the trees
> and a blue true dream of sky; and for everything
> which is natural which is infinite which is yes
>
> (i who have died am alive again today,
> and this is the sun's birthday; this is the birth
> day of like and love and wings: and of the gay
> great happening illimitably earth)
>
> how should tasting touching hearing seeing
> breathing an – lifted from the no
> of all nothing – human merely being
> doubt unimaginable you?
>
> (now the ears of my ears awake and
> now the eyes of my eyes are opened)
>
> e. e. cummings

Beside me Hedy was crying. I put my arm around her. A wind picked up and the cool autumn day turned cold.

They were lowering the coffin to the ground, when something primeval woke in me. It screamed out in the hollow recesses of my primitive self – 'NO, NO! Not my son, my beloved son – No, they can't put him in that cold damp ground. NO, NO!' it shrieked.

I knew that I was calmly standing at the graveside, I knew that only my grasp on Hedy's shoulder had tightened. But within me a wild woman was shrieking and throwing herself against the smooth walls of my self-control.

In my hand I held two red roses. With determination that was like fighting an overwhelming head wind, I handed one rose to Hedy. I moved in slow motion, while the distraught woman within me howled with grief and despair. To the graveside I walked. Why so deep? Why so very deep? My hand threw in the rose, but she, the wild one, wanted to throw herself in the grave and claw the coffin with her bare nails. My hand threw in the rose but my eyes did not see it fall, for a mist passed over them.

People were turning to go. There were people whom I did not know, friends of Tristan from the Paddon Home, perhaps. I went up to the members of the school staff and thanked them individually for coming, remembering not to hug one who had always said he disliked that sort of physical contact.

The wind whipped about now and everyone dispersed like the leaves blown away by that same wind. A white birch grew on a little knoll not far from where our car was parked. Around it grew redberries in profusion nestled in a thick green carpet of moss. I stared at them till Hubert came and steered me back to the car.

On returning home I understood for the first time why there are 'wakes'. The house was bright with lights and friends. A wordless hug from a dear friend broke the chill hold of the wild woman within me. Tristan would have liked this, good friends, abundant food, jokes being told, laughter. Eating seemed an unfamiliar activity and I wondered how many meals had been missed in the last few days. It was good to be alive and among friends; it was good to talk and to laugh.

Hedy and Dorothy offered to clean up after everyone left. Hubert and I went to bed. For awhile we talked in the intimate darkness, then finally we slept.

Suddenly I was sitting up wide awake.

'What is it?' Hubert asked, waking up.

'Do you remember the song in "Emmet Otter's Jugband Christmas" that Moose liked so much?'

'Yes . . . yes, I think so. Why?'

'He always wanted me to sing it for him, but neither of us could ever remember all the words.'

'The one that went . . . "We're closer now than ever before . . ."?'

'Yes, that's the one. Someone was singing me the song now, in such a lovely clear voice!'

'Was it Moose?'

'I don't know. But whoever it was he *knew all the words*.' I hummed the last refrain . . . 'Love is teaching us how . . .'

'What time is it?' Hubert wanted to know.

'It's three . . . why, that makes it exactly twenty-four hours since Tristan died.'

Thanks, Tris, thanks for letting me know.